Philanthropy and Voluntary Action in the First World War

This book challenges scholarship which presents charity and voluntary activity during the First World War as marking a downturn from the high point of the late Victorian period. Charitable donations rose to an all-time peak, and the scope and nature of charitable work shifted decisively. Far more working class activists, especially women, became involved, although there were significant differences between the suburban south and industrial north of England and Scotland. The book also corrects the idea that charitably-minded civilians' efforts alienated the men at the front, in contrast to the degree of negativity that surrounds much previous work on voluntary action in this period. Far from there being an unbridgeable gap in understanding or empathy between soldiers and civilians, the links were strong, and charitable contributions were enormously important in maintaining troop morale. This bond significantly contributed to the development and maintenance of social capital in Britain, which, in turn, strongly supported the war effort. This work draws on previously unused primary sources, notably those regarding the developing role of the UK's Director General of Voluntary Organizations and the regulatory legislation of the period.

Peter Grant is Senior Fellow in Grantmaking, Philanthropy and Social Investment at the Cass Business School, City University, London.

Routledge Studies in Modern British History

Philanthropy and Voluntary Action in the First World War

Mobilizing Charity

Peter Grant

Routledge
Taylor & Francis Group
NEW YORK   LONDON

First published 2014
by Routledge
711 Third Avenue, New York, NY 10017

and by Routledge
2 Park Square, Milton Park, Abingdon, Oxon OX14 4RN

*Routledge is an imprint of the Taylor & Francis Group,
an informa business*

Library of Congress Cataloging-in-Publication Data
Grant, Peter, 1955 February 21–
   Philanthropy and voluntary action in the First World War : mobilizing charity / by Peter Grant.
      pages cm — (Routledge studies in modern British history ; 10)
   Includes bibliographical references and index.
 1.   World War, 1914–1918—Civilian relief—Great Britain.
 2.   World War, 1914–1918—War work—Great Britain. 3.   World War, 1914–1918—Social aspects—Great Britain. 4.   Charities—Great Britain—History—20th century.   I. Title.
   D638.G7G73 2014
   940.3'1—dc23
   2013038347

ISBN13: 978-0-415-70494-6 (hbk)
ISBN13: 978-1-315-89021-0 (ebk)

Typeset in Sabon
by IBT Global.

Contents

Figures

Tables

Abbreviations

ASC	Army Service Corps
BAOFH	British American (Overseas) Field Hospital
BEF	British Expeditionary Force
BSF	Belgian Soldiers' Fund
COS	Charity Organisation Society
CPWC	Central Prisoners of War Committee
CRB	Committee for Relief in Belgium
CWRCC	Central War Refugees Committee for Croydon
CWSCH	Croydon War Supplies Clearing House
DGVO	Director General of Voluntary Organizations
DPP	Director of Public Prosecutions
FA	Football Association
FANY	First Aid Nursing Yeomanry
FRF	French Relief Fund
IWGC	Imperial War Graves Commission
LCC	London County Council
LGB	Local Government Board
LMA	London Metropolitan Archives
LSE	London School of Economics and Political Science
MCC	Marylebone Cricket Club
NCSS	National Council of Social Service
NCVO	National Council for Voluntary Organisations
NRF	National Relief Fund
NUWSS	National Union of Women's Suffrage Societies
OTC	Officers' Training Corps
PDSA	People's Dispensary for Sick Animals
QMG	Quartermaster General
QMNG	Queen Mary's Needlework Guild
RSPCA	Royal Society for the Prevention of Cruelty to Animals
SSFA	Soldiers' and Sailors' Families Association
SWH	Scottish Women's Hospitals
TNA	The National Archives (Kew)
VAD	Voluntary Aid Detachment

VRL	Voluntary Recruiting League
WAAC	Women's Auxiliary Army Corps
WEWS	Westminster Entertainments for Wounded Soldiers
WNC	Workers' National Committee
WRC	War Refugees Committee
WSF	Workers' Suffrage Federation
WSPU	Women's Social and Political Union
WVR	Women's Volunteer Reserve
YMCA	Young Men's Christian Association
YWCA	Young Women's Christian Association

Foreword

Professor Gary Sheffield

In writing *Philanthropy and Voluntary Action in the First World War: Mobilizing Charity* Peter Grant has made a very substantial contribution to the history of Britain in the traumatic years of 1914–18. The vast voluntary effort used in creating the New Armies in 1914–15 has long been recognised, and analysed in a series of books and articles, not least in Peter Simkins's seminal *Kitchener's Army* (1988). Other aspects of the military voluntary effort, such as the wartime Volunteer Force, have also been studied (see K.W. Mitchinson's excellent 2005 book *Defending Albion*). Hitherto, the vast topic of the civilian counterpart to Kitchener's Army and the like has been curiously neglected, to the detriment of our understanding of Britain's war experience 'in the round'. Dr Grant's work has put the civilian voluntary sector on the historical agenda. It brings some welcome balance to the familiar picture of the First World War bringing about an unprecedented level of control and intervention by the British state; as he makes clear, this was paralleled by a huge voluntary and philanthropic effort. To use Dr Grant's analogy, the relationship between philanthropy and the state is like that of religion and science. Just as religion fills in the gaps that science is unable to explain, philanthropy likewise complements the work of the state.

This book is especially timely in that it appears on the eve of the centenary of the outbreak of the war, at a moment when public and media interest in the conflict is extremely high. The long discredited idea that the First World War was an accident, that no state wanted conflict, has resurfaced, along with the equally erroneous view that Germany did not really pose a threat to Britain. There is plenty of evidence to refute both of these notions. One immensely important factor is the response of the British people to war. The level of voluntary effort was a measure of the gravity with which the German threat was regarded. As Peter Grant argues, just like the Second World War, the 1914–18 conflict was a 'people's war'. Both were total wars, conflicts in which mass mobilisation of people and resources were essential. People can be coerced into contributing to a war effort, but the striking point about the British in both world wars was that very high level of consent among the people. This book illustrates and helps to explain why millions 'bought into' Britain's war effort. Not the least of its importance lies in the way social capital provided a solid foundation for the war effort. The war broke up some societies, but British society proved to be remarkably cohesive. Grant sees voluntary action as 'an integrating mechanism' that in a very class-bound society brought together people from very different socioeconomic backgrounds, not least in changing the relationship between philanthropy, which by its very nature is a 'top-down' phenomenon, and grass-roots mutual aid.

Such changes reverberated long after the end of the war, influencing the society that evolved in the 1920s and 1930s. This was a remodelled British society in which the state played a greater role than before 1914, but the voluntary sector played a critical role. As Deborah Cohen showed in her 2001 book *The War Come Home,* in contrast to Weimar Germany's state-centric welfare policy towards war veterans, in Britain much less generous state provision placed a heavy burden on charities. Had the voluntary sector been less vibrant, it is conceivable that British ex-servicemen would have been much less politically docile than was actually the case. In short, social capital was of critical importance in enabling Britain both to fight and win a total war and to adjust to and cope with its consequences.

Dr Grant's work, based on intensive archival research, also has much to tell us about the 'nuts and bolts' of the way that philanthropy, charities and the voluntary sector worked and changed during the First World War. In particular, Sir Edward Ward emerges as a previously underrated hero of the voluntary war effort, and Grant effectively consigns the notion that it was all about sock-knitting by upper class women to the wastepaper basket. *Philanthropy and Voluntary Action in the First World War: Mobilizing Charity* is an innovative piece of history that enables us to look at Britain in the First World War in a new light. It deserves a wide readership.

Professor Gary Sheffield
September 2013
Chair of War Studies
University of Wolverhampton

Preface and Acknowledgments

This book examines the role of non-uniformed voluntary action on the home front during the First World War. The history of voluntary action is now assuming greater prominence but is still a significantly underresearched area. The impact of philanthropy and charity in Britain during 1914–18 was profound; indeed it may have been greater than at any other time in our history. Though the book shows that the contributions made by thousands of men and, even more so, women has been significantly underrated by previous historians of the war the book also resurrects the profile of one outstanding figure. Sir Edward Ward undertook the role of Director General of Voluntary Organizations during the war but was also a major figure in the history of army logistics, civil military relations and management education. Ward is so little regarded by historians that they make the persistent error of undervaluing his contribution to the army reforms of the pre-war period, saying he occupied the position of Under Secretary of State at the War Office when he had in fact been the Permanent Secretary since 1901.[1] I therefore make no apologies for examining his career in some detail.

The book began life as my doctoral thesis and I would like to thank my ever-optimistic and enthusiastic supervisor, Professor Jenny Harrow, for her support. I would also like to gratefully acknowledge my debt to my two external examiners, Professor Bernard Harris and, especially, Professor Gary Sheffield who has also kindly provided the Foreword. My thanks also go to my fellow members of the Voluntary Action History Society, especially Dr George Gosling, who have listened critically to various versions of the arguments put forward.

I would also like to thank the following: Leanne Green for research and ideas on illustrations; Andrew Gill whose Burnley in the Great War website is the source of the illustrations of 'Little Kitchener' and the 'Hieland Lassie'; to the Croydon Local Studies Library, the National Army Museum, the London Metropolitan Archives, the National Portrait Gallery and the Imperial War Museum for permission to use illustrations and to all the other archives and libraries whose resources I have utilised.

1 Introduction

VOLUNTARY ACTION AND TRANSFORMATION

The day after Britain declared war on Germany in 1914 the Labour Party called an emergency meeting of the Labour and Socialist movement 'to consider the industrial and social position of the working classes as affected by the war.'[1] The outcome was not a condemnation of the war but the establishment of a new grouping, the War Emergency: Workers' National Committee (WNC). The WNC soon comprised thirty-five members including leading figures from the trades unions (such as Ben Tillett), members of the Parliamentary Party (including Ramsay MacDonald), the Co-operative Movement, Fabian Society (one of whose representatives was Sidney Webb), the British Socialist Party and four women members (including Margaret Bondfield).[2] They issued what amounted to a 'war manifesto' to protect working class interests and drew up a programme of twelve demands:[3]

1. All war relief should be merged and administered by the Government.
2. Labour representation (both male and female) on all national and local committees established in connection with the war.
3. Full provision out of public funds both for dependant allowances and comforts for soldiers and sailors.
4. Rates of allowances and war pensions should be adequate (these were given in some detail).
5. Establishment of cooperative canteens in all camps and barracks.
6. Provision of public works for the unemployed displaced by the war.
7. Active government encouragement to increase home-grown food supplies.
8. Protection against exorbitant price increases, especially for food.
9. A comprehensive programme of municipal housing.
10. The establishment of maternity and infant centres for workers.
11. Provision of free school meals.
12. A continuation of state control of the railways, docks etc after the war.

At the time, depending upon one's political persuasion, these demands were either utopian or a dangerous socialist threat. Yet by 1918, virtually all of them had been achieved and most had happened without direct popular action and many with the support of those entirely opposed to socialism.[4] Moreover, the innovations were carried out either initially or entirely by voluntary organisations rather than government. In the process, the relationship between charities and the state was transformed.[5] The transformation included the first direct state control of charities, through the creation of a Director General of Voluntary Organizations (DGVO) and the first compulsory registration of non-endowed charities. How this came about and what legacy it left is the subject of this book.

The First World War saw the greatest act of volunteering ever in Britain. Two-and-a-half million men volunteered to fight in a conflict that cost more than 700,000 of them their lives. There was, however, another act of volunteering between 1914 and 1918 on at least the same scale, though without the same life-and-death consequences. This was the voluntary effort at home especially to support the men at the front, in health and sickness, but also to aid numerous other causes. In 1929 one commentator on the war suggested, in relation to wartime voluntary activities that 'a book might be written on the conduct of these activities, which, as social life ceased to exist, absorbed the energies of people in all ranks of life.'[6] Yet it remains a phenomenon about which little has been written. Even in the relatively few publications that cover the home front, it is not given significant space. Most scholarly works also give little account of non-uniformed voluntary action, its immediate impact on the war effort nor its longer-term effects on social welfare.[7] Though there is a mountain of memoirs written by men at the front there are few recording the lives of those who stayed at home.[8] Where charity is mentioned (usually fleetingly) it is seen in terms of an outbreak of sock knitting in 1914 carried out exclusively by middle and upper class women and having no impact whatsoever on the course of the war. This misrepresentation began during the war itself with *Punch* quick to satirise the aristocratic lady fumbling with her needles and has been repeated ever since. Early culprits include Vera Brittain in *Testament of Youth* and she has been followed by E.S. Turner's *Dear Old Blighty* which, where it does mention charity, does so disparagingly.[9] Gerard DeGroot in *Blighty* repeats the comments and Samuel Hynes too is patronising and derogatory.[10] Even very recent works suggest the impact of philanthropic activities was negligible.[11] The approach of much of the existing literature to non-uniformed voluntary action has, therefore, been superficial at best. Its conclusions are consistent across the literature and can perhaps be summed up as concluding that charitable activity mushroomed on the outbreak of war being primarily directed towards the National Relief Fund, Belgian Refugees and the Red Cross. It was mainly a middle class phenomenon characterised by those ladies who undertook a frenzied spate of sock knitting. Overall, it was an amateurish exercise that had little real impact either on the home front or with the troops. As the war dragged on charitable activity significantly declined and there was little long-term impact either on individuals or upon the transition of social welfare from the private to the state realm.

It is certainly true that there was a phase of frenetic knitting and stitching which spread throughout the country in 1914 and what they produced was sometimes not exactly what was needed. However, even shoddily produced goods could be helpful because 'many men in the trenches used these unwanted, and often unsuitable, items for cleaning their rifles and wiping their cups and plates.'[12] Yet despite the tone of condescension in some contemporary writings on the subject, the production of most comforts quickly became better organised. To characterise First World War charitable activity as a whole in terms of middle class sock-knitters is akin to depicting the British Army's approach to the war solely in terms of its organisation in August 1914. A key perpetrator of this image has been Arthur Marwick, still perhaps the leading historian to cover the home front of 1914–18. His seminal work *The Deluge: British Society and the First World War* was published in 1965 during the intense revival of interest in the war that encompassed the mammoth BBC television series *The Great War* (1964) as well as the Theatre Workshop's highly influential musical entertainment *Oh! What a Lovely War* (1963), later filmed by Richard Attenborough (1969). *The Deluge* has little to say about charitable voluntary action other than in relation to work for Belgian refugees and prisoners of war and is dismissive on the topic, considering it too trivial to be worth recording or investigating in more detail. Even in 1977 when Marwick wrote *Women at War 1914–1918* to accompany the major Imperial War Museum exhibition on the subject he was still, largely, condescending.[13]

One could perhaps forgive these misreadings if the primary sources available to refute them were non-existent or even hard to find. Yet this is not the case. Though archives generally do not have easily referenced sections on 'Charity' or 'Voluntary Action', many key documents from the period survive. The National Archives, for example, contain copies of the application forms of (virtually) every organisation that registered under the 1916 War Charities Act. These forms give the names, addresses and, sometimes, occupations of the officers of the charity. These can be supplemented by searches through the census records, thus building a picture of the gender and class of these people. In London the Metropolitan Archives contain eighty-nine volumes of correspondence and documentation relating to war charities in the capital. Here, the archivist confirmed that I was the first person to use the collection systematically.

A prime purpose of this book is to demonstrate that the middle class, sock-knitting image of First World War charity is yet another of the myths that has surrounded that traumatic period of British history. There was a massive increase in charitable voluntary action during the First World War. Around 18,000 new charities were created, a 50 percent increase on the number in existence pre-war. The value of their fund-raising was

Figure 1.1   Sir Edward Ward in the uniform of Commandant-in-Chief of the Metropolitan Special Constabulary (Artist: Walter Stoneman; © National Portrait Gallery, London).

Figure 1.2 Sir Edward Willis Duncan Ward, 1st Bt (printed by Vincent Brooks, Day & Son, after Sir Leslie Ward, chromolithograph, published 30 May 1901; © National Portrait Gallery, London).

Figure 1.3   Sir Edward Ward and his staff at Ladysmith, Ward seated centre right (one of sixteen photographs collected by Arthur Hutton, the Reuters representative at Ladysmith, 1899–1900; courtesy of the Council of the National Army Museum, London).

significantly more than £100 million (probably reaching at least £150 million), equivalent to the income for 'good causes' through today's National Lottery, and their legacy was significant. Charitable activity in the war was, especially in many industrial towns and cities, a manifestation of working class solidarity with many more organisations run by ordinary women and men than by well-to-do matrons. It was easily the most significant charitable cause that had ever been supported in Britain and it had profound effects upon both the war effort and the relationship between voluntary organisations and the state.

Though there were moves in the direction of state control of charitable activity in support of the war effort, this was not a coherently developed policy of government nor was it by any means a steady, linear process. Rather it was motivated by specific events, or crises, such as concerns as to wasted effort or lack of coordination in the supply of comforts for the troops. In 1915 this, together with public pressure and embarrassments over perceived shortages, led to the establishment of the post of DGVO under Sir Edward Ward. However, Ward's remit was coordination of supply, not regulation of abuses. Legislation, in the form of the 1916 War Charities Act, was almost a last resort entered into when abuses of the charitable system became a significant public issue. Where state intervention did occur, it was often due to a failure to integrate the dual charitable impulses of mutual aid and philanthropy with the requirements of a budding state welfare system.

Philanthropy and voluntary action also provided Britain with a distinct advantage over her main adversary, Germany, in the reservoir of social capital on which it was able to draw. In relation to this issue I examine the notion of philanthropy as a means of social control. Did it act 'as a means by which the dominant professional and commercial classes confirmed their power and status'?[14] There is some support for this thesis in the pre-war context but I argue that voluntary action in Britain during the war acted as an integrating mechanism between social classes that helped initiate changes in the relationship between 'top-down' philanthropy and 'bottom-up' mutual aid and that this trend continued into the post-war period. Voluntary action contributed significantly both to maintaining morale at home (a visible sign of 'pulling one's weight') and with troops and prisoners of war. Contrary to received opinion, through war poets such as Siegfried Sassoon and Robert Graves and writers including Paul Fussell and Eric Leed, the vast majority of troops welcomed charitable efforts on their behalf and were kindly disposed towards benevolence on the home front. In contrast German social control of voluntary action strengthened under an increasingly militaristic government and this led to a serious weakening of social capital.

CHARITABLE VOLUNTARY ACTION IN PREVIOUS CONFLICTS

The earliest charitable support connected with Britain's armed conflicts was not the result of voluntary action but of state intervention. In 1681, Charles II established the Royal Hospital Chelsea for army veterans. This was followed thirteen years later, during the reign of William and Mary, with the equivalent institution for seamen at Greenwich. The first notable public support had to wait until the Napoleonic Wars, the first time since the Civil War that a conflict impinged upon the daily lives of significant numbers of the British public. The Lloyd's Insurance Market raised the Lloyd's Patriotic Fund in 1803 to support impoverished servicemen and their families, a role it continues to provide to this day.

In many respects the Crimean War of 1854–56 was a watershed in the conduct of modern warfare, not least in its relationship to charitable causes. The graphic despatches of *Times* correspondent William Russell exposed the gross mismanagement of the war together with its impact on the welfare of the troops. The most famous humanitarian response was that of Florence Nightingale and her Sisters of Mercy and their activities were substantially paid for by public subscription. *The Times* established the Soldiers' Sick and Wounded Fund after a spontaneous outpouring of donations in the wake of Russell's reports and a sum of £7,000 was collected in a few weeks. It was this fund rather than any official channel that managed and resourced Nightingale's mission.[15] Other Crimean War funds included such descriptive bodies as the Central Association in Aid of the Wives and Families of Soldiers Ordered on Foreign Service and the Association for the Relief of Widows, Orphans, Wives and Families of Seamen and Marines.[16] These organisations raised significant amounts and even the fund established in New South Wales for the dependants of British soldiers contributed over £60,000 to the cause.[17]

The second Anglo-Boer War was the first where a significant number of volunteers joined the professional army. The roughly 90,000 volunteers were supported by a far more extensive network of charitable organisations than had been the case in the Crimea.[18] The Mansion House Fund was one of the first in the field soon after the outbreak of hostilities in 1899. Started by the Lord Mayor of London, its purpose was to bring financial relief to Uitlander refugees made destitute by the war.[19] Funds in excess of £200,000 were raised in Britain and South Africa with their disbursement in the hands of a Central Committee in Cape Town. An Imperial Patriotic Fund was established and again colonial contributions were significant, £100,000 coming from Australia alone.[20] A number of funds were organised by newspapers, both national and provincial, and considerable sums were raised in this way including £254,000 by readers of the *Daily Telegraph*.[21] Even more significant was the work of the Soldiers' and Sailors' Families Association, which raised more than £1.2 million to provide support for 200,000 dependants of servicemen.[22] Perhaps the best-known example of fund-raising during the Boer War was Rudyard Kipling's poem 'The Absent-Minded Beggar'. The poem was commissioned by Alfred Harmsworth, publisher of the *Daily Mail,* and achieved huge popular success, especially after Sir Arthur Sullivan set it to music. Heavily promoted by the *Mail*, an 'Absent Minded Beggar Relief Corps' was set up to aid wounded soldiers and sailors and their families and send medical supplies and comforts to South Africa, raising £250,000.[23] Despite such popular and dramatic interventions Andrew Thompson has noted that the charitable efforts of the Boer War are another forgotten chapter in British philanthropic history. Six million pounds was estimated to have been raised during the war by voluntary effort, a figure Thompson describes as 'staggering . . . equivalent to just under £410 million [in today's prices] and to be compared, say, to the £40 million raised worldwide by Bob Geldof's Band Aid and Live Aid appeals in 1985, and the £170 million raised by Comic Relief since its inception in 1988.'[24] I would agree with Thompson's conclusion; however, it should be considered in context when compared to the sums raised during the First World War which were (at least) twenty times as much. Thompson is astute in his summary of the meaning of this significant public support. It was essentially humanitarian in nature (there were even a few instances of pro-Boers making donations), but was bolstered by feelings of patriotism. 'Above all', he concludes, 'the war funds are testimony to the dynamism of provincial philanthropy at this time, to the strength of civic pride, and to the depth and public sympathy and solidarity with British soldiers.'[25] These traits were still present in 1914–18 but, if anything, had become more complex. In summarising service charities prior to the First World War Adrian Gregory has suggested that they were narrowly focussed and followed highly traditional views of charity both in their forms of fund-raising and in distinguishing in moral terms between 'deserving' and 'undeserving' cases for support.[26] This was soon to change.

2   Charity, Philanthropy and the Voluntary Sector in 1914
A 'Golden Age'?

VOLUNTARY ACTION BEFORE THE WAR

Several writers on Victorian and Edwardian philanthropy in the UK have argued that it marked a golden age of charity with levels of giving expanding significantly in the later part of the nineteenth century.[1] The scale of charitable giving was certainly significant; however, there are grounds for questioning the received wisdom that voluntary activity in the nineteenth and early twentieth centuries was exceptional in its scale, growth, redistributive effect and supremacy over the poor law.[2] Examination of successive editions of *Howe's Classified Directory to the Metropolitan Charities* reveals that the income of London charities in 1883–84 was £4,447,436 and there were 1,013 charitable institutions in London. By 1912, this total had reached about £8.5 million and in 1913 just under £9 million per annum, which meant that voluntary income grew approximately in line with national income.[3] David Owen gives roughly similar figures gleaned from the *Annual Charitable Register and Digest*, published by the Charity Organisation Society.[4] The Poor Law Commission estimated that London charities accounted for 57 percent of national charitable income, which, in 1913, was therefore around £14 million a year. By far the largest proportion were charities connected with the propagation of Christianity (especially overseas missions) who accounted for over 40 percent of the income. These activities, as noted by Alan Kidd, 'often reflected the enthusiasms and anxieties of the charitable rather than the practical needs of the poor.'[5] Excluding religion, total charitable income in 1913 was about £8 million a year. These figures are significant when one considers that they are approximately two-thirds of the sum distributed at this time for national poor relief through the Poor Law by local authorities; however, they indicate that there was no dramatic expansion of income during the last decade of the nineteenth and first decade of the twentieth centuries. But this did not mean that the ground for potential rapid expansion of voluntarism was not fertile. Clearly conditions must have existed which could account for the extraordinary response, not least to Kitchener's call for a new national army, with 1.2 million recruits by the end of 1914, an act which has rightly been described as 'one of the most impressive mass movements ever witnessed in British history.'[6]

It is helpful here to distinguish between different types of charitable activity or voluntary action. It is a distinction specifically expressed by William Beveridge in his lecture entitled 'Voluntary Action for Social Advance', where he defined voluntary action as comprising two main types—mutual aid and philanthropy. Beveridge explained that 'it is Mutual Aid when consciousness of a common need leads to combined action to meet that need, to helping oneself and one's fellows together. It is philanthropy when the driving force is not consciousness of one's own needs, but what I have described as social conscience.'[7] If philanthropy was not on the increase in pre-First World War Britain, mutual aid certainly was. The late Victorian and Edwardian periods were marked by an upsurge in mutual aid bodies, clubs and associations:

> People in the lost world of pre 1914 were much more sociable and lived in a society with much more obviously defined communities, groups, extended families and even neighbours. Clubs and institutions of every kind flourished to an astonishing degree, for all classes and conditions of men and women, before the First World War. . . . In 1914 people 'belonged'. The men who went off to war in 1914 were from a generation of 'joiners'.[8]

The clearest and most widespread of mutual aid organisations for ordinary people were the trade unions and friendly societies, and the war years saw a significant increase in their membership. By 1914 union membership had doubled from under two million at the turn of the century and was to double again, to eight million, by 1920. Friendly societies were in their heyday. In 1900 the membership of affiliated and ordinary friendly societies was 5,400,000, more than 20 percent of the entire United Kingdom population.[9]

Whereas the union and friendly society movements stemmed from a clear motive for personal gain, many other organisations had more altruistic motives, for example, the powerful drive to better oneself and others through education. This had been fuelled by increasing educational standards and far higher rates of literacy, and indeed it has often been noted that the First World War itself was a uniquely literary war.[10] Educative self-help was encouraged by many from the upper and middle classes who realised the political benefits of certain manifestations of voluntary action. Jonathan Rose has commented that 'especially in the late nineteenth and early twentieth centuries, after the achievement of mass literacy but before radio and television, working-class culture was saturated by the spirit of mutual education. Every day, information and ideas were exchanged in literally millions of commonplace settings—parlours and kitchens, workplaces and shops.'[11] Better education led to an increasing propensity for sections of the working class to engage in more altruistic charitable activities and Frank

Prochaska suggests that 'the respectable working class, often identified with church and chapel, was particularly noticeable in its charitable activity. . . . Philanthropy was a test of respectability, and one had to be far down the social ladder . . . to be altogether free from social obligation.'[12] One massive voluntary movement was the Sunday Schools. By the mid-nineteenth century three-quarters of working class children were attending and in 1901 six million people were enrolled. Sunday Schools were not all religious in nature as there was a significant Socialist Sunday School movement, with well over thirty of them in Glasgow alone just before the war.[13]

The impetus to voluntary activity was stimulated by organisations that were aimed at developing the healthy body and mind in accord with late-Victorian concepts of educational improvement, manliness and athleticism. Nowhere was the mechanism more clear than in the transformation of sport during the second half of the nineteenth century into a rational recreation.[14] From its genesis in the Victorian public school the principles of athleticism were proselytised in an explosion of organised sports clubs in the later decades of the nineteenth century. These clubs fostered the organisational and leadership skills of a section of society who, through the extension of voting rights, were achieving a greater political role. Britain became the first modern sporting nation in which codification and institutionalisation transformed fragmented and localised 'games' into national 'sports'. This included

- The formation of national administrations for individual sports;
- Regulation through the adoption of standard written rules;
- The formation of clubs and, in many sports, the proliferation of local, regional and national league and cup competitions.[15]

This was not only a leisure revolution but a bureaucratic and managerial one too.

Uniformed boys' organisations were also influential in spreading the gospel of athleticism. It has been claimed that these organisations 'assisted in producing a working class that, like the middle class, was trained for war, in Orwell's phrase "not technically but morally."'[16] The degree of militarism inculcated by these organisations is debatable but the extent of athletic education they exhibited is not. Of these, the best known was the Boy Scouts founded by Boer War hero Sir Robert Baden-Powell as a response to the ill health of recruits for South Africa. Within two years of its establishment, in 1908, the Scouts claimed 100,000 members and by 1914 over 40 percent of boys belonged to some kind of youth organisation.[17] The Boys Brigade, founded by Glasgow businessman William Alexander Smith, was especially active in promoting what has become known as Muscular Christianity. It was one of the first voluntary movements to introduce working class boys to organised sports, which had previously been the preserve of the public schools. In Smith's perfect world, boys would talk 'to each other in the most perfectly natural way about the Company Bible-Class before all their comrades on the football field.'[18] The Church Lads' Brigade, the organisation of the established Anglican Church, was another body that used military-style training within a religious context. Its success at instilling spirituality amongst its members is questionable but its military aspect proved a national asset, as it contributed 120,000 of its current and past membership to the forces during the First World War. The Bishop of London, Arthur Winnington-Ingram, was especially proud of the Church Lads' Brigade. Under his presidency its London branch recruited a battalion of 1,000 men that subsequently earned a personal commendation from Lord Kitchener.[19] The support of extreme nationalists such as Winnington-Ingram has led some writers to suggest that 'youth movements were, for the most part, developed as instruments for the reinforcement of social conformity . . . part of what the sociologist might term the culturally organised processes of formal and informal social control mechanisms.'[20] John Springhall argues that these organisations were formed for negative reasons, to prevent deviance, rather than for positive ones, to promote social cohesion. He supports this contention by reference to the fact that, in seeking to extract funding from middle class supporters, youth movements suggested that they had a deterrent effect on deviance. One needs to be very careful in making the assumption that it was actually true just because the organisations said they had this effect. Many youth charities today promote their activities to potential wealthy supporters as diverting young people away from crime. However, there is little research evidence to demonstrate the truth of this assertion and these charities would certainly not say that this negative outcome was their main objective; they would use far more positive terms like 'raising self-esteem' or 'promoting cohesion'. Springhall's entire argument is somewhat ahistorical, using modern values to interpret the past. He considers it patronising for Edwardian youth organisations to have stressed middle class behavioural norms and denigrate working class life and 'street culture'.[21] Such an approach would not have been seen as patronising at the time. It would more likely have been viewed as a good thing, bettering oneself. It is Springhall's approach that is patronising, or certainly belittling, as it suggests that working class recruits to these bodies were too foolish to realise that they were being controlled and patronised. The alternative is that they knew that one purpose of the movements was to change their values but that they willingly colluded in this process because it brought benefits to both sides of the exchange of values. Springhall's misuse of hindsight ends with a regret that there were no radical left-wing youth organisations until the advent of the Woodcraft Folk in the 1920s.[22] This is to miss the point; of course the youth organisations were not formed to challenge the status quo in society, but equally they did not make the working class 'content with their lot'. In that they were mechanisms for instilling class values, they were also encouragements to social mobility within the system. It would therefore be wrong to overemphasise the militaristic

nature of the uniformed boys' organisations or cite the Scouts, and especially the Boys Brigade, as examples of how militaristic British society as a
whole was and thus that it was itching to go to war in 1914.[23] Whilst not
entirely without foundation, in that Britain was certainly *more* militaristic
in 1914 than in 1939 or today, it is an exaggerated view. Firstly, the army in
1914 was still more or less the preserve of the very highest and very lowest
stratas of society and viewed at best with suspicion, at worst with contempt
by both the business and respectable working classes.[24] Secondly, the key
motivation of men like Smith and Baden-Powell was to build overall character (body *and* mind), not simply martial qualities. It is instructive that
when, in 1910–11, the government tried to incorporate both bodies into
a homogeneous national cadet force, and despite the offer of substantial
financial aid, they both refused.[25]

Research into boys' organisations of the period demonstrates that their
members were predominantly the sons of the respectable, upper-working
class.[26] These movements were part of a major national trend, encouraged
and supported by those in power, as a natural and positive development
towards political inclusivity in the years preceding the war. An approach
purely based on a paternalistic, philanthropically inclined middle class eager
to improve the condition of their fellow citizens would not have been successful if the working class members had not cooperated. Some commentators
see this as a clear case of social control and there are some examples where
the working class resisted the leadership of their 'betters'. One example is
'the day in the 1870s when Christ Church Football Club walked out on the
local vicar, crossed the road to the Gladstone Hotel and formed Blackburn
Rovers Football Club', leading to the development of professional football.[27]
However, the integrative trend, part philanthropy, part mutual aid, of sport
and boys' organisations was, at this point in history, more prominent than
the 'social action' model of the Christ Church footballers though both trends
contained the fuel for an upsurge of voluntary action in 1914.

Whilst sport and uniformed organisations were almost entirely restricted
to the male population there is equal, if not greater, evidence of the potential
for voluntary action among the women of pre-1914 Britain. In the 1890s,
Prochaska has estimated that half a million women volunteers worked full
time in charity and another 20,000 were paid officials in philanthropic societies.[28] Again though, the greatest potential lay in the middle and upwardly
mobile working classes through organisations 'which imbued them with
leadership skills, civic consciousness, and a commitment to service.'[29]
Many of these reflected traditional paternalism, or in this case maternal-
ism, and the relationship noted with respect to men and boys above. The
largest was probably the Mothers Union and although membership figures
are fragmentary, Prochaska has suggested that a million women and children attended their meetings in the Edwardian period. There were though
many voluntary organisations with a significant membership of working

class women, such as the Co-operative Movement and the non-conformist churches, but again it was women from the 'respectable' working class who were dominant.[30]

SOCIAL CONTROL OR SOCIAL CAPITAL?

A key aspect of the entirety of voluntary action, and especially philanthropy, and one that is still the subject of considerable debate today is the extent to which it was a means of social control. By social control is meant 'a conscious attempt by the establishment to *impose* middle-class values on the working class and thereby avert negative consequences for the dominant class.'[31] The crucial factor here is *imposition*, manipulation of the working class for negative rather than positive, educative motives. It is self-evident that the first part of this theory is true—there was a desire by the middle and upper classes to provide a rational alternative to negative pursuits and this was mirrored by many mutual aid organisations controlled by the working class themselves. It is the second part that is more contentious, i.e. was this a deliberate attempt to reduce radicalism? There is certainly some evidence that supports this view with many statements from the mid-nineteenth to early twentieth centuries suggesting that without political reform or positive action the working class would turn to extreme politics. However, it is possible to argue that in the period before the First World War things changed. As the nineteenth century moved on and it became increasingly certain that the working class would play a greater role in the political life of the country, establishment attitudes changed, and they changed to an even greater extent in the decade before, and most especially during, the war. Those who propound the social control view see very little difference between the two strands of voluntary action, philanthropy and mutual aid. This view ignores the fact that many of those most prominent in propounding mutual aid were also among the most radical politically, including the Fabian Society and prominent members of the Labour Party. Mutual aid certainly had an element of 'bettering oneself' but it also sprang from the necessity for the working class to defend itself against the worst excesses of capitalism. This aspect is one recognised by John Bourne in his discussion of the composition and beliefs of the British Army during the war.

> The existence of this rich diversity of [pre-war] working-class 'civil society' is indicative of much wider community solidarity. . . . Working-class people did not choose community solidarity because of their innate moral superiority to the thrusting, individualistic, selfish bourgeoisie. They were forced into it by the demands of their situation. Community solidarity was the product of shared adversity. This produced a quite extraordinary degree of mutuality.[32]

One reason the social control thesis has been reinforced was the clash between many radicals and established charitable organisations that occurred during the decades leading up to the war. The leading charitable organisation of the day was the Charity Organisation Society (COS), founded in 1869 with two prime motivations. The first was the coordination of charitable activity in order to avoid duplication and waste—a laudable if ultimately futile goal. The second was the propagation of their view of 'scientific philanthropy', itself comprising two main ideas. The first was that the poor could be divided into two categories, those who through no fault of their own had fallen on hard times and who, with some assistance from charity, could re-establish their place as respectable members of society and those who refused to help themselves and were therefore beyond assistance. The second view, based on this assumption of the deserving and undeserving poor, was that there should be a rigid division between which category was helped by the state and which by charity.[33] Whilst the state had an obligation to prevent total destitution, it was charity's role not to waste their resources on undeserving cases. It is very easy to criticise this view as both reactionary and misguided. Poverty, then as now, was more often caused by unemployment, sickness or simply old age; it had little to do with freedom of choice. Consequently this second major plank of COS philosophy was as doomed as the first. Hardly surprisingly the COS's ideas brought philanthropy into direct conflict with both revolutionary and reforming socialists.[34] The latter, who were the considerable majority, rightly saw state intervention as being of far greater efficacy in tackling social issues than even 'organised' charity. Despite these clashes the COS view was remarkably persistent and it took the First World War finally to lay it to rest.

It is from this battle, and the work of the reforming Liberal government of the post-1905 period, that a closely related idea to that of social control has developed amongst commentators on voluntary action. This is the proposition that in the early twentieth century the state, coming to a realisation both of the extent of social problems and their responsibility for them, extended their remit to the social sphere and that, as a result, voluntary action declined into insignificance. Such a proposition was re-enforced by social reformers anxious both for the state to take on this mantle and to emphasise their own role in the development of state intervention. There are again some difficulties with this proposition. Firstly, as has been shown, the role of charity in the nineteenth century has tended to be overemphasised. Equally, the role of the state in the social sphere has been underestimated. True the Liberal government significantly speeded up intervention but, as Justin Davis Smith has noted, 'there was a well-established tradition of statutory support for voluntary action going back well into the early years of the [nineteenth] century.'[35] Secondly, the failure of 'scientific philanthropy' and the advance of state control of social services has misled many writers into a belief that voluntary action *as a whole* significantly declined.

Invariably this is a 'fact' that is asserted with little concrete evidence beyond the obvious one that the state was intervening more in the realms of health, education and social welfare whereas private philanthropy was doing less. What these commentators have not done is look more systematically at the *resources* of charity in the post-1914 period. The questions they should have been asking were 'did the income of charities decline or rise?' and 'did the numbers of people involved in voluntary action decrease or increase?' This book only looks in detail at the war and its immediate aftermath but it is clear that neither resources nor activity fell. We should not be surprised at this. In the post-1945 euphoria, following the full creation of the welfare state, there were many, especially on the left, who confidently predicted the death of charity. With institutions like the National Health Service and free education, they argued, what would be the need? Inevitably though standards change, the material possessions of the poorest families today would be considered luxuries by those of a few decades ago and, as needs change, so does voluntary action to meet it. It will be the contention here that voluntary action did not decline; instead it adapted to new needs and new circumstances, sometimes in response to extensions in state intervention, sometimes in advance of them.

When it came the First World War acted as a catalyst to further, massive voluntary action re-enforcing many of its positive, integrative elements and, in some cases, this began to break down the class barriers that inhibited others. This was especially true for many women and Jacqueline De Vries has suggested that it was the 'pre-war membership boom in women's social, service and political organizations' that had a significant impact in that it 'provided . . . the "social capital" necessary for winning the war.'[36] This is a crucial comment and one that is examined in detail later. This involvement of women in war was something entirely new. These 'women volunteers came from a portion of society untapped in earlier wars, the vast network of organised women's groups and associations that had been growing for several decades before the turn of the twentieth century.'[37] During the war, women ran a host of voluntary organisations. Even where the nominal figurehead was a man and men dominated the executive committee, it was often the women who did the day-to-day work, and it was not only leisured middle and upper class women who acted in this capacity.

The wider impact of the pre-1914 explosion of organised sports clubs, boys' organisations, clubs, societies, associations and women's organisations is beyond the scope of this book but the influence of pre-war voluntary action during the war itself was profound. Not only did it predispose a large cross-section of society—especially the upper-working and middle classes—towards charitable endeavours, it had many other effects. These ranged from the positive and progressive, unified bodies working across class boundaries, to the less altruistic, including restrictive trade union measures to prevent the use of unskilled, especially female, labour. Most often, the positive predominated. The massive voluntary effort of 1914–18 was the basis of a strength in social capital that gave Britain a distinct edge over her main adversary, Germany. In Britain voluntary action survived and even flourished under the somewhat half-hearted attempts at state control both during and after the war. In Germany state control under military direction after 1916 stifled what began as an almost equal flow of voluntary effort.

The unique and cataclysmic nature of the war also brought about a greater fusion, or integration, of the two elements of voluntary action breaking down many of the barriers that had previously existed, most often identified through class differences. This integration was sometimes quite explicit and deliberate but more often, accidental and unstated. Nevertheless, many of the voluntary and charitable movements of the war years combined the two impulses, often in harmonious partnership but occasionally producing class or culture clashes that had repercussions at national level. It was often where integrative partnership broke down that state intervention was required. After the war, though there was a moving apart of the trends, the two strands were never as distinct again. The developments in voluntary action through the years of war also cemented the transformation of the accepted view of what charity was 'for'. In 1914, the Victorian view of charity as being there to treat the worst excesses of the industrial state probably had equal status with the more modern conception that charity should treat underlying causes. By 1918 the new idea, which was much more comfortable with charity working hand-in-hand with state welfare, had decisively gained the upper hand.

Case Study 1
Newspaper and Sporting Appeals

The First World War occurred after the bulk of the population became literate and before the era of radio and television. Newspapers therefore played a highly significant role in communication and their influence on public opinion during the war was significant. In 1914 total sales for the eleven national daily newspapers were over 4.5 million. If one includes evening papers the figure reaches 5,890,000.[1] If one assumes two or three readers per copy 'most of Britain's adult population came within Fleet Street's orbit.'[2]

As in the Boer War patriotic articles and numerous press-initiated appeals stimulated philanthropic efforts. It was good for circulation and helped:

> Keep in touch with readers at home and at the front, and of course show their patriotism. They were often for cigarettes and tobacco for local lads at the front, although the *Daily Telegraph's* was for Belgian refugees. *Sporting Life's* appeal was, naturally enough, for footballs, boxing gloves, and playing cards. And *Musical News* intended to send out mouth organs.[3]

The appeal by the London *Evening Standard* was typical in that it supplied eleven million cigarettes as well as 50,000 tins of Nestlés milk, even if their published testimony from the front under the by-line 'A Sergeant's Letter' smacked a little of hyperbole:

> Dear Readers of the *Evening Standard*,—Your very welcome present of milk has been received by the N.C.O.'s and men of the 27th Div. Supply Column. I can assure you that it will always be remembered. Twice a day, for the next few days (and long after). We shall think of you when we drink our tea, sweetened and made by your generous gift.[4]

The *Standard* also raised the funds to found the St Nicholas Home for Raid Shock Children, opened in Chailey, Sussex, in 1917. Here 590 London children recuperated from the effects of the Gotha bombing raids, one of the first responses to this new form of warfare.[5] The *Daily Graphic's* scheme was a little different with a concentration on providing greatcoats for Boy Scouts on patrol duties on the East Coast (which realised £1,880 in two weeks) and assisting sick and injured horses through the Royal Humane Society (which collected £7,300). The *Daily Sketch* 'collected over 20,000,000 cigarettes, a quarter of a million pairs of socks, ten thousand "Jack Tar tins" (each worth five shillings), forty-two thousand scarves, and hosts of other articles.'[6]

As one reads more about troop comforts or soldiers' diaries and memoirs it sometimes seems that the First World War was fought on Woodbines. Probably the leading tobacco fund was the Smokes Soldiers and Sailors Fund which distributed 492 million cigarettes and 456,000 pounds of tobacco during the war.[7] Cigarettes may not have done much for the men's long-term health but even if this had been appreciated it would have been the last thing on a soldier's mind and gifts of cigarettes were clearly hugely appreciated, and not only by the soldiers. So vast was the increase in cigarette consumption during the war that it had brought in more than £1 million in additional tax to the exchequer by April 1915.

Inevitably, many of the newspaper schemes had more than an eye on publicity or taking advantage of a commercial link-up than in discovering and meeting the real needs of servicemen. The *Daily Express* 'Cheery Fund', under the management of 'Orion', was certainly successful. By July 1915 it had supplied (among other things) 18,000 sets of boxing gloves, footballs and mouth organs; 10,000 handkerchiefs; 2,500 games and puzzles; 600 briar pipes; 520 cricket bats and balls; 700 whistles; 66 violins; 60 banjos; 28 auto-harps; harmoniums; roller-skates; golf outfits and fishing tackle. The stated purpose of the fund was 'to oblige everybody at the front who asks for things, and cheer up those who do not want anything.'[8] This hints not a little of disorganisation and you can perhaps hear the poor soldier at the front saying 'Oh no, not another harmonium / pair of roller-skates / pair of plus fours.' As with some press appeals today the connection between what was supplied and the actual needs of the beneficiaries could be out of line. This problem was significantly addressed following the establishment of the DGVO in late 1915 who stuck much more closely to what the men really needed. The list compiled by one PoW was probably fairly accurate in its priorities: boots, socks, underclothes, flannel shirts, tobacco, cigarettes, chocolate, packs of cards, Keating's Powder (a contemporary insecticide), books, and Coal Tar or Carbolic soap.[9]

Local newspaper appeals spread throughout the country and the social commentator and journalist W.E. Dowding noted in June 1915 that, though much smaller, their contributions were just as valuable, perhaps more valuable, in cementing a sense of involvement in the war effort in communities up and down the land.[10] Local papers were perhaps better able to coordinate men's requests with actual supplies. The *Croydon Advertiser*, for example, ran a regular column in 1915 of 'Tommie's Wants' with individual requests for items from troops. These relied on the requests actually reaching the paper, but it was at least less haphazard. Typical examples included a wristwatch for a hospital orderly or an electric torch for an artilleryman as well as the usual musical instruments and footballs. In addition, newspapers played an extremely important role in advertising, often at no charge, the activities of other wartime charities. Dowding, himself the treasurer of a war charity, recognised that 'the editors of our British newspapers have played a fine part. Without publicity the war funds could never have been raised: and publicity has been given with more open-handed generosity than any of the organisers of funds could ever have believed possible.'[11]

As befitted sport's popularity and status in society games equipment was a popular theme of many appeals, often run by sports bodies and clubs. Both Liverpool and Everton sent footballs and kit to fans in France and the MCC sent cricket equipment to seventy-six military and naval units, as well as to prisoners of war.[12] As the issue of disabled servicemen became more prominent the Football Association established a fund for wounded or disabled footballers and the dependants of those killed. It transferred its existing Benevolent Fund into the scheme in February 1918 and, within a year, the Football National War Fund exceeded £13,000.[13] There were regular collections at matches or donations of gate money, sometimes raising substantial amounts. In the first post-war season the two games between Everton and Nottingham Forest realised £1,418 and in 1920 half the proceeds of the Charity Shield between West Bromwich Albion and Spurs, £1,414, were donated to the FA Fund. Annual payments to veterans were around £1,200 a year in the early 1920s but had fallen to about £800 towards the end of the Fund's life in 1938, when it reverted to its original purpose of assisting any former footballer in need. The FA's scheme may have come about partly to atone for what many saw as its tardy response to the outbreak of war. Unlike amateur-dominated sports like cricket, professional football was not halted in 1914 and continued to be played until the end of April the following year. The fact that the clubs had contracts with players until the end of the season was not thought a sufficient excuse and football was compared unfavourably with other sports such as cricket, rugby and rowing.

More unusual were the fund-raising efforts of women's football teams. Women's football blossomed during the war, especially at munitions factories, and they often utilised their matches for fund-raising purposes. Teams associated with the Armstrong Whitworth Company (of whom there were six from the Scotswood locomotive factory alone) raised in excess of £1,500 for war charities over three seasons up to the Armistice and after the war the famous women's team, Dick Kerr's Ladies, from Preston, was founded for the object of helping ex-PoWs.[14]

3 The Outbreak of War and Early Charitable Efforts

In the first weeks following the outbreak of war two immediate and significant problems were the focus of attention for charitable and fundraising efforts. The first was the initial depressive effects of the war on British industry and the second the influx of thousands of refugees from Belgium. In many ways, these first responses also set the pattern for the sometimes uneasy relationship between voluntary and official action that was to characterise the entire war. The effect of rapid increases in prices and unemployment affected mainly two categories of people—firstly, the needy dependants of servicemen, especially reservists and territorials and, shortly thereafter, those of volunteers and secondly, those whose trades had been disrupted such as cotton workers, builders or those working on luxury goods. Parliament saw unemployment as their first concern and on 4 August a Cabinet Committee was established under the chairmanship of Herbert Samuel, President of the Local Government Board (LGB), 'to advise on the measures necessary to deal with any distress that may arise in consequence of the war'. A special department was formed at the LGB and it quickly began to organise work at local level. Local authorities were called on to form their own committees with representatives of the municipal authorities, boards of poor law guardians, trades unions and philanthropic organisations. Four sub-committees, dealing with London, Agricultural Districts, Urban Housing and Women's Employment, quickly followed with their individual remits. Unemployment amongst women was more serious than amongst men as they were overrepresented in both the cotton and luxury goods trades and by September nearly a million were unemployed or on short time.[1] Disastrous, and long-term, unemployment was widely expected to follow the outbreak of war by those of all political hues. Ramsay MacDonald warned that 'there are places like West Ham, where the whole population will encamp on the doorstep of the workhouse before the month is over.'[2] In fact, concern about the depressive effects of the war proved unfounded. Very quickly, the agricultural sub-committee was disbanded 'owing to the absence of distress among the rural population.'[3] Even in the parts of the country thought most likely to be affected, such as the cotton towns of Lancashire, the situation was not anything like as serious as had been expected. After 'a good deal of unemployment in the first few months of the War, the contrary proved to be the fact later, and the cotton trade, particularly the heavy goods section ... experienced a period of prosperity such as had never been known before.'[4] By the end of the year Samuel's Committee was able to report that 'happily, the fears of a widespread dislocation of trade which were entertained in some quarters at the beginning of the War have not been realised. Except in a few districts and in a few particular industries unemployment has proved to be much less serious than was anticipated.'[5]

The various measures undertaken were very much an extension of the social welfare principles already employed by the Liberal government and, though charities assisted, were met largely through government action. The wartime depression of employment was a temporary phenomenon and 'the period of depression in England that followed the outbreak of war gradually disappeared as industry adapted itself to new demands [and] early in the year 1915 a shortage of labour rather than unemployment had become a matter of public concern.'[6]

PATERNALISTIC PHILANTHROPY—THE NATIONAL RELIEF FUND

The situation regarding dependants of servicemen was more problematic, partly because it was not the province of a single government department. Both the War Office and Home Department had some responsibility and coordination between them was often fraught as was the case later with the regulation of charities. On the outbreak of war the only organisation concerned with allowances and pensions for servicemen and their dependants was the Commissioners of the Royal Hospital at Chelsea. Their rates of relief remained unchanged from the Boer War and the massive demands of the new conflict were way beyond their means. The only other source of immediate help came through local Poor Law Guardians and the existing mechanisms, rules and rates of relief were again unsuited to such emergency needs. There were also two other charitable organisations in existence who provided some assistance to servicemen's families, the Soldiers' and Sailors' Family Association (SSFA) and the Soldiers' and Sailors' Help Society, but on the outbreak of war they had very few resources.

It was clear that if something were to be done quickly this would have to be through charitable means. Indicating the somewhat haphazard and spontaneous response to the outbreak of war there were *two* royal appeals. The first on 6 August was under the name of the Prince of Wales for a National Relief Fund (NRF), whereas the second, on behalf of his grandmother, Queen Alexandra, was specifically for the SSFA. This rather embarrassing situation was quickly remedied when on 11 August it was agreed to amalgamate the two schemes under an Executive Committee.[7] Though the Fund was established to help alleviate all distress caused by the war, in practice 60 percent of the proceeds were directed towards naval and military distress.[8] The NRF utilised the network of 300 Local Relief Committees established by the LGB in towns with a population of 20,000 or more, or counties for smaller population centres, to coordinate relief efforts. These committees, though closely involved with the NRF, were also at liberty to raise their own funds and were not centrally controlled.[9] They had significant autonomy and this could lead to disagreements with the NRF in London. In some areas, due to the boom in industry later in 1915, their work became less critical though their early efforts were considerable. One such area, Todmorden (then in Lancashire, now in West Yorkshire), was typical in this regard where the council responded by calling a public meeting on 14 August to elect a Relief Committee and set the fund going by utilising £104 left over from the Distress Fund raised at the time of the Boer War. The meeting provided a foretaste of many of the NRF's future problems in that the proceedings were lively on the question of the constitution of the committee with significant debate regarding the representation of capital and labour but 'eventually a large and representative committee was appointed.'[10] They unanimously agreed to join the national scheme and to request an immediate £250 grant to meet urgent cases but later also agreed to form a local fund that eventually raised four times the amount contributed by the NRF. Initially the committees had a great deal of work. 'During September, October and November the Central Committee sat every night dispensing relief, except Saturdays and Sundays, the meetings usually lasting from 6.30 to ten o'clock or later.' However, the Mayor was able to announce on 4 December that 'for the time being no further subscriptions were required as the fund in hand was sufficient for some time to come.'[11] The subscriptions to that date were £1,904 16s towards the local fund and £549 18s 5d for the National Fund.

Though some charity leaders, in the existing COS, Guild of Help and Social Welfare movement, were quick to see that the local representation committees had major implications for the relationship between charity and the state there was no existing national organisation that could identify and recommend potential beneficiaries and administer the NRF on the ground.[12] This role was vital, as the increase in work was so massive with 'the number of wives in receipt of allowances at the outbreak of war [increasing] in a fortnight from 1,500 to 250,000.'[13] The only bodies that fitted the bill were the previously mentioned SSFA, created in 1885 to help support dependants of those participating in the Egyptian expeditionary force, and the even smaller Soldiers' and Sailors' Help Society, formed in 1899. They became highly significant social welfare networks within a short time from the outbreak of war. Elizabeth Macadam, no great lover of unregulated charitable activity, praised the mobilization of the SSFA saying that 'the resurrection of this moribund body at lightning speed is one of the triumphs in the history of voluntary effort.'[14] Just how rapid this increase was is revealed by its work in Liverpool where 'the Soldiers' and Sailors'

Family Association rose from a body of 13 members . . . to a body with 29 district heads, some 700 voluntary workers and an expenditure of £1,000 a week within the first few weeks of war.'[15]

The system was a somewhat uneasy alliance for many reasons, not least the confusion between entitlements and charitable gifts. Marwick has called the NRF 'an attempt to integrate private charity and public appeal into Government action' but this led to an unsurprising backlash when Labour leaders criticised the SSFA for treating payments as charity, to be given only if working class women met their expectations of good behaviour.[16] They insisted the money was a right and should be administered by the state. Most of the fieldwork for the SSFA was done by middle class 'lady visitors' who 'acted as the advocates, disciplinarians, trouble-shooters, and morality police of soldiers' wives.'[17] There was considerable debate and controversy as to whether benefits should be extended to 'unmarried wives' and whether they should be withdrawn if women were found to be spending too much time in public houses.[18] Not surprisingly many women resented this intrusion and the officious and patronising manner of some visitors. Even more outrage was caused when the police were given powers to supervise the conduct of soldiers' wives as, in the words of Harold Baker MP (Financial Secretary at the War Office), a 'timely warning to those particular individuals who would by misconduct forfeit their allowances.'[19] To the members of the WNC Baker's tone conveyed the very worst aspects of outdated philanthropy and provoked an angry resolution protesting against the order which they characterised as a document 'full of gratuitous insult to all British women and to every man fighting for his country [and which] holds the women of Great Britain up to the contempt of all other nations.'[20] Even at this early stage in the war, it was clear that these attitudes could not be maintained and, with working class support considered essential, the order was not carried out. Despite a continuing uneasy relationship between labour and the NRF, the left did see some merit in its method of organisation. The *Daily Herald* wanted to make local relief committees into 'citizen organisations', rather than mere dispensers of charity.[21] This was a far-sighted comment. The committees did become more representative and inclusive and gave the working class an entrée to local corridors of power. The initial NRF mistake of failing to include trade unionists and other representatives of working people was, generally, not repeated. As the war went on, working class membership of official committees at both local and national level became the rule rather than the exception, for example with conscription tribunals and war pensions committees.

Because the NRF was not state controlled, the exact remit and powers of the SSFA were also ill-defined. Individual branches or even individual officials had wide discretion in how they applied the funds and this led to major inconsistencies. The other main problem, one still common to emergency appeals to this day, was that of delays in the distribution of the funds. There was even criticism that the Fund itself was unsure of its role and wasteful of resources with 'business firms [pouring] money into the fund, some several times repeating donations of thousands of pounds, notwithstanding the fact that nobody knew for what object it was all to be used.'[22] By April 1915 the NRF had realised the remarkable sum of £5 million but only £2 million had been handed out. Both the press and the WNC persisted in their criticism and some of the more militant areas outside England were on the verge of open revolt at the dictates of the London-based body.[23] Something of a crisis was reached in April 1915 when the South Wales Miners' Federation decided to discontinue contributions and Glasgow declared independence, setting up its own fund because they were dissatisfied with NRF administration.[24] Despite placatory letters from the Prince of Wales himself to the Lord Provost of Glasgow, the die had been cast and movement towards full state intervention followed. A Select Committee, under Sir George Murray, was established which recommended that 'the care of soldiers and sailors disabled in the war should be assumed by the State.'[25] His report led to the Naval and Military War Pensions Act of 1915 and in 1916 the Ministry of Pensions also took over the administration of separation allowances. There were still some clashes, both over the use of funds and when the new state-controlled system 'borrowed' money from the NRF to meet its early obligations.[26] Though the WNC was unable to fully overturn either of these decisions their criticisms were being taken far more seriously by the government who realised the problems of the NRF and its ad hoc nature. Increasingly thereafter, the state was assumed to be the natural home for such major issues.

The National Relief Fund was too much an expression of outdated approaches impinging on an area ripe for integration into the embryonic welfare state. More than anything else it was the moral issue of paternalistic middle and upper class 'do-gooders' passing judgement that doomed the entrepreneurial approach. Even at this early stage in the war, there had been decisive changes from Victorian values of philanthropy. Women were simply not prepared to 'go through humiliating processes modelled on the charitable assessments of the Charity Organisation Society' and George Robb is therefore perfectly correct in his view that 'the traditional philanthropic ideal of moral reform was out of step with wartime democratic sentiment.'[27] Nevertheless, the NRF raised an enormous sum from all sections of society, though mainly in the early part of the war. The total was just under £7 million of which over 70 percent was raised in the first nine months.[28] It was also a significant precursor for state intervention in the social welfare field and demonstrated that even at a time of enormous expenditure on the war the British economy could sustain the cost. Separation allowances ultimately cost the government almost half a billion pounds, nearly as much as soldiers' pay, and it was 'the unprecedented circumstances of the war that had made such massive social spending possible.'[29] It could therefore be said that the NRF, by its coming under state control, brought the potential of a welfare state a step closer and, by the reaction of labour that now had to be taken far more seriously to maintain national unity, it put another nail in the coffin of paternalistic philanthropy.

'MIGHTY AND GENEROUS GREAT BRITAIN'—BELGIAN REFUGEE RELIEF

'The readiest opportunity for private philanthropy was provided from the very beginning of the war by the Belgian refugee problem.'[30] The response to this influx demonstrates many similar aspects to wider issues of voluntary and philanthropic activity during the Great War. There was an initial explosion of voluntary effort, some attempts at coordination and, later, state intervention, partly in reaction to expressions of public disquiet. In common with the NRF, the coordination of relief began with private enterprise but increasingly came under state direction. However, unlike the case of the NRF much of the voluntary effort was immediate, spontaneous and 'bottom-up' rather than initiated from above. The first work of registering Belgian refugees and of providing French and Flemish interpreters was done by a voluntary organisation—the London Society for Women's Suffrage, a branch of the National Union of Women's Suffrage Societies (NUWSS); 'it provided 150 interpreters for this work in a few days, and work was carried on at all the London Centres from early morning till midnight.'[31] The example of the NUWSS was quickly followed by many others so that 'within a matter of days of the first refugees arriving, a network of relief charities sprang up, most of which were very small and only cared for one or two Belgian families, usually in houses donated by local well-wishers.'[32] Very quickly there was more concerted action. On 24 August two eminent women, Lady Flora Lugard and Dame Edith Lyttleton, joined forces with Viscount Herbert Gladstone to form the War Refugees Committee (WRC) to coordinate relief efforts. The prominent pro-suffrage Tory peer Lord Hugh Cecil became its chairman and 'on the first day of its operation the Committee received 1,000 letters offering accommodation for the refugees, and within two weeks offers of hospitality for 100,000 people had been made by all social classes.'[33] At its peak the WRC directly employed over 500 people, virtually all of them volunteers, and there were over 2,000 local committees in existence.[34] However, the WRC suffered from the same problems as the NRF.[35] It was criticised for inefficiency and 'rapidly forfeited the advantages of massive public sympathy by its initial mistakes.'[36] It had a huge number of volunteers but was unable to organise them coherently so that many were turned away disillusioned. This is recognised as a problem in today's relief funds and was also an issue in volunteering for the army in the early days of the war. Even Viscount Gladstone described the first week of the WRC as a period of hopeless confusion.

The sheer numbers—the 265,000 Belgians in the country by June 1915 constituted the largest refugee movement in British history—coupled with the role Belgium had played in Britain's entry into the conflict ensured that there was an almost immediate government response. The first inclination of Home Secretary Reginald McKenna had been to build huge camps for the refugees, possibly in Southern Ireland.[37] This idea, with its overtones of Boer concentration camps, was rapidly dropped though some large venues were utilised. For example, Earls Court exhibition centre was in use throughout the war accommodating over 100,000 Belgians for short periods.

As early as 9 September the WRC was placed under the auspices of the LGB. The fact that the local committees formed to relieve industrial distress had less to do than anticipated meant that they could be utilised for this new role. At Herbert Samuel's suggestion, 'the machinery for relieving English victims of the war's economic disruptions was finally put to use relieving foreign victims of its military campaigns.'[38] At the same time, the government was keen to ensure that it was not seen as in any way favouring refugees over the needs of British citizens and thus discouraging voluntary activity. It therefore stressed the voluntary element in its official reports both during and after the war.[39] However this cooperation between government and the voluntary sector was another step towards the kind of partnership that many non-COS theorists had argued for and became increasingly familiar as the war continued.[40]

Despite official intervention, most organisations helping our 'gallant allies' remained entirely voluntary; 'the great majority . . . were the spontaneous creations of local people. Very often an individual or group of friends and neighbours began by offering to take refugees and then enlisted the entire community to help.'[41] This led to a mushrooming of activity with hundreds of communities across Britain establishing funds. It was again women who usually supplied the driving force for local activity and many of them had learned their trade in the pre-war campaign for the vote.[42] Folkestone, the major port of entry for refugees, became almost Belgian in character but many other towns all over the country also did their bit. One that more than pulled its weight was Croydon, south of London. A Belgian Refugee Committee was formed in the town in mid-August but, after the WRC started work, a local branch was quickly established under the official title of the Central War Refugees Committee for Croydon (CWRCC). They held their first meeting on 27 October 1914, with a view to coordinating local activity or stimulating it in areas where nothing had so far been organised. They were, however, at pains to point out that they did not want to step on the toes of existing work. The CWRCC was formed under the auspices of the Guild of Help (one of the major existing national charities for the support of the poor and needy) and their main task was finding accommodation. There was some discussion about whether or not they should fund-raise as there was initial confusion about what financial support the local authority would provide. It was ascertained from the LGB that the Corporation had no powers to use its own funds for the refugees

and so, over the next eighteen months, it was the CWRCC who were responsible. By December the Committee had assisted in establishing twenty-eight
hostels (defined as those establishments with five or more refugees) with
423 inmates and a further 139 accommodated in forty-four private houses.
These figures rose to a peak of forty-seven hostels (643 refugees) and forty-six houses (120 refugees) by 12 January 1915. The 'Greyhound' pub
was converted into a reading room with free Belgian newspapers and there
was a local branch of the refugees own organization, the 'Comité Belge',
who sought the CWRCC's assistance in acquiring wool for refugees to knit
socks for the Belgian army. Even so, support for legitimate refugees did not
always mean that the CWRCC was immune from concerns about 'dubious
foreigners'. In February 1915, they became concerned that German spies
may have infiltrated the refugee community and 'agreed that the notice
about the two families suspected of being German should be given to the
Police.' Suspicions apparently fell particularly on two girls but, before they
could be traced, they had left the area and so it is impossible to say if this
was simply a manifestation of the spy scare of the early days of the war or if
there were genuine grounds for suspicion.[43] Though the CWRCC remained
in existence until April 1919, the Committee did not hold a meeting after
April 1916, suggesting that the refugee issue had largely been solved by the
second year of war.

Even small towns far removed from the ports of entry did their bit.
Todmorden received their first refugee on 16 October and by February 1915 over fifty were accommodated in the area. Here too activities
started to run down by 1916 when 'several of the refugees returned to
Belgium, others to France, while others found employment elsewhere in
the country, with the result that by the end of 1917 very few remained in
the Borough.'[44] Not far away in Saddleworth, the first Belgian refugees
arrived 'on a black night, wearing sabots and with their worldly possessions wrapped in a large cloth, two families were welcomed by Edwin
Hudson of the Distress Committee in a language of which they understood nothing.'[45] Reaction in Saddleworth was probably typical of many
practical, but caring, working class communities:

> Although the newly established Belgian Fund had swollen consider-
> ably, it was reported that some people were hesitant about giving too
> much before they had actually seen what they were getting for their
> money. The Committee was assured that once the Belgians had been
> seen on the streets, donations would swiftly follow.[46]

There were few significant problems encountered between the British and
the Belgian refugee community though there were some examples of tension. Perhaps the most acute was in Barrow-in-Furness in 1917. It came
after some refugees purchased houses and tried to evict the tenants but this
was, perhaps, more an expression of discontent about housing conditions

than about Belgians. The Commission on Industrial Unrest visited the town and were addressed by a local magistrate:

> This is a very sore point. As sure as you and I are here, there will be Satan's row if Belgian people are allowed to buy houses and the working classes in Barrow-in-Furness are turned out into the streets. There will be a riot.[47]

After threats of strike action, Barrow was designated a special area for housing, tenants were protected and new temporary accommodation for workers were hastily constructed.

There were also some comments about the ungratefulness of certain refugees (many of them from the upper and middle classes). The good people of Eye, in Northamptonshire, had some of their confidence undermined by the indolence of a refugee family. Employing a subscription list for Belgians with weekly collections being made by Boy Scouts, they had rented a house. However, their refugees left when charitable support ceased. When the father, Pierre Sinnaghel, had refused to work, despite the intervention of a Belgian priest and Belgian schoolmaster, this was described as 'a very sad end to what was a promising beginning, and a great disappointment to those who worked so hard for them and gave so willingly of their support.'[48] Saddleworth too had its problems, finding some of its guests sullen and ungrateful.[49]

The issue of the refugees faded later in the war as other causes came to prominence and the experiences of Eye and Saddleworth were exceptions to the general rule. Of those local histories commenting on the Belgians nearly all report positive relationships, with many refugees expressing extreme gratitude for their reception. Valedictions such as the following from the de Bruyn-Vermeulen family of Antwerp are typical:

> During the ten months [of their stay] we have been able to appreciate the character of the English people, their patriotism, and their compassion for us and our unhappy countrymen. During all this time we have felt among friends, and often we forgot our sorrow. We shall always remember Britain as the country of generosity, the country of hospitality, freedom and ardent patriotism—the country that will make every Belgian refugee say:—'I have two countries—my own dear Belgium, and this country: mighty and generous Great Britain.'[50]

There were, however, few attempts at integration and the overwhelming majority of refugees, like the de Bruyn-Vermeulens, returned home after the war.

Obviously the largest number of Belgians remained at home, the vast majority behind enemy lines. As one refugee commented, those in Britain were in many ways the lucky ones: 'we were so happy in England! We were in paradise compared with those who stayed in Belgium.'[51] The huge international effort for their assistance has many similarities with Band Aid and other campaigns for famine relief in Africa today. The main driving force came from the United States under the weighty patronage of future president Herbert Hoover. Hoover established two committees on 22 October 1914: The Commission for Relief in Belgium (CRB) under American direction and the Comité de Secours et d'Alimentation (Comité National) under Belgian control. In March 1915 relief operations were extended to France and a third committee established, the Comité d'Alimentation du Nord de la France (Comité Francais), and in May 1917 a further group, the Spanish-Dutch Committee for the Protection of the Relief in Belgium and Northern France, under the Spanish Ambassador in London, was added. The CRB set themselves three tasks: provisioning of the entire population, conduct of financial relief and exchange operations and care of the destitute, of which it was estimated there were around three million out of a total civilian population of seven million. The CRB's overall fund-raising was huge, with a very significant proportion coming from Britain. Eventually they had 55,000 voluntary members on the distributing committees in all countries. The largest proportion of their income came from government sources: $387m from the United States Government, $109m from the British and $205m from the French. However, there were also significant contributions from voluntary sources with the largest cash sums donated by Britain and the Empire, $14m in cash, $3m in kind. Americans gave $6m in cash, $28m in kind.[52]

If there were few problems with individual refugees the same cannot be said about the administration of some of the charities established for the benefit of Belgium and its people. The profusion of organisations created significant difficulties. Unlike the main Belgian charities some of these bodies were on or over the borderline of legality; the WRC also clashed with the British branch of the CRB, headed by the Comte de Lalaing, the Belgian ambassador in London. The WRC lacked funds whereas the CRB did not (it was especially supported through the *Daily Telegraph's* appeal). Though there was a clear difference between the two, the former for Belgian refugees in Britain, the latter collecting funds solely for use in Belgium, many people seemed to think the two were linked or even one and the same. The outcome of this rivalry was that 'an unalterable hostility developed between the two bodies' and 'the experience with the [CRB] Fund was to spur the [War Refugees] Committee towards energetic support for the tighter control of war charities.'[53] Mirroring the concerns expressed over the NRF, the press began to find examples of what they saw as maladministration. Prominent among them was Robert Donald, editor of the *Daily Chronicle*; his leader article of 12 February 1916 proved highly influential in the debate over the control of charitable activity that followed. After investigating Belgian relief charities Donald had concluded that there were far too many of them (over fifty) and that they were run on 'exceedingly unbusiness-like lines' with no audited accounts and, often, not even a proper committee. Anyone could set up a fund and easily, it seemed, assemble an impressive list of patrons, none of whom had any idea about how the funds were being administered. He called for government action to introduce 'vetting' of Belgian relief funds and suppress those that failed to meet adequate standards.[54] Some action was taken almost immediately. The Charity Commissioners established a Belgian sub-committee and later on the LGB was given the power to regulate Belgian relief charities.[55] The LGB report on their work refers to the *Daily Chronicle* campaign, but the regulations were permissive rather than compulsory. Therefore the LGB scheme was not quite what critics had been demanding and fell well short of the *Chronicle's* plea for closer scrutiny and legislation, which led Donald to throw his weight behind calls for the regulation of all war-related charities.

The pattern set with regard to both initial distress, through the NRF, and refugees followed a similar course, which was to be repeated for later charitable efforts. There was an immediate, and significant, voluntary response to the problem with some attempts at national coordination. Later there was criticism of the operation of the bodies involved and demands for official or legislative action. As the war continued, the problems of unemployment and Belgian refugees declined and other philanthropic causes rose to prominence. These first two causes also came very much within the category of top-down philanthropy whereas many later initiatives were far closer to mutual aid or, at least, looking after one's own.

Case Study 2
'Private Tom' and Other Animals

From 1914 charities of every size and description sprang up. Some were for very specific purposes such as those for the relief of air raid victims and even potentially unpopular causes such as the dependants of conscientious objectors (though there were only two of these, one in London, the other in Watford) or distress among enemy aliens. Though there were only four bodies formed for this latter purpose one was the highly efficient Prisoners of War Information Bureau which was the official body dealing with German PoWs and internees in the UK.[1] Most charities were for humans in need but many animal casualties (especially horses) were provided for, most notably by the RSPCA Fund for Sick and Wounded Horses, Our Dumb Friends' League Blue Cross Service and the Purple Cross. There was an early dispute for recognition with the British Army but it was resolved when the Blue and Purple Cross agreed to provide their services to the French Army.[2]

Unsurprisingly the RSPCA was the largest animal charity operating during the war. There were ninety RSPCA Inspectors serving with the army who 'look after the animals they come across on the march. They tend the neglected cows. They befriend the lost dogs. They painlessly destroy starving and suffering creatures.'[3] There was even a home for lost dogs at the British Army Base at Boulogne. However, the RSPCA's main task was to help care for the hundreds of thousands of horses used by the BEF. Partly because of their work the 'wastage' of horses was reduced from the 60 per cent of the Boer War to a tenth of that figure.[4]

The National Canine Defence League (now the Dog's Trust) stepped in on the home front. By May 1915 they had provided 1,650 dog licences and were supplying regular food for 155 dogs left at home by reservists who had been called up or those who had volunteered. On 14 October 1914 they received what has to be one of the most genuine and touching letters of thanks to any wartime charity:

Dear Sir
   I now have pleasure in writing to thank you for your kindness to my wife in her recent trouble about the keep of the dog [sic] whilst I was serving my King and country in Belgium and France. Having the

misfortune to be wounded at the Battle of the Aisne on Sept. 13th, 1914, I was sent to the 5th Northern General Hospital, Leicester, for operation [sic], and then invalided home for a few days on Oct. 5th, 1914. My wife then showed me your letter telling me of your gift of food. The so-called City Aid had interviewed my wife and told her it was her duty to destroy the dog; even told her the place and fee, 1s, for destroying same, for every penny spent on food was money wasted.

Having fought at Mons and the retreat to within a few miles of Paris, our regiment had the satisfaction of saving a large number of dogs that had been forgot by their owners that had to leave their homes in a hurry and move for safety, and some of them had forgot their dogs. We had several of them follow us all through our trying time, and it would teach some of the so-called City 'Aid' Society a lesson if they could see them in the firing line with us. It was a common sight to see them lick their new owners' hands and faces and lying between our legs; they shared the same dangers as us and several of them got killed one way or another. You could not help, whilst lying there, wondering what your own dog would do, that you had brought up and taught to do your bidding. Then to receive a letter from my wife asking me what to do about destroying the dog, as the City Aid had been on to her about it. But a friend of mine had seen your advertisement in papers [sic] and told my wife about it. If you would like to show this letter to any of your subscribers you are at liberty to do so. I hope I have not took up much of your time in reading this.

I remain, yours truly

W.J. Astell

T. Company, 1st East Lancashire Regt.[5]

As Private Astell suggests, animals could even provide companionship in the trenches. Official mascots ranged from the conventional dogs or goats to the more unusual cows or even a bear, though he stayed in England and later became the model for Winnie-the-Pooh.[6]

At the end of the war the RSPCA stepped in to assist soldiers who wanted to bring back dogs they had rescued. A typical plea for help ran thus, from a Private, 1/7th London Regiment:

He has been a faithful animal to me both in holding the line and attacking. I have had him about twelve months, and he was with me all through the retirement of 1918, and with me all through the late attacks since August 1918. He has been slightly wounded twice in going over the top with me, but he has been inoculated by a friend in the RAMC each time. . . . I think he deserves to come with me, as he has stuck to me through thick and thin, and when I was wounded and could not walk he stayed with me all through the attack under a heavy barrage for nearly three hours, so you can understand how attached I am to him.[7]

The Council agreed to cover the quarantine expenses of all of these animals and built 500 special kennels for the purpose and the Society's 'Soldiers' Dog Fund', which was supported by the *Evening News*, ended the war with a surplus of £5,304.[8]

Most of the animal charities were already operating before the war and, like the RSPCA, Blue Cross and Dog's Trust, continue their work to this day. Some, including probably the most remarkable of all, were a response to the patriotic fervour the war engendered in many people. The story of the Dogs and Cats of Empire Fund is best told in the words of its founder, Maud Field, in a letter of 10 July 1915:

> In reply to your letter I shall be pleased to tell you all I can about 'The Dogs and Cats of Empire Fund'. I saw in the paper one day that the Kaiser said Germany would fight to the last cat and dog—This made me think that the dogs and cats of the British Empire ought to do something for their country—I therefore issued an appeal to them through my fox terrier 'Tom', asking every dog and cat to give 6d. There was a great response, and in four months Tom had collected £1,000 for a Y.M.C.A. Soldiers Hut at the Front. The Hut is now in full swing, it is a large double one, and I am told it is the largest and the best equipped Hut in France—Every dog or cat who gave £5 could have his or her picture hung upon the wall of the Hut—A great many sent £5. Two gramophones were also sent by dogs!
>
> I also made an album of subscribers photographs and letters to amuse the men who use the Hut—Tom's master, my brother, Captain Stephen Field, died in April as a prisoner of war at Wittenburg, and since then Tom has been collecting for British prisoners of war imprisoned in Germany—Tom's life sized picture with the inscription 'Private Tom R.A.M.C.' adorns the wall of the Hut.[9]

Subscribers to the Fund included guinea-pigs, 'Solomon a chicken hatched in October last', a cockatoo aged thirty from Argentina, 'a ginger coloured cat without a tail', a spider, sixteen horses, a 'school of teddy bears', a 'naturalised dachshund formerly called Herr Rufus von Pop' and some cocks and hens who contributed 'with much glad crowing'. It was no wonder that the *Daily Chronicle* said of the Dogs and Cats of Empire Fund 'it is, in a way, the most remarkable of all the funds which have been started since the war began.'[10]

4 Supporting Tommy
Charity Goes to War

Having responded to the initial demands caused by the threat of significant unemployment and the influx of Belgian refugees voluntary effort decisively shifted. As Britain's armies expanded exponentially, charitable activity concentrated on British and Empire troops both at the front and when they were wounded or invalided. Almost as quickly as the establishment of the NRF, other bodies, both existing and new, sprung into action. Medical supplies were a priority as the government had made few plans for supplying hospitals with necessities and providing comforts for soldiers. The Regimental Associations, British Red Cross and Order of St John performed some of these services but were soon overwhelmed by the level of need. Entire communities mobilised to support their local regiments and area hospitals with many of the early responses initiated by middle and upper class women, often the only direct way they could support the war effort. A typical example was that of the Duchess of Bedford who established a hospital at Woburn Abbey. In common with many upper class ladies this entailed something of a change from her pre-war lifestyle: 'the Duchess is herself the Matron-in-charge . . . keeps all the records, is up at half-past five in the morning, and spends her day in the endless doing, thinking and contriving that such a hospital needs.'[1] The Duchess's example was followed by many other aristocratic and landed families and Mary Ward estimated that 'altogether about 700 country houses large and small have been offered to the War Office' for use as military hospitals, rest homes for troops or other war-related functions; 112 were loaned to the Red Cross alone for such purposes.[2] Another group of privileged ladies, Americans married to Englishmen and resident in this country, established The American Women's War Relief Fund. They rapidly provided a fleet of motor ambulances, founded the American Women's War Hospital in Paignton and operated an Economic Relief Committee in London running work schemes employing 405 unemployed women producing clothing and equipment for the hospital. To support all this work they had, by August 1915, raised £62,000 in cash.

Bodies who already possessed the equipment and expertise were the first to react. Among existing organisations quickly, and literally, into the field was the Salvation Army, who dispatched an advance party to Brussels in

August 1914.[3] The YMCA too rapidly mobilised its resources calling on its previous work in South Africa. The principle architect of the YMCA's wartime mission was its dynamic national secretary, Sir Arthur Yapp, who rebranded the organisation the 'Red Triangle'. They opened more than 250 recreational centres in Great Britain within ten days of the outbreak of war and the first YMCA secretaries to serve with the BEF arrived in France long before they had received official permission from the War Office.[4] The public face of the YMCA on the home front was the dozens of huts and canteens providing free refreshments, many adjacent to main railway stations, which remained open day and night.[5] The Euston Station buffet, organised most prominently by Miss Margaret Boulton (as fund-raiser) and Miss Marietta Feuerheerd (as manager), had 30,000 customers a month by December 1915 and by 1916 there were 30,000 women working in YMCA huts at home and abroad.[6] Later in the war the Red Triangle was joined by the Blue Triangle, organised by the YWCA to support the newly created WAACs.

ROYAL PATRONAGE AND LADIES OF LEISURE

The war's most significant 'knitting and stitching' organisation was Queen Mary's Needlework Guild (QMNG) which was established immediately on the outbreak of war following the Queen's letter to the press on 4 August. Because it enjoyed royal patronage and produced a lavish history with a foreword by John Galsworthy, the QMNG is sometimes seen as the archetypal war charity.[7] It was, in fact, only partially representative of even early efforts and no more representative of the bulk of war charities than, say, Robert Graves's *Goodbye to All That* was representative of the bulk of experience of the British army.

Though its stated purpose was 'to alleviate all distress occasioned by the war', it concentrated mainly on the production and distribution of clothing and other items to servicemen and hospitals. With the prestige of the Queen's endorsement branches of the Guild blossomed all over the Empire, from Canada to Ceylon, in Britain and on the continent where there was a branch in The Hague. In November 1918 there were 630 branches with 1,078,839 members, excluding those in North America. The total production of the Guild by 1918 amounted to 15,577,911 articles with an estimated value of £1,194,318. St James's Palace was utilised as a clearing depot turning it, in the words of the Guild's official report, into an enormous 'dry-goods store'. The significant work-force of the Guild could quickly be put to use in emergencies. Following the first German gas attack at Ypres in April 1915 'workers of the Guild in St James's Palace cut, at fever-speed, three million eye-pieces for gas masks, out of cinema film.'[8] It was clear that some of the 'leisured' women who joined the Guild were unused to the work as it was commented that 'many women of these sewing parties have no idea how to put the garments together.'[9]

More serious was the potential for the work of the Guild to exacerbate unemployment amongst women working in the textile and clothing industries. There was 'vigorous opposition from the working women's organizations' to their activities as they were seen as providing many of the same items made by women who were now unemployed.[10] Opposition was also expressed by the WNC whose executive included several well-known and influential women from the Labour movement such as Mary Macarthur (of the Women's Trade Union League), Margaret Bondfield (later the UK's first female Cabinet Minister) and Susan Lawrence (of the London County Council). In a resolution drafted by Sidney Webb, the committee urged all 'benevolent persons' to 'avoid doing positive harm' by confining themselves to activities that would not impinge upon work done by working women.[11] Their reaction shows the tension that existed in these early days between well-intentioned but disorganised voluntarism and the Labour movement. The committee 'took a firm stand in opposition to appeals which were being sent out urging women to volunteer for work rendered necessary by the war when more than half a million women were out of employment.'[12] Their appeal produced a swift reaction from the Palace that would have been unlikely even a month before. On 17 August, the Guild made an announcement in the press to indicate that the intention was to work in partnership, not opposition. Representatives of working women were called in for consultation to ensure that everything possible was done to safeguard the interests of women workers.[13] The 'Queen's Work for Women Fund' was started with the funds raised being turned over to the Central Committee on Women's Employment to provide work or assistance for unemployed women. The Central Committee also began to issue contracts for the provision of army uniforms and though there were some teething problems (existing patterns had to be modified to take account of the women's inexperience) 'the result was that the manufacturing difficulties were removed, full employment in the tailoring trade began at once, and the Army Supply Department was also greatly benefited by the prompt fulfilment of orders.'[14] The Queen further poured oil on the waters by placing a personal order through the Central Committee for 75,000 woollen body belts that were to form part of her Christmas gift to the troops. These were produced by women formerly employed in the carpet trade in Kidderminster, Belfast and elsewhere who had been badly hit on the outbreak of the war.[15] Despite this, some problems remained as the wages paid to those working for the Guild were sometimes extremely low and, until the employment situation stabilised, relations between the Guild and the Labour movement remained tense.[16]

As well as the female members of the Royal Family, most of the wives of the BEF's commanders involved themselves in voluntary work. Lady Smith-Dorrien, wife of the then commander of 2nd Army, made a valuable contribution, of which the WNC did approve, as being additional to existing paid labour. In April 1915 she heard from a nurse that it was proving impossible to safeguard the valuables of sick and wounded soldiers close to the front. She contacted her husband to ask whether the supply of closable bags for this purpose would be useful and 2nd Army's Assistant Director of Medical Services, General Porter, replied in the affirmative requesting an immediate 50,000. The first depot was established in Lady Smith-Dorrien's house at 5 Eaton Gate but in 1916 moved to larger premises and a further expansion in 1917 led to another move. Besides the London HQ depots were established in Scotland, Bedford and, eventually, the U.S. with over 12,000 people contributing to the scheme. The bags themselves were initially of unbleached calico but this was soon changed, as bright colours were more easily distinguishable and popular amongst the men who gave them the nickname 'Blighty Bags'.[17] Bags were distributed through the official DGVO scheme with 40,000 a month going to Medical Stores depots and smaller quantities direct to hospitals and Casualty Clearing Stations. Activities were uninterrupted by Sir Horace's removal from his post after Second Ypres and by the war's end Lady Smith-Dorrien's Hospital Bag Fund had produced over two million items.[18]

Overall, activities led by upper class women were more typical of the early months of the war and certainly had their drawbacks. The first, the danger of voluntary labour replacing paid work, has already been noted. The second was the entirely uncoordinated nature of the activity. Both were a concern to the WNC, which was 'quick to point out the counter-productive tendencies of the rash of "Lady Bountiful" proposals to make and donate clothing and necessities to the British Army and the poor.'[19] It was thus by a slightly stumbling mix of royal patronage, voluntary effort, working class agitation and central control that the situation stabilised into a reasonably efficient, and certainly extensive, system of clothing production. QMNG was one organisation that was considered sufficiently independent, or more likely prestigious, to be excluded from the coordinating scheme undertaken by the DGVO.

EGGS FOR THE WOUNDED, CONKERS FOR THE GUNS—SCHOOLCHILDREN DO THEIR BIT

Middle class girls were also giving their time towards the national voluntary effort from the first days of the war. The Girls' Patriotic Union was formed under the auspices of the Association of Head Mistresses and by November 1914 boasted a membership of 290 Girls' High and Public Schools. The Union's first report included many activities indicative of the class of 'young ladies' involved and, though well intentioned, might not have had a significant impact on the war effort:

> Girls in a boarding school have asked that they may have no sugar in their tea. Others have asked that they may not have customary prizes.

Many have given up their weekly pocket money, thus denying themselves sweets; and so on. . . . And in some places outside hockey and
net-ball matches have been given up and the money thus saved has been
devoted to the relief of distress.[20]

Very quickly more pragmatic and effective work began to be carried out,
often in direct cooperation with less privileged partners. Schools linked
with local hospitals to provide supplies; older girls from London volunteered their time at a former workhouse processing Belgian refugees whilst
others translated newspapers for French-speaking refugees and 'one school
sends its contributions regularly to the local Labour Bureau to provide paid
employment.'[21] Later on the Girls' Patriotic Union supplied four recreation
huts for France (one each for the army, navy, airmen and the WAAC). They
also became involved in the founding of the 'greatest of the wartime charitable institutions', the 'Star and Garter' Home for Disabled Sailors and
Soldiers.[22] They raised the considerable sum of £5,500 which endowed
fourteen rooms at the new establishment in Richmond.

Schools efforts were by no means confined to the upper classes. It was not
long before every school in England was regularly and directly engaged in
war work. Even the smallest schools, such as Stanbury Board School in the
Yorkshire village of the Bronte sisters, Haworth, with a roll not far above
100, played its part. In November 1914 thirty shillings were raised by selling national flags painted by the children. In April 1915 a first hamper of
comforts for soldiers knitted by the children was despatched containing six
large scarves, three wool helmets and seven pairs of socks. The wool was
provided free of charge by a local spinner and production soon reached an
industrial scale. Knitted comforts were supplied to Keighley Military Hospital and, later in 1917, sixty soldiers from the hospital were entertained
in the school. The programme including a whist drive, tea, a walk on the
moors (conducted by the headmaster) and a concert. The appearance of
no fewer than fifteen motor cars at one time to convey the invalids caused
'quite a sensation' in the village. By the time of a visit by Miss Cockshott, a
member of the Worth Valley Education Sub-Committee, in June 1917 hundreds of under vests, mufflers, helmets, hot-water bottle covers and other
items had been sent away either to the Keighley Hospital or direct to the
front. On this visit Miss Cockshott pressed the boys to knit and sew as well
as the girls.[23]

In East Anglia the headmistress of St Matthew's District School, Ips-
wich, reported that 'the girls really put their backs into the war effort.'
On 4 August 1914 a branch of the 'League of Young Patriots' or 'Princess
Mary's League' was started and by 9 October three-quarters of the girls
had joined. They began by knitting socks for Belgian refugees but by 1916
even the youngest children were contributing directly to war production.
On 2 July (the day after the commencement of the Battle of the Somme) the
Young Patriots despatched forty-two rifle covers and forty-two sandbags.

The logbook also records that on 2 May 1917 'the First Class Girls [aged 7 and 8 years] spent the whole time in making sandbags', a task in which the boys of the school also joined. By 5 December 1917 the school could boast that 'today we have sent off the last consignment of sandbags and grenade bags, making a complete total of 931 sandbags and 2,209 grenade bags.'[24] Participation in these activities was stimulated by many visits made by servicemen to the schools they had attended. All the logbooks speak of frequent talks by soldiers either home on leave or invalided out. Many returned to thank the children for their assistance in the supply of comforts for the troops and sometimes they expressed their appreciation in more direct ways such as at Tattingstone National School, Suffolk, where a soldier and former pupil visited in December 1916 and left enough money at the village shop for every child to have a farthing's worth of sweets. In Kent, some children were even luckier when 'no doubt against all the rules, children living near Broomfield [near Maidstone] enjoyed occasional flights in exchange for cigarettes and home-made cakes.'[25]

Children even contributed to the production of explosives. It was discovered that the horse chestnut could be used as an alternative to acetone (an essential element in the manufacture of cordite) and an experimental factory was established in Kings Lynn. It was in this experiment that the children of Tattingstone participated and on 30 November 1917 'two sacks of chestnuts weighing 3 cwts 2 qrs were sent this week to the Minister of Propellants.'[26] Nobody really knew why they were collecting. The government was, naturally, reluctant to reveal the motive behind its scheme because the Germans could very well copy this novel form of production. A question was asked in the House of Commons but the answer given simply stated that they were required for 'certain industrial purposes' and promoted as aiding food production rather than killing Germans. The veil of secrecy drawn over the horse chestnut's final use even led to accusations that voluntary effort was being used to provide personal profit.[27] The horse chestnut scheme was not one of the great successes of the war. Despite somewhere between 3,000 and 4,500 tons being collected, the Propellant Supplies Branch of the Ministry of Munitions was slow to organise the collection from depots and the Board of Education received many complaints. Corsham Council School in Wiltshire alone collected seven-and-a-quarter tons but their county authority wrote to the Board on 31 January 1917 stating that, owing to the failure to collect the nuts, 'the children are greatly disappointed, and will obviously attempt similar efforts in the future with reluctance.'[28] As a result, only 3,000 tons reached the King's Lynn plant and letters in *The Times* tell of piles of rotting horse chestnuts at railway stations. Another accusation that the Ministry of Munitions and Board of Education had to scotch was that the nuts were being used in the production of poison gas.[29] Even so the chestnut scheme spread nationwide, and beyond schoolchildren collectors, as the Croydon War Supplies Clearing House minutes for 21 November 1917 show when 'it was reported that 4-and-a-half tons of acorns and chestnuts had been collected.'[30] It is likely that the acorns would have ended up as pig feed, but perhaps not, as they too could be utilised for acetone production. On 7 September 1917 a conference was held between officials of the Agriculture Food Production Department, Sir Frederick Nathan of the Ministry of Munitions, Captain Desborough of the Admiralty and Mr Ainsworth of the Board of Education. The Admiralty thought acorns potentially even more productive than chestnuts and both they and Munitions wanted to utilise schoolchildren in their collection. Mr Ainsworth resisted this as there would be payment by the Ministry to farmers and his superiors supported him. Clearly it was acceptable for children to be involved in explosives production but not if it was a commercial scheme.[31] An unintended outcome of the chestnut programme was an inundation of suggestions to the Board of Education for collecting dozens of other products that correspondents considered beneficial to the war effort. Some of these were relatively sensible, for example, sweet or Spanish chestnuts as a food source, but it was difficult to think of a use for the stalks of Jerusalem artichokes recommended by the Rev C.R. Garnett-Botfield of Oswestry.[32] Unsurprisingly, the great chestnut collection was not repeated in autumn 1918.[33]

Rather more prosaic was the cultivation or collection of food products. On 24 July 1918 R.H. Carr of the Ministry of Food wrote to the Secretary of the Board of Education asking that children become involved in the systematic collection of blackberries and offering 'substantial remuneration' of 1d per pound.[34] This time the Board overcame their scruples regarding commercial operations (no doubt because there was no private intermediary) and so agreed to the proposal and children were released from school to take part, but not for more than three half-days. One school, Tattingstone, reported that 'half a day [was] given this afternoon under the National Blackberry Scheme. The result was very good. 364lbs being sent to Burton and Saunders [a factory in Ipswich].'[35] By far the largest of the food schemes involving schools was the National Egg Collection to provide fresh eggs for wounded soldiers. Started in November 1914 it reached a peak of 1.4 million eggs a week. One hundred thousand honorary collectors, many of them from schools or members of the Scouts, Guides or Church Lads' Brigade collected these at over 2,000 centres. Often the children wrote short messages or just their name and address on the eggshells and received notes of thanks back from the men on the receiving end of the gifts. Typical was this from a Wiltshire soldier pleased to get a reminder of home:

> In the battle of . . . I had the misfortune to be shot through the head; I was taken to hospital, and after being made comfortable in bed my first meal consisted of an egg bearing your address, and as I come from Wootton Bassett I thought I must write and thank you for it. I wish you could see the joy on the poor fellows' faces when they get the eggs; it would fully repay you for all your trouble. Again thanking you, Yours truly, T. Tucker.[36]

One girl, Kathleen Sawyer from Swindon, was surprised to receive an egg-shell back from France in 1917 from an egg that had been eaten by her own uncle and the 3 November edition of the campaign's magazine *Eggs Wanted* carried a picture of Kathleen on its front cover holding her uncle's eggshell. Wounded soldiers got a steady supply of nourishing food from various voluntary sources though sometimes it might have proved just a little too rich if the efforts of Lord Selborne and Edward Carson (among others) in September 1915 was anything to go by. They helped amass 3,000 brace of grouse, partridge and pheasants for war hospitals, perhaps reserved for officers.

Outside school, the war gave the uniformed boys' organisations even greater scope for direct contributions with Baden-Powell's Scouts in the forefront. Their duties included guarding against sabotage, acting as messengers, organising relief measures, establishing first aid and dressing or nursing stations, assisting refugees and soup kitchens, working as bellboys on Birmingham's trams, helping with the flax harvest and acting as air raid wardens. All of which helped release large numbers of men for more urgent tasks and for military service.[37] Upper and middle class boys from the public and endowed grammar schools also carried out a huge range of war work. The High Master of Manchester Grammar School listed just some of the activities taken up by his pupils by mid-1916, noting that those in the Boy Scouts were most prominent in the work. They included acting as orderlies in recruiting offices and hospitals; Saturday collections of waste paper; coastguard patrols; distributing recruiting posters; manufacturing leg rests, bedside tables and other items to furnish a house for Belgian refugees; packaging troop comforts; forgoing school prizes to donate funds to the Red Cross and YMCA and postal work at Christmas. For the last of these they were paid 6d an hour but donated much of this to funding a Scouts motor ambulance for France. In the summer holidays they worked in munitions, in YMCA huts or at fruit picking and they even made artificial limbs in the school workshops.[38] By replacing men in this way, Scouts performed some of the same roles as women during the war and if a young woman was not clipping your tram ticket a Scout was probably doing so. There is no doubt that the Scouts played a very significant part in the war and Paul Wilkinson goes so far as to consider that 'it is no exaggeration to say that Kitchener's New Army depended on a boy-scout spirit and resourcefulness for its morale, and on the dissemination of public school loyalties and values among lower middle-class and working-class men.'[39]

Some individual children went even further. In Burnley, Lancashire, two young girls performed heroic deeds on behalf of local charities. Amy Foster became known as the 'Hieland Lassie' on account of the Highland costume she wore when collecting funds for soldiers' parcels. One of eleven children of Teddy and Maud Foster, Amy also worked tirelessly for St Dunstan's both during and after the war. Jennie Jackson, daughter of a miner from Towneley Colliery, was born in 1907 and, as 'Little Kitchener', became

Figure 4.1   Jennie Jackson, 'Little Kitchener'.

Figure 4.2 Amy Foster, the 'Hieland Lassie'.

perhaps the best-known child fund-raiser of the war. 'Her role began when, shortly after the outbreak of war, her mother saw two soldiers sharing a cigarette while walking in Towneley Holmes, which prompted her to think of ways of supplying tobacco to the men in the trenches.'[40] Her mother Kate made a perfect replica military uniform for Jennie and, after gaining permission from the Chief Constable, Jennie began collecting coppers at the corner of Market and St James's Streets but soon gravitated to touring local pubs, clubs and factories as well. Her phenomenal success was such that in February 1916 Jennie decided to collect for a field ambulance, which was built in Burnley and handed over to the army by Queen Alexandra, with Jennie proudly present. In all she raised a total of £4,000 (roughly equivalent to £200,000 today) and received the War Medal of the British Red Cross Society. At the 1919 Great March of Peace in London Jennie received her highest honour, becoming the only child to be permitted to join the march and witnessing the unveiling of the Tomb of the Unknown Warrior in Westminster Abbey. Her mother went on to become head of the women's section of the Royal British Legion in Burnley and Jennie herself lived to the age of eighty-nine, dying in 1997.[41]

TECHNIQUES AND TYPES OF SUPPORT

One needs to draw a distinction between the work done by organisations new to the field (such as Lady Smith-Dorrien's Fund, newspapers or school-children) and those undertaken by existing charities, often national bodies (like the Red Cross). Existing organisations, like the NUWSS and the YMCA, were in a much better position to refocus their activity to war help and the improvisation so typical of the early months of the war was far easier for bodies with an existing organisation and trained volunteers. You could perhaps equate these two strands of charity with the small, but well-trained and organised, regular Army of 1914 as against the hastily impro-vised and, initially, enthusiastic rather than efficient Kitchener battalions.

In all there was an enormous range of charitable activity undertaken, but with a significant bias towards comforts for troops and medical supplies. There were also very significant local variations in the nature and type of support. For example, in December 1919 Croydon had nineteen organiza-tions registered under the War Charities Act. They included four of a gen-eral nature (including the Croydon War Supplies Clearing House); three for Belgian refugees; three workplace related; two for the Red Cross; two for hospitals and one each church related, for Christmas gifts, for children and a local branch of the Comrades of the Great War. Todmorden, though one-sixth the size of Croydon, had twenty-eight: seven for soldiers' comforts (there was less coordination than in Croydon); six for general purposes; five church related; four workplace related; two each for hospitals and Belgian refugees and one each politically connected, for the YMCA and a Sewing

Table 4.1   Main Categories of War Charities

Comforts for British and Empire Troops	28%
Medical support (including hospitals and supplies)	25%
Support for disabled servicemen	13%
Relieving distress at home	11%
Post-war remembrance and celebration (including war memorials)	9%
Aid for refugees and overseas	8%
Assistance to prisoners of war	7%

Source: War Charities Act 1916: Index of Charities Registered under the Act to March 1919 (London: HMSO, 1919).

Guild.[42] Todmorden also had no fewer than seventy-two unregistered war charities in addition. Unregistered charities were smaller organisations usually confined to the employees of a single street, a church or chapel or a workplace and they were far more numerous in industrial, working class areas (Croydon only had a handful). Of those in Todmorden, eleven were based on a single street or small neighbourhood, nineteen on churches and no fewer than thirty-eight on workplaces. By the end of the war charities fell into the main categories indicated in Table 4.1.

Between them these organisations used an astonishing range of fundraising techniques, many still in use today, such as flag days, which, though not invented during the First World War, mushroomed after 1914. Direct mail to potential donors was used for the first time to any significant extent. The YMCA and Church Army employed it extensively to attract donors along with leaflets proclaiming '£25 will buy this, £50 that' etc. Subscription lists (which had a long history) were published for many of the larger funds in the national press, most notably for *The Times* appeal, thus acting as an incentive to the better off to keep up with their peers and payroll giving, though again not new, increased significantly. In Birmingham weekly collections were made in most of the large factories and 50,000 people contributed over £20,000 to the NRF.[43] Those employed by the City Council in Manchester utilised a similar method, 'the officials taxing themselves on the amount of their salaries, the taxes varying from 2¾ to 5 per cent.'[44]

The annual *Times* 'Our Day' in aid of the Red Cross was a forerunner of appeals like Comic Relief and Children in Need, a single day on which everyone was expected to do something for charity, the more unusual or eye-catching the better. Dressing up in silly clothes, performing prodigious feats of endurance or eating for charity is by no means a modern invention.[45] Our Day was not just a British affair as activities took place throughout the Empire. Though the Dominions were most prominent, other countries also played a part. For example, in the Dutch East Indies the Samarang and Mid-Java committee raised 78,372 guilders in 1917, a total they were determined to better a year later. So on Saturday 19 October 1918 at 9pm they held a 'Concert and English Comedy' which comprised songs followed by a production of *The Importance of Being Earnest*. Britain's allies joined in the fun with Algernon being played by M.R. Dubois St Marc, Chef Francais of Peek and Co. Helpfully the committee provided a plot synopsis in Dutch. Fund-raising from overseas was commonplace. In addition to the significant national examples already given (such as Our Day and the American Women's War Relief Fund) there were many small-scale local groups. To support the efforts in Saddleworth a Colne Valley Society was established in Holyoke, Massachusetts, by a former Saddleworth painter and decorator, William Escott. Escott's relatives in Saddleworth and Mossley were serving in the 7/Dukes and, in late 1916, he and his supporters collected £25 to endow a bed in Netley Hospital. There were still sufficient funds remaining to send to Saddleworth for distribution to sick and wounded soldiers of the district.[46]

At the other end of the scale came some of the massive events of the Red Cross, including a number of sales of donated valuables at Christies. The 1915 sale brought in £50,000 but the largest of all was in 1918 over a period of sixteen days from Monday 8 to Thursday 25 April. It included porcelain, silver, jewels, furniture, sculpture, manuscripts (including a Beethoven score and letters from the Brontes, Dickens, Elizabeth I and Nelson), drawings and etchings (including a collection donated by the King) and many paintings. These included works from old masters, such as Gainsborough's *Portrait of Captain Thomas Cornewall* and Bassano's *Christ Mocked* donated by the Duke of Norfolk, through giants of the Victorian era such as Lord Leighton, Burne-Jones, Alma-Tadema's *The Staircase* and G.F. Watts's *Ariadne in Naxos* to contemporary artists such as William Orpen, Augustus John, Glyn Philpot and C.R.W. Nevinson. The final two were available for hire to the highest bidder to produce a specially commissioned work. Philpot, perhaps best known today for his striking portrait of Siegfried Sassoon, offered to do a portrait whereas the often irascible Nevinson would paint anything 'except a pet Pekinese or a fashionable portrait.'

Pageants with plenty of dressing up were extremely popular and often highly elaborate. These also had the bonus of being able to mobilise the entire community from the youngest to oldest, often playing patriotic characters like Britannia or Robin Hood but also with villains, most notably the Kaiser himself, portrayed as well. In an era where people were used to producing their own entertainment and many could sing or play an instrument such fund-raisers were a natural recourse. Then there were the slightly more quirky ideas. For example, 'women all over the country subscribed in name-groups, according to their initials, from A to Z, so that each group might give money or present an ambulance, a bed or a canteen. . . . The Marys subscribed a fully-equipped motor kitchen.'[47] Examples involving animals give a flavour as to just how memorable these quirkier ideas could be. In Wiltshire it was noted that 'everyone will recollect the interest excited in the streets of Swindon when Mr Hoare appeared with his Shetland pony, "Kitty", who soon became quite proud of her collecting-box and the attentions lavished upon her, or when Mr Tarrant turned out with his organ and monkey.'[48] However, for inventiveness and generosity it would be difficult to beat the example of Forfar's 'Mons Cat':

> There were many novel ways and devices for raising funds at the Free Gift Sales, but few were as popular and effectual as the repeated sale of the Mons Cat. This cat was found at an old farmhouse near St Quentin and came unscathed through nine engagements including Hill 60. It was brought to Forfar from Belgium by a wounded soldier and purchased by Mr William Lamond, cattle dealer, South Street. It was 'snowballed' at all the sales and always bought back by Mr Lamond himself. The cat had to its credit, thanks to the generosity of its owner and others, no less than £3,000.[49]

As this would today be the equivalent of around £150,000 this was some cat.

Case Study 3
'My Good Lady, Go Home and Sit Still'—Militant Women

Alongside Irish independence, the outstanding piece of unfinished politi-cal business on the outbreak of war was the question of women's suffrage. As Marwick has noted, 'one of the most interesting psychological phe-nomena of the war is the way in which the suffragettes, who for ten years had been waging war on the Government and the community, now out-shone everyone in their patriotic fervour and stirring appeals for national unity and endeavour.'[1] Whilst a minority of feminists formed part of the pacifist opposition throughout the war the majority of suffragists flung themselves wholeheartedly into war work. This caused a split in the more militant of the major suffragist organisations, the Women's Social and Political Union (WSPU). Sylvia Pankhurst voiced stringent opposition to the war but most of the rest, including her mother, Emmeline, and sister Christabel, ranged with the patriots. Sylvia formed her own Workers' Suffrage Federation (WSF), which maintained a resolute opposition to the war, but despite this she still made a significant contribution to wartime charity. On 15 August 1914 to alleviate unemployment amongst women in the East End she set up her own employment exchange in Old Ford and a week later her first milk distribution centre. 'Soon she was running four mother and baby clinics.... During 1915 her restaurants served 70,000 meals, 1,000 mothers and babies were seen at her clinics [and] over £1,000 was spent on milk distribution.'[2] Given the over-jingoistic nature of much of Emmeline and Christabel's rhetoric, there is a strong case to be made for Sylvia's works having had a far more positive impact on the home front than that of her mother and sister despite her vocal opposition to the war itself.

There was greater unanimity among the members of the less radical National Union of Women's Suffrage Societies (NUWSS), led by Millicent Garrett Fawcett.[3] Though Fawcett was initially opposed to the war (she was principal speaker at an anti-war meeting at the Kingsway Hall on 2 August 1914) Britain's entry quickly changed her views. As Fawcett herself described, and as we saw in relation to Belgian refugees, the NUWSS had the advantage over many other bodies dedicated to war charity of having a strong existing structure:

We were a tolerably large band of organized women—over 50,000 members, and about 500 societies—scattered all over the country, accustomed to work together in a disciplined, orderly fashion for a common end; we felt, therefore, that we had a special gift, such as it was, to offer for our country's service—namely our organizing and money-raising power.[4]

The NUWSS organised a network of hospitals in France, five in Serbia and one in Salonika with a total of 1,800 beds as well as lending the services and paying the salaries of nearly 150 trained workers for local relief committees all over the country. 'The NUWSS also sent the Millicent Fawcett Unit . . . to Russia in 1916 to work among the Polish refugees, especially to do maternity nursing and work among the children.'[5] They set up a maternity unit in Petrograd, a children's hospital at Kazan on the Volga and another hospital for both refugees and local peasants at Stara Chilnoe.

A key figure in overseas medical work was the Honorary Secretary of the Scottish Federation of the NUWSS, Dr Elsie Inglis, who has strong claims to being the greatest heroine of the war. Sadly, the British authorities were less than appreciative of her outstanding abilities during her lifetime. In September 1914 she went to the War Office and offered to equip and staff a fully operational hospital in France. She was told by an, unnamed, War Office official, 'my good lady, go home and sit still.'[6] Undaunted by this misogynist response she repeated her offer to the French Red Cross who responded positively. The NUWSS Scottish Women's Hospitals (SWH) were entirely run by women, from the surgeons down to the orderlies, drivers and domestic staff. Though initiated by Inglis the project was enthusiastically taken up by the whole NUWSS. The first hospital, at Royaumont, was quickly joined by one at Troyes, financed by the students of Newnham and Girton women's colleges. Satellite committees of the SWH were formed in Canada, Hong Kong, Australia, New Zealand and South Africa and by 1919 £428,905 had been raised for the scheme. Sadly Dr Inglis herself, and many of her staff, did not see the culmination of her work as she died just three days after bringing her unit out of Russia in November 1917.

Memorial services were held in her honour at St Margaret's, Westminster, and in St Giles's Cathedral, Edinburgh. Those who were there speak of it not as a funeral but as a triumph. The streets were thronged; all Edinburgh turned out to do her homage as she went to her last resting place. The Scottish Command was represented and lent the gun-carriage on which the coffin was borne and the Union Jack which covered it.[7]

One might say too little, too late.

It was in Dr Inglis's work in Serbia that she encountered two of the war's most remarkable women, who also ran their own fund. The Hon Evelina Haverfield and Sergeant Major Flora Sandes' Comfort Fund for Serbian

Soldiers and Prisoners might have had the longest name of any wartime voluntary organisation but its founders certainly deserved to be commemorated in its title.[8] Evelina Haverfield was the daughter of the third Baron Abinger. She was a keen sportswoman who, during the Boer War, collected abandoned horses from the battlefield and nursed them back to good condition. She was among the first London women suffragists to be sentenced to imprisonment (for 'storming' the Houses of Parliament) and organised a branch of the WSPU. One of her publicity stunts was parading on horseback dressed as Joan of Arc in full armour. She was one of the original members of the Women's Emergency Corps in August 1914, which 'was soon joined by many women from the higher classes and was in the early days an unlikely mix of feminists and women who would not normally have mixed with such dangerous types.'[9] She then founded and organised the Women's Volunteer Reserve (WVR) and was President and Commandant-in-Chief of the Women's Reserve Ambulance (Green Cross Corps). In the WVR Haverfield insisted that drill practice was essential to 'train women for their own defence in the last extremity' and that 'if women made themselves really efficient they would be recognized when the time came.'[10] As Nicoletta Gullace has pointed out this was a highly controversial viewpoint and attracted 'scathing ridicule' from both men and many women. Despite this 'the marching and drilling of uniformed women and the adoption of military "rank" gained an astonishing popularity among women on the homefront.'[11] The WVR became involved in several ventures, not least of which was in providing, until 1918, a uniformed group called the Lady Instructors Signals Company, who trained Aldershot army recruits. The WVR was rather expensive to join—one had to pay for one's own uniform that, at more than £2, could not be afforded by poorer women—though it was a significant influence in the establishment of the Women's Legion, which had a more widespread appeal.

In April 1915, Evelina went to Serbia as administrator of one of the Scottish Women's Hospital Units at Valjevo and remained, with Dr Inglis, working for the Serbs as prisoners of the enemy from November to February 1916. In August 1916, she went to Russia in charge of the transport column of Dr Inglis's unit. It was on her return to Britain in November 1917 that she organised the Serbian Comforts Fund with Flora Sandes and became Commissioner for the Serbian Red Cross Society in Great Britain. Haverfield went back to Serbia in August 1919 and at her instigation another fund was raised, for Serbian children, with which she established an orphanage at Baiyna Sachia on the borders of Bosnia. It was there in March 1920 that she succumbed to pneumonia brought on by fatigue and exposure. She received the Order of St Sava, St George's Medal for bravery under fire and was made a member of the Serbian Order of the White Eagle after her death.[12] The work of Dr Inglis's team in Serbia was summed up by the Prefect of Constanza who remarked that 'it is extraordinary how these women endure hardships; they refuse help, and carry the wounded themselves. They work like navvies. No wonder England is a great country if the women are like that.'[13]

If Evelina Haverfield was remarkable then Flora Sandes was unique. She was the only British woman to serve as a front-line fighting soldier during the First World War. Flora, the daughter of Samuel Sandes, a Scottish clergyman, was born in 1876. Even though she was nearly forty years old on the outbreak of the war, she joined an ambulance unit in Serbia. She described her experiences in a newspaper interview in 1918:

> 'I went to Serbia . . . in August 1914 being one of the first to go to the help of that little nation. After the terrible retreat I joined the regimental ambulance, but, being cut off from the unit I asked permission to join the Serbian Army as a private, and was accepted. For two years I have taken part in all the fighting, and was badly wounded at the taking of Hill 1212. On this occasion a hand grenade exploded near me, and I sustained 24 wounds. I ordered the men to fall back, but they refused saying "We are not going unless we can take you". One of the officers crawled through the snow, dragging me along, while the men remained behind and fought a gallant rear-guard action until I was carried into safety. The next day, when our troops attacked and occupied the Bulgarian trenches, they found a number of our men who had been taken prisoner. Every one lay dead in the trench with the throat cut from ear to ear. That is the Bulgar way of dealing with prisoners.'
>
> Sergeant-Major Sandes has been awarded the highest decoration for which Serbian soldiers are eligible. Having been granted a few weeks' leave of absence she is devoting her time in this country to collecting funds for the Hon. Mrs Haverfield's Society for providing comforts for the Serbian soldiers and Serbian prisoners of war.[14]

Sandes wrote and published *An English Woman-Sergeant in the Serbian Army* (1916) to help with the fund-raising. The book is an extraordinary narrative of physical bravery and endurance. For example, she describes having bullets extracted from her body without anaesthetic and having to act as chief surgeon for her unit after all the doctors died from typhus, performing operations such as toe amputations with a pair of blunt scissors. Despite these gruesome episodes Angela Smith astutely sums up *An English Woman-Sergeant* as being totally different from later, better-known memoirs such as those of Sassoon and Graves, calling it 'rather jolly and romanticised, making the whole experience sound like fun.'[15] Sales of the book realised over £5,000 of which the first £2,000 was sufficient to provide 108 tons of supplies to be shipped to Serbia. Sandes also undertook an extensive speaking tour to aid fund-raising. She thus provided 150,000 men with tea, lemonade and cigarettes, as well as clothing the whole of her army division.[16]

Sandes's active service was still not over because 'despite her success in London, she returned to the front in time to help recapture Serbia from the enemy in the great offensive of September 1918.'[17] After the war Sandes remained in the Serbian Army and had reached the rank of captain by the time she retired. In 1927 she married Yurie Yudenich, a Russian sergeant in her platoon and a former White Army officer. She lived with him very happily in Belgrade where they ran a taxi service until he died in 1941. Sandes even briefly rejoined the Serbian Army at the age of sixty-five to fight the Nazis. After World War Two she became, rather incongruously, a chaperone and wardrobe mistress at the Folies Bergere in Paris before finally returning to England where she died at her Suffolk home in 1956.[18]

Inglis, Haverfield and, most definitely, Sandes were exceptions among women but though they were exceptional it would be wrong to dismiss their importance. Their activities were given a great deal of publicity and despite criticism in some, conservative, circles they were generally treated as having made a heroic contribution to Britain's cause. Praise for such 'unfeminine' activity from the mainstream British press would have been impossible before the war; indeed it is remarkable how the exploits of Sandes were reported so matter-of-factly and without adverse comment. Gullace is correct in her conclusion that 'because only one British woman saw actual combat in World War I (although several succeeded in enlisting only to be unmasked at the front), the achievements of women like Evelina Haverfield and Flora Sandes are largely symbolic—but their symbolism was significant.'[19] Janet Lee is prepared to go further, suggesting that Sandes 'modelled resistance to female subordination and enhanced women's claim to personal and collective power.'[20]

5 The Comforts Crisis and the Director General of Voluntary Organizations

THE COMFORTS CRISIS

Following the first flush of response to the war, especially concerning the hardships of soldiers' dependants and Belgian refugees, there was a flourishing of voluntary activity geared towards medical supplies and troop comforts. Medical services were already systematised and state controlled, or quickly became so, and voluntary action could be directed to existing medical support agencies. These included Voluntary Aid Detachments (VADs), which had been in existence since 1909 and were administered by the Joint War Committee of the British Red Cross and Order of St John; the Women's Sick and Wounded Convoy Corps founded by Mrs St Clair Stobart in 1907 and the First Aid Nursing Yeomanry (FANY), founded in the same year by Captain Edward Baker. By 1912 the VADs, of whom two-thirds were women, had a strength of 26,000, reaching 90,000 by 1918. Even so, with the enormous demands created by the war there were immediate shortages of medical supplies and comforts for wounded men both abroad and at home.

There had been organised comforts for soldiers during the Boer War and some formations had existing voluntary support bodies, usually in the form of Regimental Associations. The St John's Ambulance had acted as a central body for the collection of gifts in kind and all subscriptions from the public had been channelled through the Red Cross.[1] The War Office was aware of the issue of troops' comforts at the outset of the war and at a Directors meeting on 16 August 1914 chaired by the BEF's Quartermaster General (QMG) Sir William Robertson agreed 'to take up the question of private packages being sent to the troops and ascertain what was done during the South African War.'[2] What they found was that the officer in charge of troop comforts, Sir Wodehouse Richardson, the Deputy Adjutant-General for Supplies and Transport, was against the whole idea of parcels being sent out for individual soldiers.[3] This was because they had often contained inappropriate items like bottles of brandy or beer, inflammable wax matches or even a decomposing pig's head. Then there was the question of profiteering by companies taking advantage of the public's patriotic generosity, by packaging items up into soldiers' gift boxes and selling them at inflated prices. Richardson's conclusions were unequivocal, that the sending and receiving of comforts should be a privilege and not a right: 'All gifts should be either for general distribution or for distribution to individual regiments or brigades. . . . I feel very strongly about this parcel nuisance, which should be stopped as soon as possible.'[4] Richardson's views were partially supported by the Red Cross in their report on the Boer War. They were concerned with the lack of coordination and stated that 'in connection with the formation of these several funds and of private committees throughout the country, there was much danger of overlapping and of undesirable competition.'[5] Sir Edward Ward, the future DGVO, was a close colleague of Richardson's in South Africa (Ward was Director of Supplies in Natal and then at Army Headquarters) and though he took on board some of Richardson's recommendations when he launched the DGVO scheme he rightly recognised that to ensure public confidence and morale the sending of parcels must be maintained as the right of both individuals and organisations.

However, the sheer scale of the current war soon caused significant problems. Did the items collected or sent match the needs of the troops? There is plenty of anecdotal information that they sometimes did not. For example, a soldier with five mufflers but no socks or, as in the case of the Second Battalion of the Royal Welch Fusiliers, too many socks: 'socks were sent from home in such quantities for the first two years of the War that men were throwing them away after only one wearing.'[6] There was duplication of effort and unfairness in distribution. Prisoners of war were a case in point as 'some lucky prisoner might receive three or four parcels a month, while his neighbour got none at all.'[7] Quality control was a further problem as not all charities produced their goods to high standards. Captain John Liddell of the Argyll and Sutherland Highlanders wrote to his family in November 1914 criticizing the oddities being sent:

> The people who send them mean very well, but apart from the fact that these huge bales stop everything else coming through the post, the Government ones [i.e. ones made to Government specifications] are far more appreciated by the men, and with reason, as they are really tophole garments, and some of the efforts that arrive are very thin and shoddy.[8]

The situation was even more critical with regard to more costly technological items funded by charitable contributions. The motor ambulances being supplied were all of different makes and types, meaning that maintenance was a serious problem.[9] One group, from the clan Mcrae, wanted to provide an ambulance solely for clan members. As Sarah Pedersen points out this 'suggests a certain naivety about the organisation of the battlefield. Presumably the envisaged ambulance would be able to "home in" on wounded clansmen while barring its doors to any casualties of inferior birth.'[10]

Captain Liddell's complaint of overloaded postal services was reinforced at a QMG Directors meeting in November 1914 when Robertson reported that 'the number of gifts was stupendous, and recently the First Army Corps had wired to him asking him not to send any more.'[11] Then there was the question of whether comforts were going to the right people. Middle class regiments, such as the Civil Service Rifles or Honourable Artillery Company, might be well provided for, but what about some of the New Army battalions? Should the supply of such essentials as warm clothing, blankets or field glasses really be left to the vagaries of charitable collections? There were many examples where the entrepreneurial spirit led to inconsistency in the supply of important items. In winter 1914–15 the War Office made an appeal for blankets and later for respirators. There was an immediate, but uncoordinated public response which quickly led to oversupply.[12] The overall situation was that 'the outbreak of war found voluntary effort on behalf of the Army entirely unorganised. . . . No societies existed for the purpose of providing comforts and gifts for combatant troops at home and abroad.' With regard to the hundreds of bodies that sprang up to fill this vacuum, 'there was no regular organisation existing dealing with the distribution of gifts. . . . A great amount of waste of time, labour and money resulted, unsuitable patterns of articles were produced and overlapping became a very serious matter.'[13] Overlapping of charities, and hence waste of effort, had long been one of the bugbears of the COS and so would have been a familiar cry.

It was not too long before official attention became focussed on the issue. In the debate on the King's speech on 12 November 1914 Sir Harold Elverston, Liberal MP for Gateshead, questioned the Home Secretary, Reginald McKenna, on the matter in the House of Commons. He referred to recent appeals for 300,000 socks and 300,000 belts but ironically extended the principle to inquire whether 'the nation would be content to leave to voluntary effort the equipment of the mechanical instruments of war?'[14] He felt a clear distinction should be drawn between what were, in reality, necessities—including clothing, bedding and military equipment and what were luxuries; 'let the public supply our men at the front with what may really be termed luxuries, but do not let them depend upon private generosity for what are real necessities.'[15] McKenna's response was somewhat superficial in that he suggested the question was better asked of the War Office, though he did promise to raise the specific issue of blanket supply with colleagues in that department. He also referred to the natural desire of many civilians to 'do something personally for the individual soldier' but in trying to distinguish between comforts and essentials his reply smacked not a little of confusion and pedantry, considering such items as scarves and balaclavas as 'comforts' as 'they perform a useful function and add to the comfort of the soldier, but they would not in ordinary circumstances be served out as part of his kit. . . . It does not increase his fighting capacity, but it adds a little to his comfort.'[16] This probably came as little 'comfort' to the sentry in the Ypres salient standing up to his knees in icy water and with no change of socks back in his dugout.

From McKenna's remarks, the Home Department appeared somewhat indifferent but the War Office *was* considering the matter seriously, and at the very highest level it began to cause significant concern. This is revealed in the correspondence between Major-General Sir John Cowans, Army QMG at the War Office throughout the War, and Lieutenant-General Ronald Maxwell, who had become the QMG at GHQ in France. It was Maxwell's view that clothing needs were being adequately met and that any significant supply of clothing comforts from home was superfluous. He was clearly irritated at the beginning of February 1915 when a letter from Lady French, wife of the Commander-in-Chief, appeared in the press appealing for comforts including shirts, socks, undergarments, woollen caps and gloves because 'there has been a very marked falling off in those gifts of late.'[17] Maxwell's suggestion to Cowans, on 4 February, was that 'the requirements of the troops at the front have been fully met, and would suggest that the sending out of gifts of clothing and necessaries for general distribution should now cease.'[18] Maxwell was taking the official military view and regarded complaints as meddling by uninformed civilians, however eminent. Cowans took a more considered, political stance, especially after an exchange of correspondence with Miss J.R.L. French, daughter of the C-in-C. She wrote to him on 5 February saying the situation was rather confused and that 'one day one is told that comforts are very badly wanted and the next that they are an encumbrance. . . . Your statement to my sister a little time back [was] that anything and everything was wanted, and that we could not send too much.'[19] Cowans therefore turned down Maxwell's request for an unequivocal press statement and instead suggested that officers in France should be told they could get warm clothes etc 'in the proper way' and not to write letters to the press.[20] Maxwell duly issued a note to Armies and the Cavalry Corps to pass down the line to all officers to this effect.[21] Unfortunately, this statement came just after the issue escalated further. It was raised in the House of Commons by James Hogge, Liberal MP for East Edinburgh and a leading campaigner for state pensions for disabled servicemen, who quoted Lady French's letter.[22] Harold Baker replied that it seemed to be a case of misunderstanding or misinformation. 'I wish to say that our most recent information about the supply of those articles at the front was that the quantity was so great that thousands had to be kept in store. There is an apparent contradiction somewhere', he responded with puzzlement.[23] Hogge put forward a possible solution asking 'could there not be some centralisation with regard to the distribution of those comforts which are collected apart from those which are supplied to the troops by the War Office? There must be an enormous wastage going on [and] there is certainly an incongruity somewhere.'[24] Whilst not making any specific promises Baker agreed that there was merit in the suggestion and that 'it will not be lost sight of.' There was little chance of this happening and, though the matter never reached the same proportions, or seriousness, as the 1915 shell scandal, the comforts scandal continued to the end of the year. An article in the *Globe* on 9 February reported that the men of the 1st Battalion, Argyll and Sutherland Highlanders, were 'in need of clothing of all descriptions.' Maxwell's enquiries ascertained that there might have been some delay in supply to the Argylls but that the commanding officer now reported 'that his unit was well supplied with warm clothing.' Maxwell's note to Cowans was that 'the reply speaks for itself. The newspapers are a nuisance. The best plan is to pay no attention to them.'[25] This was a little suspicious in that the Argylls' needs had been fulfilled on 10 February, the day after the *Globe* article had appeared. There was also correspondence on the issue of boots for the Royal West Surreys (1st Queens) in March but then things appear to have settled down until the autumn. In late March, Lord Kitchener finally approved a communiqué that no further supplies of warm clothing need be sent and that Lady French was closing her appeal (no doubt there had been some embarrassment between the Field Marshal and his wife over their less than complementary statements). This was followed in June by an Army Council Instruction forbidding officers 'to advertise their personal wants or to make any such appeal to public charity on behalf of the troops.'[26] This, of course, did not prevent officers from making indirect appeals in their private correspondence.

Two cases, the second probably the most serious to date, occurred in October and November. Though the latter was after the creation of the DGVO it happened before his reforms could take effect and was based on events in October. The first concerned the supply of shirts and sweaters for the 1st Somerset Light Infantry about which their second in command wrote to a comforts fund. The second began after Lt V.E. Reynolds, an officer of the 10th Battalion, West Yorkshire Regiment, part of 17th Division, wrote to his wife. She wrote to Thomas Marlowe, editor of the *Daily Mail* with a view to publication but, realising the potential embarrassment immediately after official action had been taken, he passed it on instead to the War Office for investigation. Mrs Reynolds claimed that 'the plight of some of his poor men is pitiable. They are most of them without socks at all, many without shirts, and their boots are in a terrible condition.'[27] Cowans immediately wrote to Maxwell asking him to investigate this and other complaints.[28] Before Maxwell could reply Cowans sent on three further letters from 'officers who have written home to say that their men are absolutely desperate' and he commented that 'it certainly is a most extraordinary thing how absolutely continuous these appeals are.'[29] Maxwell completed his investigations and replied on 21 December. Again he concluded that there were really no difficulties and that 'every complaint received has proved to be without the slightest foundation and the waste of time involved in the investigation is lamentable.'[30] On the latter point he was certainly justified and, in addition to the time taken to investigate complaints on the ground, this matter had now taken up considerable amounts of the time of two of the country's most senior Generals for a period of some ten months. However, on the first point, he was being somewhat economical with the truth. This is confirmed in his

own correspondence, for Maxwell enclosed a letter written to him by Brigadier General Harold Tagart, Deputy Adjutant and QMG Third Army, in
which Tagart noted that the problem was partly due to the official allowance
of only two shirts and three pairs of socks per man and that the soldier would
'continue to want more. So should I in his place.'[31]

The Reynolds incident was a considerable irritation to the War Office
and GHQ and could have become a major scandal if the *Daily Mail* had
published the letter. As it was, the unfortunate Reynolds was made to write
a contrite apology to his Adjutant in which he stated that 'the letter referred
to was a private one to my wife, and I had no intention whatever that it
should be used for publication. I much regret that this was done and have
taken steps to ensure that this shall not occur again,' which he no doubt did
by admonishing his, rather public-spirited, wife.[32] It is interesting, though,
what this letter does *not* say, i.e. that his original contention of a lack of
clothing was untrue, which you would have expected him to do and his
C-in-C demanded, if it were the case. What was the truth of the matter?
There is probably room for both Maxwell's assertions of exaggeration and
the officer's individual complaints to have some validity. A letter from one
sapper on the Western Front is perhaps indicative of this situation:

> The things most suitable for us out here are eatables and Camp Coffee,
> Cocoa, Oxo. These are things we can easily make under such difficulties
> as are experienced in war time. Regarding woollen goods we are fairly
> well off, but shirts are very much needed as we cannot get much washing
> done and one never knows how quickly one may have to move.[33]

Mismatches in supply were almost inevitable, a shortage in one item
reported in the press leading to an upsurge in either official issues or donations that, in turn, led to a glut in supply. Such problems are well known
among today's disaster relief funds. However, there certainly *were* some
shortages in some units and Maxwell's irritation is probably less defensible
than Cowan's more measured approach.

In September a *Times* leader demonstrated the situation had become
close to a national scandal:

> There have admittedly been many drawbacks to the efforts which have
> been made by numberless private individuals since the war began. In
> some cases things have been supplied for which there was no demand;
> in other cases the wrong kind of the right thing has been made and
> sent to the front. . . . It should not be a task of insuperable difficulty to
> devise some scheme which will dovetail the work and money of volun-
> teers into the normal official sources of supply.[34]

These incidents led Cowans to consider what action the War Office could
take both to solve the problem and remove public criticism. In this he was
assisted when the office of Financial Secretary to the War Office was taken

up at the end of May 1915 by Henry Forster, the former first-class cricketer and future President of MCC and Governor-General of Australia. Forster had been pondering the issue for some time and he instigated enquiries into the supply of troops' comforts to ascertain whether greater coordination was required. Forster conferred with Cowans before he reported on his findings and made the following announcement in the House of Commons on 18 November 1915:

> When I was appointed to my present office I made inquiries as to whether or not there was any real waste in connection with the splendid work which people had undertaken. I found that there was waste of effort on the part of voluntary workers, and, what I thought more regrettable, waste of a great deal of material. I thought it would be a good plan, if it could be done, to organise the bodies of workers who are good enough to give their time and trouble to the provision of comforts for the troops, and to see whether or not we could not systematise the whole movement throughout the country with a view to the prevention of waste.[35]

By the time of his announcement the scheme had been in operation for over a month. The first official notification had been on 20 September:

> The Army Council hope shortly to announce the formation of a central organization under the direction of Colonel Sir Edward Ward . . . for the purpose of co-ordinating the work of the various committees and individuals now engaged in supplying comforts and luxuries for the troops and of directing into the most useful channels their kindly energies.[36]

Notices had appeared in the press on 11 October and Sir Edward Ward had been given the impressive title Director General of Voluntary Organizations. On 1 October, he took up his post charged with 'coordinating and regulating all voluntary organisations throughout the country.'[37]

The choice of Ward was inspired. No one combined his knowledge of army supply, Whitehall politics and managerial competence. Yet he is today an almost entirely forgotten figure. It is therefore highly worthwhile to examine his career and the unique skills he brought to his new role.

THE GREATEST SUPPLY OFFICER SINCE MOSES—SIR EDWARD WARD, DIRECTOR GENERAL OF VOLUNTARY ORGANIZATIONS

The Saviour of Ladysmith

Edward Willis Duncan Ward was born in Oban on 17 December 1853, the only son of Captain John Ward RN and Mary Hope, daughter of John Bowie. He was privately educated and in 1874 entered the commissariat of the Control Department. This was the precursor of the Army Service

Corps (ASC) but at that time, though comprising military officials it operated separately from the army. In 1885 he was promoted Assistant Com-
missary General and saw active service in the Sudan campaign where his
work was commended by Sir Garnett Wolsey. When the ASC was formed
in 1888 he was commissioned with the rank of Major, being promoted
Lieutenant Colonel in 1890. The now Lord Wolsey assisted Ward's career
and he was posted to Ireland until 1895, holding a staff appointment in
Dublin from 1892. In 1895–96, he was Assistant Adjutant General for the
Ashanti expeditionary force in West Africa to suppress the slave-raiding
and human sacrifices practised by the Ashanti chief Prempeh.[38] The expedition leader, Sir Francis Scott, summed up the logistical problems Ward
faced. In hostile conditions 'a rapid advance had to be made through 150
miles of tropical forest in a country practically destitute of supplies. And,
above all, the perils of a climate notorious for its unhealthiness had to be
encountered.'[39] In Ashanti, Ward demonstrated an early flair for innovative
management techniques, overcoming the difficulties with aplomb and being
particularly sensitive in his handling of the 100,000-plus 'native' carriers.
Another senior officer on the expedition was Robert Baden-Powell who was
appreciative of Ward's efficiency:

> The whole of this mass of usually blundering natives was working just
> like clockwork all along the line within three days of its organisation
> in the hands of Colonel Ward and his never-tiring staff. Not a load gets
> lost or even delayed, not a man is in arrears of his daily pay.[40]

Ward achieved this by the simple, but effective steps of giving 'native' over-
seers greater responsibility for managing porters and by using local labour
rather than 'trusted' workers from further afield who had less immunity
to local strains of disease. This had not been done before because it was
felt that local labourers might be more prone to mutiny or desertion, but
Ward's view was that this was more usually caused by bad management
and poor conditions, both of which he improved. Ward had previously set
out his key guidance in the handling of 'native' labour:

> Labour should be as local as possible;
> Immediate superiors should be drawn from the natives themselves;
> Pay should be fair and remitted to the labourers families;
> It was imperative that all British officers dealing with the labourers
> should both speak their language and understand their culture.[41]

The *Army Service Corps Journal* noted that, operating on these principles,
'our dealings with the large number of native carriers etc were conducted
both amicably and cheerfully, and the kindest feelings existed on all sides',
concluding that the expedition had considerably added to the ASC's reputation.[42] Ward's summing up stated that 'as far as my researches have led me,

I cannot find that on any previous expedition have the wants of the soldier been so well provided for as on this occasion' and this view was clearly shared by his superiors as, on his return, he was made a companion of the Order of the Bath.[43]

Back in London, Ward was made Deputy Assistant Adjutant General Home District and for the next five years was given charge of the annual Royal Military Tournament, in those days held at the Agricultural Hall in Islington, which raised funds for service charities. Under his guidance, 'the success and popularity of the Military Tournament went forward by leaps and bounds.'[44] In its early days the Tournament had made a loss but by 1896 was returning a profit of £4,000. In the first year under Ward profits tripled to £12,000 and though this declined to £7,500 in 1900, the year Ward relinquished his role, there was an immediate drop in the following year to just £2,000 and five-figure profits were not achieved again until 1923.[45]

Ward's strengths lay in his managerial and organisational skills and in 1897, he published his approach in the then definitive handbook for military supply services, the *Handbook of Army Service Corps Duties in Peace and War*. When, in September 1899, war loomed in South Africa, he was appointed Chief Supply Officer for Natal.[46] On 9 October 1899 the Boers gave the British an ultimatum that they withdraw their troops from the borders of the South African Republics. The British refused and two days later the Anglo Boer War commenced. The mounted Boer commandos

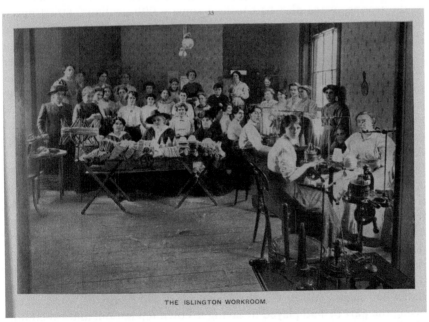

THE ISLINGTON WORKROOM.

Figure 5.1 The Islington workroom of the American Women's War Relief Fund (courtesy of the City of London, London Metropolitan Archives).

immediately swept into the British Colony of Natal, pushing back the British troops. In only twenty-one days they were at the doors of the town of Ladysmith, the last major obstacle facing them before they reached the coast, where Ward was in charge of supplies. The British troops, under the command of General Sir George White, were told that their duty was to stand firm in the town and to prevent it from being taken. So began the Siege of Ladysmith. Pitted against 12,000 British troops, 21,000 Boers encircled the town. Realising the possibility of a siege, Ward had 'caused enormous quantities of supplies to be sent up from the base to Ladysmith. The articles were not even tallied or counted as received, in spite of the remonstrances of the consignors; but by means of Kaffir labourers, working night and day, the trucks were off-loaded as fast as possible, and again sent down the line to bring up more food.'[47]

The siege began in early November and lasted three-and-a-half months. Ward's skills were tested to the limit but he was more than up to the task. Despite attempts by General Sir Redvers Buller to raise the siege, it continued into the New Year by which time the supply situation was getting desperate and 'the fate of Ladysmith now lay in the hands of Colonel E.W.D. Ward.'[48] The Boers were amazed that the town was holding out for so long. On 6 January when they met a delegation from the Imperial Light Horse during a truce, the Boers asked how it was that the British were 'as fat as pigs' when they were meant to be starving. Ward had specially selected the plumpest, healthiest-looking men to form the delegation.[49] In addition to the troops, Ward also had to feed some 6,000 civilians. Dried peach leaves were utilised instead of tobacco and horsemeat became a 'valuable and much relished addition to the pitifully scanty rations.'[50] Meat was in especially short supply but there were plenty of horses, for whom fodder was rapidly running out, and so 'about the middle of the siege they had to kill horses in the town for consumption. The patients were allowed the soup that was called "Chevrill". They liked it very much.'[51] To help raise morale Ward also took responsibility for editing the short-lived periodical the *Ladysmith Lyre,* his qualification for the job being, in his own self-deprecating analysis, that he was the only person with a supply of paper.[52] Finally, between 20 and 27 February 1900, Buller fought a successful battle at Pieters and on 27 February 1900, the British pickets on Wagon Hill saw the Boer besiegers trek away across the veldt as Buller's troops marched into Ladysmith. The siege was over and there were tremendous celebrations in the town.[53] Though there were outbreaks of disease, especially typhus, not a single person—military or civilian, black or white—had died through malnutrition. Without Ward's organisational expertise it is likely that supplies would have run out and the garrison forced to surrender (which indeed Buller had suggested). Sir George White was full of praise for Ward, recognising the part he had played in saving his own reputation, and called him 'the best commissariat officer since Moses'. In his despatches he wrote that 'I cannot speak too highly of this officer. . . . I consider him an officer of the highest administrative ability. . . . He is unquestionably the very best Supply Officer I have ever met, and to his resource, foresight and inventiveness, the successful defence of Ladysmith for so long a period is very largely due.'[54]

Ward was promoted to the post of Director of Supplies for the entire South African field force, where he was one of the first to realise the advantages of mechanical transport. In this position too he was a considerable success. Ward's colleague in the ASC in South Africa, Sir Wodehouse Richardson, was highly complimentary about his skills as noted in his diary:

> Colonel Ward has done very well indeed. He is tactful and a *persona grata* with the headquarters staff or, at any rate, with many of them, and that goes a long way. Anyhow, I hear no complaints from officers who come down country, and generally the first thing one complains about is one's food.[55]

Ward's obituarists agreed, *The Times* stating that overall 'the energy and foresight which he . . . displayed . . . contributed largely to Lord Roberts's final victory' and a fellow officer concluded that 'it can truthfully be said that his burly form, with his magnetic personality, unfailing good temper and geniality, ready to face any trouble or worry, no matter how great, with a cheerful smile, was one of the outstanding features of the siege.'[56] In his despatch of 2 April 1901 Roberts himself fully concurred in this view: 'His readiness and resource, his imperturbable good temper, his power of organisation, and thorough knowledge of his duties deserve the thanks of all ranks in the Army. Colonel Ward is an officer who stands quite by himself as a Departmental Officer of genius and character.'[57]

On his return to England in late 1900 Ward was created a full Colonel and knighted and was one of only a handful of officers singled out for praise in the otherwise highly critical Royal Commission report on the war. The report complimented the work of the ASC:

> Much of the success of the war is to be credited to officers whose names are not much known to the public, such as . . . Sir Edward Ward [of whose] direction of food supplies Lord Kitchener said, 'I consider that the soldier was better fed than in any previous campaign,' and this statement is supported by a mass of other evidence.[58]

Ward and the Modernisation of the War Office

On his return Ward became First Secretary to Sir Ralph Knox, Permanent Secretary at the War Office. At first, his duties appear to have been somewhat mundane but in 1901 Ward succeeded Knox under Secretary of State for War William St John Brodrick, becoming the first military holder of the role since the 1870s. Ward remained at the head of the War Office clerical establishment for thirteen years controlling an organisation several sizes larger than that of his civilian predecessors, 'the smooth working of which was obviously due in no small measure to the organizing capacity of the man.'[59] His military obituarist concluded that 'it is doubtful . . . whether any more popular high official had ever retired from Government service.'[60] It may be argued that this praise is no more than the usual hyperbole of the obituarist but it is strongly supported by the evidence and significantly underplays Ward's organisational skills. These were rooted in his service experience but also in his far-sighted, indeed innovatory approach to the use of business methods in military management.

His tenure coincided with 'the first major reorganisation of the War Office since the Crimean War.'[61] These changes took place in the aftermath of the South African War and the Commission of Enquiry chaired by Lord Elgin but gathered pace with the establishment of the Committee under Lord Esher late in 1903. Ward was ideally placed to both contribute to and enact the reforms. In 1902–03 he chaired the Committee that reorganised the establishment of the Civil Department of the War Office, although for a time things did not go smoothly in his new role as a senior civil servant. Brodrick's attempted reorganisation of the home army into six districts was a fiasco and he was replaced by Hugh Oakley Arnold-Forster, a former journalist, who had written extensively about army reform. Balfour, however, made Arnold-Forster's appointment conditional upon accepting the assistance of a committee, under the chairmanship of Esher, charged with the task of reorganising the department.[62] On a number of occasions the Committee and Minister found themselves in profound disagreement. Though in an uncomfortable position, Ward sided decisively with Esher and the reformers.

In February and March 1904 there was a complete overhaul of the War Office. The Commander-in-Chief, Lord Roberts, was removed as were the heads of the four military departments, to be replaced by an Army Council and a properly constituted General Staff. Ward was the only member of the Army Council to retain his post in the reorganisation. As one commentator has noted 'the result was friction-free government in army and defence matters in which Arnold-Forster was the only loose part, rattling ominously but without damage to the rest of the machinery.'[63] Despite Ward's usually genial personality there were a number of clashes between the two men. In early 1904, Arnold-Forster objected to an apparent conspiracy between Ward and Sir George Clarke to announce appointments without the Secretary of State's approval. In September a more serious breach of confidence occurred over Arnold-Forster's proposals to make all enlistments in the army for nine years (instead of the current three). Ward leaked the Army Order to Esher saying it was for his 'secret information, as I am not supposed yet to have seen it.'[64] Clearly Ward realised that what he was doing could be construed as a breach of trust and there was some suggestion of him leaving the War Office to return to South Africa as Governor of Natal. At the end of 1904 there was an even more serious clash between Ward and his chief. As Secretary to the Army Council all decisions published by it were under Ward's signature and yet many of them were taken without his knowledge or input. Ward sent an irritated memo to Arnold–Forster in which he pointed out that he had not seen relevant papers and that, as things stood, he 'was therefore unable to carry out what the report of the Esher Committee described as my "main function", viz "to correlate the business of the War Office and to secure the harmonious action of the administrative machine as a whole."' He pointed out that he had raised this issue on a number of occasions and had made recommendations that would have prevented the problem occurring 'and I wish accordingly to place on record a disclaimer of any responsibility for the accuracy or completeness of decisions circulated for the information of the [Army] Council.'[65] This was strong stuff and it could easily have become a resignation issue but, in the event, Arnold-Forster compromised and agreed that papers had to pass through the Secretary who 'will, where necessary, add any information as to procedure or precedent.'[66]

This was not however the end of the matter. In early 1905, Arnold-Forster produced new proposals for the chairing of War Office Directors meetings, up to this point chaired by Ward. Under the new scheme, the meetings would be chaired by whoever was the senior Director present. This was again a recipe for disaster. At a time of significant change, what was required was a strong coordinating role which Ward, with his foot in both political and military camps and proven diplomatic skills, was ideally placed to perform. Arnold-Forster's lack of grip on his department was indicated by the fact that the proposal was rubbished by his own deputy, the Under Secretary of State the Earl of Donoughmore, Civil Member of the Army Council.[67] This memo was not at all complimentary about the way his superior was running the department. Ward added his own comments to Donoughmore's note and a complete set of alternative proposals.[68] Arnold-Forster was clearly losing the battle and quickly compromised. His handwritten conclusion to these notes agrees to most of Ward's proposals with Donoughmore taking the Chair at Directors Meetings. In reality, the Under Secretary attended few meetings, leaving Ward in the Chair.

Fortunately Ward's frosty relations with his political superior improved dramatically following the fall of the Conservative government in December 1905 and Richard Burdon Haldane's appointment to the post of Secretary of State for War in the new Liberal administration. Haldane 'possessed the skills and personal characteristics that Arnold-Forster lacked' and is often cited as the greatest of Britain's peacetime holders of the post. His modernisation required 'reforms which would amount to little short of revolutionary' and in achieving them Haldane had, from the first, much greater faith in Ward and gave him significant additional responsibilities.[69] From May 1906 Ward officially chaired the weekly Directors meetings where important operational issues were discussed and actions decided. Like several other key army officers (notably Douglas Haig), Ward shared

Haldane's views on the need for significant reform and reorganisation to turn the army into a modern fighting force. He threw himself enthusiastically into these tasks which included officer recruitment, plans for mobilisation and the reorganisation of the Army Medical Department and that of the War Office itself. Ward was responsible for the compilation of the original 'War Book' which set out, in detail, the actions required on mobilization. Though it was later revised it was on Ward's basic plan that subsequent versions were based and that things eventually went so smoothly in 1914 was again testimony to Ward's organisational skills. In 1908–09 he worked with Douglas Haig on the production of 'a codified set of manuals dealing with administration and training' which became *Field Service Regulations Parts 1 and 2.* 'It was very largely his [Ward's] hand which guided Mr Haldane in his efforts to create the Expeditionary Force and the Territorial Force between 1906 and 1908. It was he who, with Sir Douglas Haig, Adjutant-General at the time, mapped out the new regulations.'[70] In 1908 Ward authored the *Territorial Force Regulations* and became Honorary Colonel of the 2nd London Territorial Division. He was also Chairman of the County of London Territorial Force Association.

Ward was a key figure in many other critical improvements. One was as Chairman of the Committee on Civil Employment of Ex-Soldiers and Sailors, a cause close to his heart and demonstrating his keen humanitarian concern. It was generally agreed that ex-servicemen were efficient workers, many employers stating that they were more satisfactory than civilians, but an overlarge network of charitable organisations did the work of finding them employment. There were nine voluntary societies as well as eight commercial agencies. The report concluded that there was much overlapping and waste of resources. Ward felt it was essential that there should be one association to take their place with an advisory council consisting of members from the more important societies and departments. There should be a central office in London acting as an employment agency, with branches in counties and large towns. It should be assisted by, but not under the control of, the Admiralty and the War Office. Local Authorities should also be urged to reserve a number of appointments for ex-servicemen. Every soldier should be required to learn a technical skill during his military career and recommendations were made regarding their training and provision for welfare.[71] The report was an important precursor for both the work of the DGVO, especially in its 'rationalisation' of voluntary efforts, and the postwar treatment of ex-servicemen.

Another of Ward's achievements was the creation of the Officers Training Corps (OTC). In other accounts this reform is credited to Haldane but it was quite definitely Ward's brainchild. Haldane had little knowledge of the armed forces and relied on advice from key specialists; in this case his chosen advisor was Ward. Ward had first made proposals along similar lines in 1903–04 (i.e. before Haldane's tenure) which envisaged the creation of an entirely new class of reserve officer.[72] Haldane recognised the OTC as Ward's brainchild by appointing him to chair the enterprise in August 1906.[73] The committee examined the schemes in existence in Russia, Japan and Germany and adapted what they saw as the best elements to the British context.[74] The new Corps would come under the auspices of the War Office and would provide a simple and effective method of counting service in the OTC as part of a candidate's training for a commission in either the reserve or auxiliary forces. This would help overcome the hindrance that military training posed to a civil career. Though a disappointment to some, particularly those like Lord Roberts, who wanted compulsory military service, the scheme was greeted with approval by most. It was enthusiastically endorsed by the Headmasters' Conference who, only five years earlier, had been against giving boys military instruction at school. Even though the number of officers produced by the OTC was hugely inadequate for the demands of the First World War, Ward's proposals had a significant and positive impact. One of its architects commented in 1915 that 'many armchair critics who looked askance at its inception, have now been forced to recognize its value' and Ian Worthington has concluded that the 'optimism surrounding the announcement of the new proposals appears to have been warranted.'[75] Between 1907 and 1909 Ward also created the framework of the Imperial General Staff which came into existence in November 1909.[76]

Though many of the reforms with which Ward was associated took place under Haldane's tenure the principles had been established before the Liberal administration took office, despite the lack of success of Arnold-Forster politically. They transformed the War Office into 'a form so effective that it remained substantially unchanged for seventy years. . . . The new organisation was uncannily like that of the board of directors in a modern service company.'[77] Michael Tadman goes further than this by suggesting that 'these advances in their appreciation of management principles paralleled the work of the great theorists [notably F.W. Taylor and Henri Fayol] quite closely, except for this vital difference—that they anticipated the published works by several decades.'[78] Tadman therefore directly links the thinking that characterised the reforms overseen by Esher and Ward to Fayol's principles, which remain the basis of modern management theory. Simon Higgens too has recognised the mechanisms of Haldane's reforms as mirroring modern management techniques by demonstrating that what was at work was a classic 'change management process'. He concludes that Haldane 'understood the intellectual complexities of institutional change' and it is clear that in his many and varied roles Ward shared the same understanding.[79]

In all of the above tasks, Ward utilised his previous administrative experience, putting forward practical managerial solutions to issues that had eluded others. His belief in sound management and business training was prominent in many of the areas under his auspices. However, in one scheme in particular these principles were taken a stage further, again anticipating much of the later work of management theorists.

The LSE Army Administration Course

The final significant change which Ward controlled was War Office reorganisation, where one of Haldane's main aims was the creation of an administrative staff for the War Office and army separate from the General Staff but with the same 'real and far-reaching' strategic control as the General Staff.[80] The subsequent London School of Economics course is again credited to Haldane, especially as he was a founder of the LSE.[81] This is only partially correct; the idea was Ward's, but its establishment at the LSE was probably Haldane's. Ward was as much the initiator as Haldane; he had been an administrative officer himself for almost thirty years, so this was his specialist subject. Ward had espoused many of the principles behind the course as early as 1893 and he put forward the idea for the scheme in a memorandum entitled 'The need for a trained administrative staff' in February 1906.[82] Clearly though, both men were of the same view on the topic and in the paper, 'Ward propounded the then revolutionary idea that modern soldiers needed training in modern administrative techniques.'[83] He enclosed a draft for a three-year staff training course, of which six months were to be spent on accountancy, commercial methods, public administration and finance, production and trade, railway administration and transport and commercial and international law. The final scheme combined Haldane's aim with Ward's conviction that management principles needed to be inculcated throughout the administration of both the War Office and the army. Ward was one of the first to apply business methods in Whitehall, some nine years before Lloyd-George utilised similar principles in his wartime coalition, and the first to introduce management training for British civil servants and the armed forces.

Ward and Haldane's conviction that business methods were needed place them within the broader movement for national efficiency that gained credibility after the Boer War. This movement was led by the former Liberal Prime Minister Lord Rosebery, who had been advocating the need for Britain to be put on a business footing since the 1880s. It was supported by other prominent Liberals and left-of-centre figures including Haldane, Halford Mackinder (Director of the LSE) and the Fabians Sidney and Beatrice Webb, who along with Haldane had helped establish the LSE. Drawing on a wider political consensus, the dining club the 'Co-Efficients' was formed by Leopold Amery and Beatrice Webb in November 1902 to air strategies that could be used to promote national efficiency. While it lasted (it disbanded in 1908 over disagreements around tariff reform), the grouping included those previously mentioned plus Sir Edward Grey, Clinton Dawkins, Bertrand Russell, H.G. Wells and George Bernard Shaw.[84]

Mackinder had already introduced programmes at the LSE to serve the executives of the railway, banking and insurance industries as well as the Indian Civil Service, and Ward had clearly already discussed the idea of a course with Mackinder and Sidney Webb because on the day he drafted his

memo he lunched with Mackinder who then wrote to Webb saying 'it is practically certain that the scheme we blocked out together will go through.'[85] In
a letter Sidney Webb described Ward's contribution to the course as 'indispensable' which is a further indication that Ward was at least as involved
in the scheme's genesis as was Haldane.[86] The scheme received the official
go-ahead six months later and immediately thereafter an advisory board
was established under Ward's chairmanship. Its senior military member was
Lieutenant-General H.D. Hutchinson, Director of Staff Duties, who was
replaced a year later by Douglas Haig when he took up that post.

Though Ward would have liked to have a period of business training
that lasted a full three years it was unrealistic for officers to remove themselves from the prospects for promotion for this length of time and so the
final agreement was for a six-month course.[87] The first ran from January to
July 1907, with the second following from October 1907 to March 1908.
Six further courses ran annually from October to March and in total 245
officers, mainly of the rank of Captain and Major, attended the course
from all branches of the army with the exception of the cavalry. Lectures
were given on fourteen subjects covering six broader areas: accounting and
business methods, commercial law, statistics, transport, banking and economics. They were supplemented by numerous 'observation visits' to such
enterprises as the offices of *The Times*, the Great Western Railway Works,
the London Docks, the London Omnibus Works, the Railway Clearing
House, the Houses of Parliament and Lloyds. Students were instructed by
eminent experts in their fields who were drawn from business, the universities and government. Haldane was a frequent lecturer along with several
others who were politically from the radical wing including Webb, who
lectured on the organisation of trade unions, Hastings Lees-Smith, later a
Labour Cabinet Minister (on economics) and the Fabian Socialist Graham
Wallas, one of the seminal figures in the development of social science (on
public administration).[88]

The course became affectionately known as 'Haldane's Mackindergar-
den' and its immediate impact was to assist the LSE's finances, allowing
them to open a refectory serving all staff and students.[89] Lawrence Dicksee,
the course's main accountancy lecturer, was in no doubt that the programme
significantly improved military efficiency and that it was responsible for the
'wonderful success of transport and supply' in the early part of the war.[90]
Those who went through the course became senior administrative officers
during the war and had a profound influence upon the supply and management of the army.[91] One aspect of the First World War that gets unanimous
praise is its logistical administration and part of the groundwork for this
success was laid in the eight courses of 1907–14. Warwick Funnell has
described the course as 'amongst the most innovative strategies to raise the
commercial awareness and accounting expertise of army administrators'
and demonstrates how it had a significant impact upon the efficient operation of the Ministry of Munitions.[92]

The LSE course demonstrates that many of the senior administrative officers and several of the senior commanders of the First World War, not least Douglas Haig, were well versed in modern business management principles, including the latest thinking from the United States on scientific management. Perhaps this information further weakens the argument that all British First World War Generals were dyed-in-the-wool reactionaries, out of touch with the modern world. D.R. Stoddart has summarised the courses as providing 'a precedent for the later university training of Army and Air Force cadets in wartime. . . . It was the beginning of the thinking soldiers army' and Funnell has suggested that it was a 'revolutionary innovation in the education of British army officers and in the approach of the War Office to army administration.'[93] There is a good case to be made that the LSE Army Class attempted, and was partially successful, in initiating a management revolution within the administration of the army.

Retirement

In June 1912 Haldane became Lord Chancellor and was replaced as Secretary of State for War by Jack Seely in a seamless transition in which Ward's cordial relations with his political superior continued. In January 1914 prior to the completion of the eighth LSE course Ward retired from the War Office intending to concentrate on his own business activities. Overall his tenure was hugely successful and set in place a more modern and robust establishment. His partnership with Haldane must stand as one of the most fruitful collaborations between a Secretary of State and Permanent Secretary in modern British history. Haldane was highly intellectual, Ward highly practical. Ward had the direct service experience Haldane needed and both men were noted for their diplomatic skills. Most crucially, the two men shared a conviction that management training was essential for a modern army and that the very latest ideas needed to be taught to officers and administrators. Correlli Barnett's summary of the period 1906 to 1914 is that 'not since the days of the Commonwealth had the British Army been so generally gripped with a sense of professional purpose in peacetime' and through that entire time Sir Edward Ward had been the senior civil servant in charge.[94]

Ward's activities did not end with his official role and his voluntary work clearly demonstrated his commitment to the welfare of both current and ex-soldiers. He helped found the Union Jack Club, providing facilities and accommodation for 'other ranks' when in London, and was its President for twenty-two years. In helping transform the War Office into an efficient department of state, he also raised the morale of its staff. He had a keen concern for staff welfare both inside and outside office hours. He organised the War Office Sports Club, where officers, private soldiers and civilians mixed as equals and, as one of them remembered on Ward's death, 'he set himself to infuse a new spirit of camaraderie into the staff under his control, and . . . accomplished work which will ever make his name memorable.'[95] He significantly improved relations between the army and the department, in many instances by replacing civilians with little knowledge by military experts, and helped in the passing of a host of reforms and improvements. His work made the British army significantly more effective and able to concentrate on its key roles. In the words of one historian Ward gave officers 'the opportunity to exercise their own judgement as to the method by which policy decisions were to be enforced.'[96] This reduction in bureaucracy may not have been as complete as it might have been but it made the army a more efficient fighting force.

In 1907 Ward had been created KCVO and, on his retirement, a baronet after which he became Chairman and Director of a number of substantial companies. However, the outbreak of war brought him back to national prominence and no one was more committed to the cause on the home front. During the war, he was an extremely active Chairman of the Council of the RSPCA where he ensured liaison with the Royal Army Veterinary Corps contributing significantly to the welfare of horses in the army and directly involving himself in cases of animal cruelty in the UK. He was Honorary Treasurer and a member of the General Purposes Committee of the West Indian Contingent Committee (which looked after the welfare of West Indian and Bermudan troops); Assistant Inspector of Shells for the Ministry of Munitions and Commandant-in-Chief of the Metropolitan Special Constabulary.[97] However, the role that was most critical prior to his recruitment as DGVO was that in relation to the 'Camps Library'. During the war this organisation provided an astonishing sixteen million books of all descriptions to every theatre of war in messes and rest huts.[98]

For his wartime work Ward was one of the first to be appointed to the highest level of the newly created Order of the British Empire, GBE, in 1919. He died, of food poisoning, in France in 1928 and is buried in Brompton cemetery. Ward's entry in the *Dictionary of National Biography* concludes that he was 'a strong but genial personality, welcoming responsibility, imperturbable, somewhat inarticulate, Ward's forte lay in execution rather than in counsel.' It would be hard to disagree and difficult to think of a man who was more fitted for the wartime role he took on.

THE OPERATION AND ORGANISATION OF THE DGVO SCHEME

In late September 1915 Ward had got to work in his new job and it had received official Army Council approval in October. The scheme's aim was coordination to reduce waste and to provide maximum support for the fighting troops.[99] A press notice was issued on 11 October and the newspapers commented favourably on both the establishment of the scheme and Ward's appointment in particular. In an editorial under the heading 'The New War Work Scheme, Business Methods Welcomed' *The Times* concluded:

> Its prime mission is to tell the people of England to make the things which
> are really wanted and to make them in such quantities as to admit of their
> being promptly handled by the transport authorities. . . . In other words
> business methods are to be applied which have hitherto been lacking.[100]

So from the first this was seen as another of Ward's schemes to improve
organisations through the employment of management principles. Another
key point was that Ward did not want his new department to stifle existing
work, just to avoid waste and coordinate it. Specifically he stated that 'the
War Office has no desire to interfere with the patriotic efforts of those who
have at the request of Commanding Officers done so much to provide comforts for individual corps.'[101] Ward identified that existing work on troop
comforts and medical supplies mainly fell into five categories:

1. Queen Mary's Needlework Guild.
2. The old Regimental Associations, working for particular Units.
3. Red Cross Work Parties.
4. Groups who had worked more or less intermittently.
5. Bodies of workers unaffiliated to any central organization—this class
   forming the great majority.[102]

It was mainly with the last two that he was concerned. With regard to the
others, he determined that he would not interfere directly with their work.
This decision was also based, no doubt, on their prestige and their desire
not to have a government official telling them what to do. Nevertheless, he
was able to ensure that their activities complemented those over which he
had more direct control.

One of Ward's first tasks was to ascertain exactly what items were
required and then to allocate responsibility for their collection based upon
each group's ability to provide them so that 'no man shall be outside the
reach of comforts.'[103] His office was responsible for keeping a central register
of organisations and issued certificates to those that it officially approved.
These were able to continue their work with the DGVO stamp of approval
and there was an official badge that could be worn to identify volunteers
working for approved bodies. Equally, he could withdraw recognition if
organisations failed to meet their quotas.[104] However, this was as far as the
scheme went; there was no intention to vet charity organisers or scrutinise
accounts. A significant early issue was that of transport and postage costs
which were a major burden for local charities.[105] Shortly before the formation of the DGVO this problem had been taken up by the WNC. They had
pressed for a reduction in postal charges for parcels sent to men at the front
and Labour MP Will Anderson had raised the matter in the House.[106] By
coordinating supplies at a national level Ward relieved local organisations
of the burden of transport costs, significantly alleviating the problem and
responding positively to the WNC's criticism.

Accompanying the announcement of its establishment, the DGVO addressed the issue of 'quality control' in its first requisition order, for mufflers and mittens. Mufflers were to be made 'of fleeced wool, drab shades, 58in long, 10in wide; Mittens of knitting wool, drab shades, with short thumbs and no fingers, 8in long from wrist to knuckle.'[107] This was quickly followed by an issue of leaflets that set out the standard pattern for sixteen items of clothing including shirts, caps, 'helpless case' bed jackets and even hose tops for Highland regiments. In December, Ward sent one of his staff to France on a fact-finding trip to report on the best method for distributing comforts and Ward himself made more than one visit to the Western Front in his Territorial Army capacity and must also have looked into aspects of comforts supply at the same time.[108] As a result of these visits, and after discussing the issue with both Sir John Cowans and the Inspector-General of Communications, Lieutenant General Frederick Clayton, Ward decided to establish a 'Comforts Pool' in each theatre of war, in the charge of the Military Forwarding Establishment, later noting the basic method of operation:

1. The DGVO was advised by the Military Forwarding Officer of the needs of the troops in his theatre. They obtained their information from Commanding Officers of individual units. Hence, a responsibility was placed centrally where none existed before.
2. The DGVO assembled these needs through the network of voluntary organisations under his auspices, requesting supplies from each according to its capacity. This ensured that there was not an oversupply of one item and an undersupply of another.
3. The organisations made fortnightly returns to the DGVO and notified him of any problems. This ensured that the DGVO was kept up to date with the capacity of individual bodies.
4. The DGVO organised transport to the required destination, ensuring that supplies emanating from a particular district were earmarked for the battalions or units the local volunteers wished them to go to. This was set out to a considerable level of detail in order to be clear who was responsible for what and thereby overcome any delays in supply.
5. Military Forwarding Officers made weekly returns to the DGVO regarding what they had received and what they had sent on to units. They were also responsible for informing all units about the 'Comforts Pool' and its operation in order to obviate any more direct requests to the home front. Again, this achieved centralised control and responsibility at senior army level where none had previously existed.[109]

From these reports Ward was able to inform local voluntary organisations that their items had reached the right destination. He realised that it was essential to maintain 'the continuance of the close connection which is so valuable between the units and the localities from which they are raised' in order not to break the bonds of mutual aid and community existing

Figure 5.2 Cover of fund-raising booklet for the British Prisoners of War Food Parcels and Clothing Fund (courtesy of the City of London, London Metropolitan Archives).

between individual organisations and 'their' troops.[110] The comforts pool was especially successful, speeding up delivery to units and significantly reducing shortages. This was even true as the number of units, together with the army, expanded dramatically.[111] This efficiency led to an elimination of complaints reaching Sir John Cowans in Whitehall. Following the episode of Lt Reynolds and the 10th West Yorks in December 1915 there is no further correspondence on file on the subject, a clear indication that in this respect Ward had done his job.

Ward's department also coordinated the distribution of supplies to the sick and wounded in army hospitals. He discovered on taking office that 'in the early days of the War ... Officers Commanding Hospitals, Matrons, and other officials, were in the habit of making application to a number of War Hospital Supply Depots and other Voluntary Societies for gifts ... which resulted in many Hospitals receiving far more stores than were required, where other and less fortunate Hospitals frequently were without Comforts.'[112] Ward was determined to end this free-for-all and put some of the blame on his partners in the Red Cross. Following discussion with the Director-General of the Army Medical Service, General Sir Arthur Sloggett, Ward wrote a stiffly worded letter to Sir Arthur Stanley, Chairman of the Joint War Committee of the British Red Cross, spelling out his scheme to coordinate activity, including how the Red Cross would need to cooperate. 'I hope that makes the situation perfectly clear', Ward concluded, atypically brusquely.[113] Stanley replied the next day to say he concurred with Ward's plans, the key being that 'Officers Commanding Hospital Units were instructed to forward indents to the Head Office of the D.G.V.O. setting out the requirements of their Hospitals.'[114] By this means Ward, unofficially, brought the Red Cross under his wing.

Another medical innovation with which the DGVO became involved was the use of sphagnum moss in treating wounds. Ward's final report explained this unusual project:

> Colonel Cathcart of Edinburgh endeavoured to bring to the notice of the medical community the great value of sphagnum moss as a surgical dressing. Considerable opposition to the general use of sphagnum moss existed, but ... the objections were gradually overcome with the result that by 1917 the vast majority of medical officers realised the possibilities. ... It was at this time that the Director General, Army Medical Service, approached me with the object that my Department's undertaking the gathering, collection, treatment, supply and distribution of sphagnum moss dressings.[115]

An entire of army of volunteers was enrolled in this, with a large number of schoolchildren involved, at least in the early days.[116] The War Supplies branch in little Ottery St Mary in Devon was heavily involved too. It had an average of eighty volunteer workers on the sphagnum moss scheme who produced a total of 240,310 dressings.[117] Though we might scoff at the amateurishness of these activities they clearly made an impact on the flow of medical supplies to the front. One contemporary commentator credited Ward with fusing the various agencies, including the Red Cross, into 'a complete and gigantic supplementary National Organization for Aid to the Sick and Wounded.'[118]

'AN INFINITY OF PERSONAL SACRIFICE'—SUMMARY AND SUCCESS OF THE DGVO SCHEME

One provision of the DGVO scheme was that those in charge of county committees were expected to ensure that local organisations were of sufficient size to ensure smooth delivery of the required items and grouping bodies together in order to achieve this. Inevitably, there were some mismatches in supply and demand. In late September 1916, as winter conditions began to set in on the Somme battlefields, the DGVO issued requisition orders for mittens. Not every organisation had produced the required number and as the minutes of the Croydon War Supplies Clearing House (CWSCH) noted, 'Miss Colam reported a requisition from the DGVO for 2,000 pairs of mittens, and as only 1,200 were in stock, it was resolved to purchase 800 pairs at 1s per pair and debit the Flag Day money with the cost.'[119] Other branches had different problems. There were a number of depots in Ireland and whilst many reported no political problems or interference (for example Limerick and Sligo) the Kilkenny (Mount Loftus) Branch account says that 'the association kept up under great difficulties, owing to political unrest in Ireland.'[120] The Lowestoft branch faced a different form of aggression as it 'was the only Depot in England to be bombarded by the German Fleet, 26 April, 1916. In spite of every pane of glass being smashed, the work was carried on that day as usual. Three 12-in shells fell within 100yds of Claremont House [their HQ], and many passed over the buildings.'[121]

In 1916 the Army Council added the task of providing comforts for the troops of Allied countries in Britain to Ward's list of duties, including U.S. troops who began to reach Europe in late 1917. The success achieved by Ward and the voluntary organisations under his department is reflected in the especial thanks they received from the officer commanding U.S. forces in Britain, Major General John Biddle. The items produced under the DGVO scheme reached prodigious totals, as Table 5.1 demonstrates. Ward placed an approximate monetary value on their production of £5,134,656.[122]

Ward summarised the work of his department in the following words:

> The work of these organizations has done more than any other movement in connection with the war to help and strengthen the morale of our men in the severe trials and difficulties through which they have passed, and has formed a great bond of affection and regard with those left at home.

When the official history of the Great War is written, there will be no more illuminating page than that which records the noble self-sacrifice of the great band of workers at home whose privilege it has been to take their share and play their part in ministering to the needs of our Army, and in having fulfilled their task loyally, faithfully, and in full measure.[123]

They also received the grateful thanks of the Commander-in-Chief. In a letter to Ward Sir Douglas Haig produced an astute assessment:

For many years, voluntary organisations of all descriptions have formed a permanent and characteristic feature of our national life. The outbreak of the war opened up a new and wide field for their endeavour, of which they were not slow to profit. Their activities have been doubled and redoubled. All classes of the community, both men and women, have vied with each other in the generous effort to ameliorate the lot of those who were fighting in their defence. Comforts of every sort and in vast quantities, running into millions have been furnished by them for the troops; at a cost of an infinity of personal sacrifice of money, time and toil.

Table 5.1 DGVO Total Items Supplied

Mufflers	1,742,947
Mittens (pairs)	1,574,156
Helmets (wool)	435,580
Socks (pairs)	3,607,959
Sweaters	123,666
Pyjamas	523,032
Bed jackets and helpless case jackets	325,188
Bed socks	351,764
Operation stockings	154,142
Hospital bags	6,145,673
Bandages of all kinds	12,258,536
Dressings of all kinds	45,503,534
Woodwork articles of all kinds	516,408
Books (via the 'Camps Library')	16,660,000
Cigarettes	232,599,181
Tobacco (lbs)	256,487
Games	62,193
Total	322,840,446

> No praise can be too great for those who assisted in the task; liberal and loving recognition of the courage and devotion of our fighting men. No words can adequately assess the value of what they did, nor sufficiently express the warmth and sincerity of our appreciation.[124]

Ward even ensured that the DGVO's office continued some of its work after the war by asking the various depots to assist in aiding the devastated areas of France with donations of clothing and other essential items.[125]

The DGVO scheme had a significant impact on reducing overlapping. When the Committee on War Charities was formed to enquire whether further legislation was required James Shaw, County Clerk of Ayrshire, wrote in evidence that overlapping had been reduced and that 'the voluntary organisation work has been put upon a complete system in the county to a very large extent' since the advent of the DGVO scheme.[126] With regard to the Croydon War Supplies Clearing House, which was clearly one of the better organised and larger bodies, switching to semi-official status caused few problems either in organisation or in donations. In September 1916, Alice Livingstone of the Croydon War Hospital Supply Depot reported on the merger with the DGVO. She commented that 'the result has been satisfactory, and orders are now received direct from Headquarters and the Croydon Branch at the Town Hall. By this means overlapping is avoided and the work goes where it is most needed.'[127]

Significantly though, it was not only the *stated* aims of the scheme that were welcomed by the press on its inception. *The Times* expected Ward's office to do rather more and stated that 'the scheme will stimulate the work of bona fide associations and will, it is hoped, check the operations of certain bodies which are conducted mainly for the benefit of the promoters.'[128] From the outset, it was clear that the press at least would expect more of the DGVO than he could deliver. It was therefore no surprise when, in March 1916, the magazine *Truth* sounded a critical note. They cited the case of the Sailors and Soldiers Tobacco Fund, which was a perfectly respectable comforts organisation. *Truth*'s ire was raised because of the proportion of its overheads:

> Every shilling contributed by the public only purchased eight pennyworth of tobacco. . . . Yet this fund is recognised by the department at the War Office under Sir Edward Ward. . . . The formation of this department was the first feeble effort to create some sort of order out of chaos, which does not appear to have had much success.[129]

This was entirely unfair criticism as control of administrative expenses was certainly *not* the responsibility of the DGVO. Ward's remit was insufficient and his powers too limited to expect him to act as a regulator or policeman. It is also important to note that the DGVO was an army-inspired programme run from the War Office. It was specifically intended to deal with issues of concern to that department and the deflection of any criticism that the army was either not doing enough or was failing to coordinate matters. The roles ascribed by *The Times* and *Truth* were not those of the War Office but of the Home Department, and Whitehall divisions and rivalries were even more significant in 1915 than they are today. In its primary aim of coordinating the collection and distribution of comforts, the DGVO scheme was successful. It continued after the passing of the 1916 War Charities Act, despite Ward's concerns that the Act could undermine his own efforts. He himself was able to report in June 1917 that 'the response to the Army Council's Scheme for the provision of comforts for general distribution to the Troops in the Field has been highly satisfactory' and the long delays previously reported had ceased.[130]

Another measure of the effectiveness of Ward's department was that it did not run into the same kinds of problems experienced by similar projects. The success of the DGVO encouraged the authorities to act with regard to coordinating comforts for prisoners of war. Following earlier abortive attempts to get the state to take responsibility, in October 1916 a Central Prisoners of War Committee (CPWC) was established under the auspices of the Red Cross and Order of St John on similar lines to the DGVO. Perhaps the problems they confronted were more complex, as they had to coordinate activities with foreign and enemy powers, or perhaps they simply lacked the organisational genius of an Edward Ward but the CPWC encountered significant criticism. The new centralised operation reduced the personal touch of local charities supporting local units and, what was worse, much of the criticism came from the PoWs themselves. In February 1917, Rifleman Bernard Britland, a prisoner of war in Germany, wrote to his mother, 'I don't know what sort of a Xmas we shall spend this time as the committee parcels are not as satisfactory as home parcels.'[131] The CPWC was severely criticised in the June 1917 issue of the *Ruhleben Magazine* representing the views of men in one of the largest camps in Germany. They repeated Rifleman Britland's reservations and contended that officers were receiving preferential treatment. The *Ruhleben* article received significant publicity in Britain, so much so that the CPWC Chairman, L.S. Jameson, was forced to issue an official statement to *The Times* refuting the allegations. His response was more than a trifle defensive, blaming several of the problems on War Office regulations.[132] That these criticisms were not simply anecdotal or media inspired is confirmed by the fact that a parliamentary committee of enquiry into the organisation and methods of the CPWC was appointed. Its report concluded that the CPWC was heavy-handed, bureaucratic and top-down in its approach. It noted that it 'evoked great discontent throughout the country' by prohibiting all private parcels to prisoners and by the rigidity of its regulations.[133] This caused resentment and the view that the army was taking over, severing ties with local PoWs and undermining local initiatives. It also privileged officers above other ranks, allowing them an unlimited number of parcels. This was the height of folly and entirely against the grain of what both the DGVO and most other official bodies were doing at the time. The report concluded the scheme had been launched prematurely and that it lacked the understanding of the workings of the War Office and army that Ward enjoyed. The report was scathing in its criticism of the CPWC, questioned the veracity of some its evidence and concluded that the public outcry regarding its work was fully justified.[134]

Comparison might also be made to the parallel scheme inaugurated in Australia. Whilst the Australian Comforts Fund operated well in many respects, it suffered from two problems. The first was that until August 1916 the supply end of the Fund was organised on a state rather than a national basis, which made coordination problematic. The second was that in the field the Fund was administered by civilians rather than being integrated into the army in the way that the DGVO scheme was. This led to clashes with the military authorities and even, on one occasion, to ACF officials being arrested as spies. The difficulty was eventually overcome by giving officials of the Fund military rank.[135]

Overall, the DGVO scheme was clearly needed and it overcame many of the supply problems encountered in 1914 and 1915. At the outbreak of war a localised approach to comforts and medical supplies was all that existed but as Sarah Pedersen has noted, 'by the end of 1915 the government had started to realise that a voluntary and localised approach to the war was not enough.'[136] Such coordination required great skill and diplomacy if it was not to alienate the mass of charitable activity that had been generated. In this, the appointment of Sir Edward Ward was a masterstroke. He was probably the only person who combined an intimate knowledge of the armed forces with a commitment to efficient management and a compassionate understanding of voluntary effort. The DGVO scheme was a halfway house between unregulated and uncoordinated activity and full legislation. It was designed to solve a specific problem, that of an imbalance in supply of troop comforts, rather than to control the entire voluntary effort of the country. Based as it was on cooperation rather than legislation it was inevitable that it worked well when dealing with well-organised, altruistic groups. What it could *not* do was deal with abuses of philanthropic principles by an unscrupulous minority of individuals who saw an opportunity for personal gain in the upsurge of charitable and voluntary giving initiated by the war.

Case Study 4
Croydon War Supplies Clearing House

We have already noted the importance of 'localism' in pre-war British society and this is a factor often ignored by historians of the period. Different parts of the country were very different in their class and work structures and, not surprisingly, reacted very differently to the strains the war placed on their communities. These regional differences and the aspects of the war they affected are well summed up by Keith Grieves in the introduction to his compilation of sources from Sussex:

> In the history of British Society in the Great War locality matters alongside the dimensions of nation, class and gender. . . . The micro-histories of individuals and communities challenge long held preconceptions, which were often generated by the interpretative lens of living through the Second World War and the Cold War. . . . The existence of local communities of volunteer soldiers, uniformed philanthropic carers, essential war workers, convalescent men, resilient relatives and mourners have become central to understanding the complex, ambiguous and sometimes paradoxical consequences of total war for the young and old, male and female, soldier and civilian, participant and bystander, propertied and cottager, and villager and town dweller.[1]

He specifically does not mention non-uniformed volunteers, not, I think, because he underrates their contribution but because their contribution has not yet become central to the debate. Grieves goes on to suggest that the study of local, primary sources can assist the historian in exploring four themes:

- Popular attitudes towards the war;
- The interwoven lives of soldiers and civilians;
- The persistent linkages of the battle front and the home front and;
- The continuities and ruptures that were experienced in local communities.

I would agree entirely with Grieves and therefore these local sources can help answer several of the questions posed in this book:

- To what extent were home front and battlefront linked?
- Did this help or hinder relationships between civilians and soldiers?
- What did this mean in supporting or hindering the development of social capital?
- What were the social consequences of the war and were they positive or negative?

One of the largest and best-coordinated local schemes was the Croydon War Supplies Clearing House (CWSCH). It was also an early attempt to prevent duplication of activity and in its final report made claim to being the blueprint for the scheme later run by the DGVO.[2] Croydon's claim is somewhat exaggerated as several other towns had followed a similar pattern. For example Eye, in Suffolk, set up a coordinating 'Patriotic Association' on 15 August 1914 and W.E. Dowding wrote in May 1915 that in many places clearing houses had been established. Formed in October 1914 the CWSCH's main function was 'to obtain detailed information respecting all appeals made by recognised organizations providing comforts for the men of the allied fighting forces.' It opened its first depot at 110 George Street in the centre of the town on 2 November appointing Mrs S.J.E. Iredell as Lady Superintendent. Its first collections were for the benefit of Belgian refugees but it rapidly expanded to fourteen depots supplying all local hospitals with comforts, hospital requisites, games, books etc. The Boy Scouts did much of the fetching and carrying and the executive of the London, Brighton and South Coast Railway agreed to transport goods in bulk free. Like the later official DGVO scheme the aim in Croydon and other towns with centralised comforts funds was coordination, not standardisation or the stifling of individual enterprise. In this the CWSCH was extremely successful and very soon assumed the characteristics of a major business enterprise. In December 1914 they held a 'shopping week' for Red Cross comforts which sent £350 of goods to France and this was followed by a Christmas Pudding appeal. In March 1915 there was a condensed milk appeal, supported by the major local employer, Nestlé, which collected 63,451 tins valued at £925. The committee felt confident enough in its finances to take out a bank overdraft that was repaid by holding whist drives and a golf tournament. In July 1915 Union Jack Flag Day raised £330 and the CWSCH funded and ran its own cinema at the Addington Park War Hospital. In October 1915 CWSCH became part of the DGVO scheme with the energetic Mr A.G. Norris assuming the role of Secretary. In December 1915 a massive sale of donated items was held at the Town Hall. Opened by Queen Alexandra the sale ran for seven days from 11am to 11pm, raising the impressive sum of £8,746, equivalent today to more than £500,000. There was another Christmas Pudding Fund that year, realising £380, but the Report recorded that many unfortunately failed to reach their destination:

It is sad to relate that a considerable portion of the puddings consigned to our local Queens Regiment stationed in India, was torpedoed in the Mediterranean, and the portion that did get through and followed the regiment to Mesopotamia, were not fit to eat on arrival, having been spoilt by excessively hot weather.

However, this was only a minor setback as the CWSCH moved on to further ventures. There were fund-raising matinees and performances at the 'Hippodrome' and appeals for footballs and boxing gloves. In February 1916 a waste collection (for bottles, rags, wool, paper and even bones) was started which over two years added a further £354 to the funds. In June 1916, Mr Norris resigned to join the army and, on his recommendation, a campaign was launched to fund a YMCA Hut for France. 'Hut Week' held in September realised no less than £6,458, which supplied several 'Croydonian' huts and even a 'Croydonian Travelling Cinema' for France. This was followed by a YMCA appeal for books. Croydon's citizens were clearly avid readers as this produced 55,000 volumes and 'besides surprising ourselves with this result, we heard the YMCA were obliged to take further premises to accommodate them.' 1918 saw only two special efforts, a matinee at the Hippodrome in conjunction with the West Croydon Cadet School (£309) and a Flag Day in aid of St Dunstan's which produced a war record for such events of £1,274.

CWSCH ceased its activities on 17 April 1919. The final balance sheet showed they had despatched 436,993 parcels to the front or hospitals and 176,823 through the DGVO. These included a motor car and driver for the Red Cross (sent out in December 1914) and a harmonium for the YMCA for religious services in camp. The total sum collected amounted to £20,683 and the final balance of just over £317 was used to endow a bed in Croydon General Hospital's children's ward to be named after the Fund and with preference to be given to children of ex-servicemen.

6 Concerns and Legislation
Scandal, Fraud and the 1916 War Charities Act

EXISTING CHARITY LAW

The intervention of the state in the operation of charities began with the Statute of Charitable Uses of 1601. The Preamble to the Statute is still used as the primary definition of what constitutes a charity in the UK. The four heads are the relief of poverty, the advancement of education, the advancement of religion and other purposes beneficial to the community.[1] Prior to the mid-nineteenth century, the only recourse for redressing irregularities in charities or restructuring or redefining their purpose was the tediously slow and inordinately costly Court of Chancery. In the first quarter of the nineteenth century publicity surrounding charity scandals produced an impetus for parliamentary reform.[2] The Scottish politician Henry Peter Brougham was the primary force behind this and Parliament established a Commission under his chairmanship in 1819. Over the next twenty years the Commission produced forty volumes of reports exposing charitable chicanery and praising good practice. The final reports of the Brougham Commission (published between 1837 and 1840) recommended the establishment of a permanent Charity Commission.[3] However, it took Parliament nearly another twenty years, a further Royal Commission and scandals in the 1840s and early 1850s to finally pass the legislation establishing the Commission in 1853. Even then, it was watered down in the Lords (who resented intrusion into areas of upper class privilege and philanthropy) and so it was defective in a number of respects. The Commission's powers only extended to charitable endowments thus excluding 'collecting charities' that were free to spend the funds subscribed as they saw fit. Also excluded were a group of rich and important charities that Tory opposition had ensured lay outside the Commission's remit. These included universities, cathedrals, collegiate churches and the fee-paying schools of Eton and Winchester. The Commission could not order that a charity's accounts be audited and any maladministration had to be gross and overt before they could act. There were severe limitations on the powers of the Commission to apply cy près schemes (for example to modernise outdated trusts) and these schemes still had to go through Chancery or be presented to

Parliament.[4] The Commission were understaffed and underfunded and suffered a 'bad press' for being slow and unaggressive.[5]

In 1860, the Commission did get an extension to its judicial powers through the Charitable Trusts Act, which enabled it to circumvent Parliament and Chancery, the only real extension of its power until 1960. They were strongly influenced by the doctrine of the COS and were 'particularly concerned to try to modernize large numbers of endowed dole charities in which neither the terms of the trust nor the policy of the trustees took any account of the need to discriminate between deserving and undeserving claimants' and, in 1881, the Commissioners were granted extraordinary powers in the case of London through the City of London Parochial Charities Act of 1883.[6] Despite these advances, the Charity Commission was not highly regarded nor did it achieve its original objectives, especially in relation to fraudulent activity; the expectations on an overstretched, under-resourced Commission were simply unrealistic. It is also noteworthy that the Commission was regarded as 'a central agency imposing its will without regard for local sensibilities.'[7] This became critical with regard to the administration of wartime charity legislation. Neither did it have any control over the non-endowed, collecting charities that exploded in number on the outbreak of war.

'AN EXTRAORDINARY BILL'

The first attempt at state control of charities during the war came within a month of its outbreak. The instigator was Sir Melvill Beachcroft, Chairman of the London County Council, but acting in his capacity as Chairman of the Social Welfare Association for London. He saw an opportunity to kill two birds with one stone: gain control over wasteful dole charities and provide additional funds for war relief. The rapidity of the official response suggests that he had already discussed his proposals with Sir Charles Cook, the Chief Charity Commissioner, and Herbert Samuel, President of the LGB. We have already seen how many people feared that the war would cause significant social problems and Sir Melvill's proposals were something of a knee jerk response to meet these potential demands. In a letter to the editor of the *Pall Mall Gazette* on 3 September 1914, Sir Melvill noted that the Royal Commission on the Poor Laws had found that the income of London charities was a significant £7.5 million a year.[8] He believed that some of these funds could be directed towards war relief and that the powers of charity trustees should be extended to allow them to divert funds into the NRF. 'Would that heroic and suffering Belgium had at its disposal but a fraction of the charitable endowments available in London alone for doles of food and money!' bemoaned Sir Melvill.[9] Within days an Emergency Bill was drafted 'to enable the income of certain charities to be applied temporarily to the Prince of Wales's National Relief Fund.'[10] The period proposed was initially three years, later amended to six months beyond the duration of the war.

The first reading of the Bill was on 9 September. Introduced by Samuel it immediately ran into problems. Questions were raised as to which charities would be affected and as to why only the NRF, seen by many as a quasi-government organisation, would benefit. To many MPs it looked as if the government were trying to get their hands on private charitable funds. This was a cause that united opinion from the right, who opposed government control, and the left, who felt they should use state funds instead. Immediately after the first reading Samuel met with the Charity Commissioners to say that he expected significant opposition at second reading unless a list of '50 or 60 particular cases' of the charities the Bill was expected to lever funds from could be cited. At the second reading the following day, he stated that there were over 6,000 charities but he suggested that the Bill might be delayed, as the Charity Commissioners would need more time to draw up an accurate list.[11] This was getting rather too much for the Bill's opponents. J.F.P. Rawlinson (Unionist, Cambridge University) summed up the mood when he attacked the 'vague' wording of the Bill, disputing both its need and its all-embracing nature. 'It looks suspiciously as if the Commissioners desired to get hold of these charities. . . . I do not think that advantage should be taken of this emergency to bring forward such an extraordinary Bill as that which is before us at the present time', he fulminated.[12] Given such vehement opposition, a vote on second reading was not taken.

Following this setback Sir Horace Monro, Permanent Secretary to the LGB, wrote to Sir Charles Cook asking whether it was worth reviving or not. Monro stated that Samuel 'feels that a very strong case will have to be presented if the House of Commons are to be induced to pass a Bill, in any shape, authorising the alienation of Charity funds towards the National Relief Fund.'[13] Sir Charles instead wrote an open letter to the press asking that charity trustees who were willing to have funds applied to the NRF should contact the Commissioners, the implication being that they would look sympathetically to amending their charitable objectives in order for them to do so. He was obviously resigned to substituting a voluntary scheme for an official one. On 15 September the *Morning Post* published a further letter from Sir Melvill Beachcroft stating that he knew several dole charities that met Cook's definition and urging others to contact the Commissioners. However it was clear that most charities had no intention of responding or had more pressing demands as by 22 October the Commission had received replies from only 287 charities pledging funds of a mere £8,707. In a further letter Sir Melvill admitted that this was a poor response. It was therefore no surprise when, in November, the LGB and Commission decided not to proceed with the Bill and, by this time, it was also clear that the NRF was receiving sufficient income from other sources. At the end of November 1915 there was a half-hearted attempt to revive the legislation. Sir Ernest Soames (of the National Debt Office) wrote to the

Commissioners saying that now there was a coalition government a bill had a far greater chance of success.[14] Sir Charles Cook didn't think things had sufficiently changed and in his reply concluded that 'the opposition last year to our very mild proposal came from all quarters and appeared to rest on a general dislike, based on very spurious grounds, for any interference with the trusts of charities.'[15]

The ignominious failure of the 1914 Bill acted as something of a disincentive to further proposed charity legislation and cannot have helped the reputation of the Charity Commission. The next steps that were taken towards government influence or legislation over wartime charitable activity did not come until the end of 1915 with the formation of the DGVO, initiated by the War Office rather than the Home Department or Charity Commission.

'ALMOST AN IMPOSSIBLE TASK'—PRESSURE FOR LEGISLATION

The creation of the DGVO dealt with the most urgent aspect of charitable support for Britain's forces. In coordinating supplies of comforts, Sir Edward Ward's department ensured there was less duplication of effort and a more equitable distribution. As such, the DGVO dealt with abuses at the supply end of charity. However, it had no influence over the collection of charitable funds, which remained open to potential mismanagement or even outright fraud. 'The professional writer of begging letters has now adapted his whine to a patriotic tune', *The Times* commented. Impostors posing as wounded soldiers frequented railway stations asking for loans of money and as charitable sentiments reached new heights, so too did the opportunities for trickery. 'The worst class of all' was the impostor who watched casualty lists and wrote to the relatives of a dead 'comrade' requesting payment of an alleged debt.[16] It was no surprise that unscrupulous individuals existed who were eager to exploit the extraordinary generosity of the public towards war-related causes and there were few legal barriers in their way. There were laws that regulated street collections in London but there was no overall regulation or registration of charities.[17] The Charity Commission only oversaw those charities with a permanent endowment and the vast majority of the myriad bodies that sprang up after August 1914 had no intention of establishing an endowment; they existed for immediate financial aid.

An indefatigable opponent of such abuse and proponent of charity control was the magazine *Truth*. Founded in 1877 by the radical Liberal journalist and politician Henry Labouchere *Truth* had made a speciality of exposing financial and charity scandals since the 1880s. It did not take *Truth* long to attack some of the manifestations of charitable support that exploded in August 1914. As early as November that year *Truth* carried a report in the 'Scrutator' column lamenting the disorganised nature of the efforts and calling for 'some sort of order to be brought to this charity chaos.'[18] This was a trifle harsh and their criticism that war-related appeals were divert-ing funds from existing causes was not borne out in reality.[19] Nevertheless, the article did contain some valid criticisms of the current scenario. They were probably correct in assuming that many of those who ran their own organisations preferred 'to be generals in their own little army of one to being useful privates in a well-organised battalion.' *Truth's* recommenda-tion was government action and control, 'a charity clearing house which should winnow the true from the false, the needful from the unnecessary, and see that the stream of contributions is directed into channels by which it would reach those for whom it is intended.'[20] *Truth* mounted an unrelent-ing campaign over the next eighteen months to bring about this type of intervention. It was also the main organ to expose one of the first charity scandals, the activities of the Belgian Soldiers Fund.[21]

Another source of pressure was the charities themselves. Recognising that fraudulent operations could have serious implications for public con-fidence and affect the income of legitimate appeals, many charities began to press the government for intervention. The mouthpiece of the COS, the *Charity Organisation Review,* made a call for action when it castigated 'all the sordid trickery of the social parasites [and] swindlers who prey on the benevolent public [and] have reaped a large harvest since the war began.'[22] The COS did their best to operate a system of self-regulation whereby legitimate charities swapped information about dubious characters.[23] Ulti-mately, though, such a system could not possibly work given the scale of wartime charitable activity.

A number of MPs also took up the cry against charity abuses around the same date. Will Anderson asked, on 16 June 1915, what was being done to avoid duplication of effort and overlapping of appeals.[24] In reply the President of the LGB, Walter Long, said that he hoped the establishment of authorised bodies dealing with pensions, allowances and disabled soldiers would help. The War Pensions Bill passed into law the following month but he agreed to consult with the Home Secretary regarding what else might be done 'for investigating and controlling organisations which appeal for public subscriptions and donations.'[25] Just six days later Laurence Gin-nell (Irish Nationalist MP for Westmeath North) asked whether, given the number of collections 'organised for personal or even criminal purposes', licensing of collections would be introduced. Sir John Simon responded that the matter was 'receiving attention.'[26] Anderson kept up the pressure the following month with a written question that queried the seriousness of some appeals and again asked for legislation in the light of two appeals supposedly by animals, 'one issued in the name of Wendy, a chestnut mare, for sun shelters for Army horses and one by Togo, a black spaniel for kennel huts for Belgian Army dogs.'[27] He was echoing one of the bugbears of *Truth* who also disliked irrational animal appeals, despite the success of 'Private Tom' and his kind. This exchange stimulated *The Times* to action which no doubt agitated the government still further. On 28 July an article appeared under the title 'Waste of Charity: The Evil of Overlapping Funds'. It reiterated previous criticisms and again urged concerted, official action.[28] Still nothing happened and Anderson was back on the case in December, asking a question of the Prime Minister, in which he quoted the estimate that £20 million had been raised to date. He said that the evidence that some of these funds were being misappropriated was clear, as a man had just received a sentence of three months in Portsmouth.[29] Again the answer was that the matter was being considered. Having had their fingers burned with the failed 1914 Bill the government was not going to rush anything.

Pressure mounted further in the New Year in respect of the various funds for Belgian relief in the wake of the Belgian Soldiers Fund case. In February the *Daily Chronicle* summarised their criticisms: overlapping effort, extravagance and outright fraud. Its editor, Robert Donald, had two main demands: firstly, it should be made more difficult for entirely bogus charities to be established; secondly, those whose motives were sound should be required to register to avoid excessive overlap and duplication. Charities should also be required to publish their accounts (which should be properly audited), have a properly constituted committee, avoid excessive administrative expenditure and have the bona fides of their promoters checked to ensure that potential patrons could be certain they were putting their names to legitimate organisations. By now the pressure on the government was reaching a critical level and it was clear that action, rather than promises, was required. The first move was that of the LGB which took steps with regard to Belgian relief funds, only sanctioning those that received the specific endorsement of the Belgian government. This rather feeble action, which had no powers of inspection or any requirement to submit accounts, was never going to answer the critics, whether in the press, Parliament or among the charities themselves.

In February 1916 the government was still resistant to legislation. James Rowlands (Liberal, Dartford) asked of the President of the LGB if the scope of the action the Government had taken on Belgian Relief Funds would be extended to all war charities. Walter Long's reply did not totally rule out action but he made it sound extremely difficult as 'we have looked into the question very carefully, and it seems almost an impossible task.'[30] It was no surprise that *Truth* pounced on his words and refuted them. In the same article that criticised the DGVO scheme, which it misidentified as a regulatory mechanism rather than a coordinator of supply, it summarised the progress to date. *Truth* considered that 'the task [was not] so difficult as it appears to be.' They cited the recent order issued under the Metropolitan Police Act forbidding unauthorised street collections, which had 'an excellent and immediate effect'. Though recognising that legislation was not 'likely to be satisfactorily accomplished by piecemeal departmental action' *Truth* bemoaned the uncoordinated nature of regulation to date, suggested some ideas that found their way into the final Act and urged cross-party parliamentary action.[31]

OFFICIAL DELEGATION AND THE WAR CHARITIES COMMITTEE

Hot on the heels of the *Truth* article the next move was taken by the charities under the leadership of the COS. A deputation of twenty-four UK-wide and English organisations headed by the Duke of Norfolk and including all the major bodies such as the Red Cross, NRF, COS and WRC, met with the Home Secretary, Sir Herbert Samuel, on 3 March 1916.[32] The aim of the delegation was to get Samuel to extend legislative control of charities so 'that in future all appeals to public benevolence in connection with any War Relief Funds should only be permitted after a licence for the purpose has been granted by the Home Office.'[33] They believed that legislation would not only act as a guarantee against corrupt practice but would 'increase public confidence in the support of those deserving organisations who are endeavouring to minimise the terrific sufferings of war.'[34] Sir Herbert was not encouraging and was supported by his officials, one of whose fears was, unsurprisingly, the additional work any legislation would cause. At one stage the Home Secretary referred to the fact that the delegation had not, up to this point, mentioned any specific cases of abuse. Rather helpfully for the delegation Sir Edward Henry, Chief Commissioner of the Metropolitan Police and part of the government team at the meeting, intervened and said, 'I can think of nine or ten funds straight away' and he described several of the cases investigated by Detective Inspector Curry discussed later.[35] Sir Herbert then raised a further difficulty. If the Government authorised charities then they could be blamed if one of these officially sanctioned organisations was found to be fraudulent.[36] He got to the crux of the issue when he summarised that 'the question is, how great the evil is, and whether it is sufficient to necessitate the creation of this new organisation [to vet and investigate charities] and the establishment of the new principle of official control of charities.'[37] Sir Edward Henry then came up with a compromise solution. The delegation wanted a positive vetting of all charities thus providing the sort of official guarantee Sir Herbert was so worried about. Instead, Henry proposed requiring registration but investigation only by exception, when doubts were raised about an organisation. This would provide 'no guarantee from the Home Office, but the public would have this much satisfaction, that if they made complaints against these Funds, they would know that their books were liable to be inspected.'[38] This was eagerly seized upon as a potential solution that could be acceptable to both sides. One member of the delegation, Aneurin Williams, Liberal MP for Northwest Durham and representative of the Armenian Refugees Fund, clearly spoke for many when he said, 'I think Sir Edward's suggestion seems to be a most excellent and practicable one.'[39] It was even supported by that outspoken critic of charity abuse, Robert Donald, attending the meeting in his role as a member of the National Committee for Relief in Belgium. He went even further than Williams by stating, 'I think it is the absolute solution. . . . It gets over the Home Secretary's difficulty of the State organised charity.'[40] Even so, Samuel was careful not to commit himself to anything at the end of the meeting. His concluding remark was that 'I am afraid I cannot do more than say that all these points will receive careful consideration.'[41]

The matter was put in the hands of Samuel's departmental officials and his private secretary, S.W. Harris, prepared a memo on 14 March. He summarised two possible scenarios outlined at the meeting: firstly, pre-investigation of organisations before registration; secondly, scrutiny of activities only after registration. If abuse were to be completely prevented then both would be required. Harris concluded that this 'would be a big piece of work. [It] would require a considerable staff and cost a great deal and I am afraid it is impossible to think of securing this maximum degree of protection.'[42] Having rejected the most complex solution Harris considered the difference between licensing, i.e. close scrutiny of organisations, and registration, which would be a looser control designed to root out worst-case abuses and which would only investigate charities in detail when abuse was reported. Registration would 'involve the minimum of work and expense . . . and would also give the minimum of protection to the public.'[43] Were this solution to be adopted, he listed four potential problems: firstly, the possibility of the Home Office being blamed when something went wrong; secondly, the potentially high level of complaints to investigate; thirdly, that registration would need to encompass every small local fund as well as national ones and including every level in between; and finally, that there was no existing branch of the Home Office that could undertake the task. He reached the following conclusions, if the registration route was the one adopted, which combined many of the points that had been raised in debating the issue in the press, Parliament and elsewhere:

- There should be a registration fee that would, partially at least, offset the cost of administering the scheme;
- Unless a charity was registered, it would be barred from making collections;
- There would be a registering authority with the power to cancel registration;
- Local funds should be registered locally at county level, national ones through a Central Advisory Committee;
- The Central Committee would have a permanent staff (possibly seconded from the Charity Commission, Board of Education or Audit Office);
- The registering authority could also help prevent overlapping by not registering organisations that overlapped with others.

Sir Edward Troup, Permanent Secretary at the Home Office, agreed with most of these recommendations but added that the Central Committee should not just be advisory; it should have the power to refuse registration. If it did not and the 'Home Secretary is responsible, it will bring refusals to register into constant discussion in the House of Commons.'[44] On receipt of this advice, which now favoured some form of legislation involving registration, Samuel decided to seek further evidence and reach some consensus. On 12 April 1916, he appointed an official War Charities Committee 'to consider representations which have been made in regard to the promotion and management of charitable funds for objects connected with the war, and to advise whether any measures should be taken to secure the better control or supervision of such funds in the public interest.'[45]

Appointed to chair the Committee was John William Wilson (Liberal MP for North Worcestershire) and its other members were Sir Ernley Blackwell (Assistant Under Secretary of State at the Home Office); Will Crooks (Labour MP for Woolwich); Lady Gertrude Emmott (from the WRC); Ewan Macpherson (Legal Member of the LGB for Scotland); James Francis Mason (Conservative MP for Windsor and a mining, iron and steel millionaire); Francis Morris (Chairman of the Children's Country Holiday Fund and the Administrative Committee of the COS) and F.J. Willis (Assistant Secretary of the LGB). They held nine meetings between 4 May and the beginning of June taking evidence from charity specialists, journalists and government officials. The first meeting quickly agreed that some form of legislation was necessary. Sir Ernley Blackwell made reference to a number of key scandals: the French Relief Fund, the War Babies Fund, Heroes Poultry Farms and the Cripples Pension Society. Though they decided that further proof of abuses was unnecessary they still took more evidence on this point and agreed a list of witnesses to call. The second meeting took place on 9 May and began the collection of evidence with the appearance of Mr G.S. Paternoster, assistant editor of *Truth*. He believed that all charities should be registered.[46] He also stated that management costs should be no more than 10 percent, a belief that has proved remarkably persistent to the present day. The Committee was working with as much speed as possible and reached conclusions as it went along, some of which it then readjusted in the light of further evidence. At this meeting they decided against the idea of an all-embracing system of regulation, thus immediately rejecting Mr Paternoster's contention. It was clear they wished to do the minimum possible to allay public fears rather than eliminate all possible abuse as supported by key critics like *Truth* and the *Chronicle*. To be fair to the Committee the regulation of *all* charities would have been beyond their stated brief. Instead they came to the conclusion that what was required was a simple scheme that could be put into force at once for preventing existing abuses, 'rather than an elaborate system of supervision which would involve the setting up of a new Government Department.'[47] Therefore they agreed that the chief question was not how far to extend registration but only whether to enforce registration under penalty or not.

Two days later they heard from Mr E.C. Price, Secretary of the Inquiry Department of the COS. True to the COS's principles he too supported the registration of all charities, one reason being the difficulty of defining in

statute what was meant by a 'war charity'. This was indeed one of the legislators' principal difficulties but his point was ignored. The next two witnesses, Algernon Maudslay, Hon Secretary of the WRC, and his colleague
Mr W.A.M. Goode, Hon Secretary of the National Committee for Relief in
Belgium, favoured compulsory registration enforced by penalty. Given their
experience, this was hardly surprising. Several of the scandals involved assistance for Belgium; there was the issue of the Belgian Soldiers Fund and its
offshoots and the WRC had been directly swindled by the multiple fraud-
ster Margaret Robertson. She had been employed in the clothing department of the Fund and had forged receipts that had cost the Committee £499.
She had also attempted to collect funds for the purchase of an X-ray motor
ambulance for the Italian army. For a while, she had been successful enough
to move from her lodging in Coram Street to the Waldorf Hotel where she
posed as the Honourable Mrs Robertson. She appeared for trial at the Old
Bailey in January 1916 and was sentenced to eighteen months hard labour.[48]
Despite the fact that she had previous convictions (for forgery) this appears
rather harsh in the light of other sentences meted out to charity fraudsters
and one suspects that it may have had something to do with her lifestyle: in
handing down the sentence the Recorder referred to her 'riotous living' and
for being so brazen in impersonating a member of the aristocracy.

The pioneering Guild of Help organiser Frederick D'Aeth, Secretary
of the Liverpool Council of Voluntary Aid, who appeared before the fifth
meeting again urged a compulsory system of registration. This session also
took evidence from the *Chronicle*'s editor, Mr Donald, who presented a fat
file of evidence with regard to Miss Carey and the Belgian Soldiers Fund. It
also contained a reference to the Immediate Assistance Committee for War
Victims, another Belgian Fund, whose general manager had committed sui-
cide 'when it was found that he had misappropriated a considerable sum
of money.'[49] Not surprisingly Donald too supported the registration of all
charities as did Mr C.F.A. Hoare (Principal Clerk to the National Health
Insurance Commission) and Miss M.H. Mason who, in common with Lady
Emmott, had bitter experience of Miss Carey's activities with respect to the
National Food Fund and who had had extensive previous correspondence
with the Home Office urging detailed control.[50] She also wrote an article
for the *English Review* stating her views on the topic and recommending
central organisation under the Home Office with local enforcement by the
police.[51] Also giving evidence at this meeting was the redoubtable Detective
Inspector Curry. He carefully listed what he saw as the 'chief evils' that
currently existed:

1. The plundering of funds;
2. Irresponsible people starting funds;
3. Funds conducted either without any committee or with bogus
   committees;
4. Insufficient checks on the expenditure of money;

5. Obtaining secret commissions on goods purchased;
6. Exaggerated appeals;
7. Patrons lending their names to charities without proper inquiry; and
8. In the case of appeals for the Allies, ignoring the Minister or Ambassador of the country concerned.

He handed over a dossier of evidence regarding seven specific war charity scandals. His main point was that control of abuse was both necessary and practicable. He said that the police 'could without any difficulty have obtained within a few days sufficient information about the promoters [of bogus charities] to shew [sic] that they were not suitable persons to have control of such funds.'[52] One point he made was extremely pertinent. He stated that where a genuine charity had been defrauded in 'many cases [they were] unwilling to prosecute for fear of reflections being made on their management' and thus losing public confidence. This is still a real problem with regard to charity fraud and it also meant that Inspector Curry was not able to give the Committee details of perhaps the clearest example of fraud with which he had been involved, that of 'Captain' Illingworth.

All the other witnesses, with one exception, also supported compulsory registration. The opponent was John Samuel, Official Secretary to the Lord Provost of Glasgow. He was 'entirely opposed to the employment of paid officials in connection with charities of any kind.' Taking a devolutionary stance he warned against overregulation, especially any system run by a centralised, national bureaucracy. Citing the example of the NRF he contended that 'there is always a danger of private and voluntary benevolence suffering where subscriptions are amenable to any system of official or red tape control or centralization.'[53] He said that in Glasgow where they had taken a very close interest in war charities, 'I can confidently say that abuses have been very few in number and almost negligible in their extent.'[54] His arguments on local control were quite persuasive and clearly had an impact on the Committee and the eventual system adopted which tried to avoid the kinds of problems that had dogged the NRF.[55]

Clearly the case for compulsory registration rested on perceptions that there were a number of fraudsters operating bogus organisations. But what concrete evidence existed to back up this assertion? The following narrative is based on detailed examination of the police files in the National Archives together with corroborative evidence obtained from the files of the London County Council, the charities own accounts and contemporary press comments.

'BEYOND THE RANGE OF ORDINARY BUSINESS'—THE BELGIAN SOLDIERS FUND

Instances of 'con artists' promoting bogus charities occurred from the early days of the war but they were generally of a very local, small-scale nature. The first scandal to reach national prominence was that of the Belgian Soldiers Fund (BSF), the brainchild of Miss Sophie (or Sophia) de Mussenden Carey, the daughter of a Lincolnshire clergyman, though of Channel Islands extraction.[56] Carey was identified both at the time and by later writers as an outright crook, and Peter Cahalan calls her 'the most indefatigable of wartime swindlers.'[57] However, there is little *definite* evidence that she did more than stretch the rules to the limit of the law and take liberties with the money donated to her fund. Carey had something of a dubious past and, as recently as May 1914, a finance scheme that she ran, the Women's Financial Information Bureau, had been the subject of an exposé in *Truth*. In a series of articles the magazine questioned the methods of her fund and those of her American financier partner, Ben Blanchard.[58] She claimed to be 'the first woman to step out publicly into the world of finance and organise and control a company dealing mainly with investments.' *Truth* questioned her credentials for running such a scheme. She had apparently gained her experience from poultry farming and breeding polo ponies and dogs, skills *Truth* clearly thought were not easily transferable to the sphere of high finance. Carey claimed she would give back £200 profit for every £1,000 invested in ten months, an extraordinary rate of 24 percent interest per annum. Carey said that the investment was done by a 'rich American banker,' named Ben Blanchard, who does it 'just to help a few friends.'[59] Blanchard sat at the centre of a network of somewhat obscure businesses and Scrutator reported a meeting with him at which 'he did not commit himself to any definite explanation of his own particular financial feats.' Despite having repaid unhappy investors in full (with interest) *Truth* concluded that 'one thing is quite obvious: the transactions are quite beyond the range of ordinary business or banking.'[60] Blanchard's tangled web of companies was each taking share holdings in the others and all appeared to be remarkably profitable. *Truth* was careful not to accuse Blanchard or Carey of fraud but the implication was clear: were there other investors who had not come forward and had not got their money back? Though there was no hard evidence, Blanchard and Carey look as if they might have been running a 'Ponzi' scheme (which depends on attracting more and more new investors to pay off those wanting to cash in their 'gains'), just like Bernard Madoff in the twenty-first century.

On the outbreak of war Carey joined the Women's Emergency Corps where she demonstrated that she had a 'remarkable flair for raising money' and organised the collection of food for refugees. 'She gained the cooperation of highly respected people like Sir William and Lady Chance, Lady Emmott and Miss M.H. Mason.'[61] After an instance of misusing the organisation's funds for a private party, Carey and three others were thrown out. Carey went off to found the BSF and another, Mark Judge (a failed hotel manager described by the editor of the *Daily Chronicle* as 'a very shady character'), later joined the equally dubious

Figure 6.1   Poster advertising Joseph Clarkson's fraudulent Belgian Canal Boat Fund (© Imperial War Museums, Q 79963).

French Relief Fund.[62] On 20 December 1914 the BSF launched a press appeal for £50,000 promoting themselves as 'the only Fund that specialises in Field Kitchen and Food Comforts and a pure water supply for the Belgian Army.'[63] They boasted an impressive list of supporters including the Belgian Ministers of War and the Interior and the President of the Belgian Chamber of Representatives. In fact, they did not have any official recognition from the Belgian government and their depiction of the plight of the Belgian Army led to the condemnation of their campaign by the Belgians as being likely to 'injure the prestige of our army.'[64] By April 1915 the BSF had raised £11,500 but doubts were being voiced regarding the administration of the Fund. In December the Metropolitan Police received a letter from a Miss Gentiar Fowler saying that she had made a £5 donation that had not been acknowledged with a receipt. Sgt Jeffrey visited the offices of the Fund in January but he was clearly reassured by Miss Carey and her team. His report concluded that 'Miss Carey is an indefatigable secretary, and of the highest character'; he was clearly unaware of the *Truth* article.[65] Despite Sgt Jeffrey's glowing testimonial doubts persisted. The Chief Constable of South Yorkshire enquired as to the Fund's credentials in late January 1915 and a note appended to the police file states that 'Miss Carey is known as running bogus charities and this particular charity is very suspect.'[66]

In May, possibly in an attempt to 'raise a smokescreen', the Fund itself complained that they had been swindled out of £1 worth of stamps by a bogus collector of funds, but it was some of Carey's acquaintances who were more suspect. The Fund was closely connected with Joseph Clarkson, promoter of the Albert Day Fund, who also ran the Belgian Canal Boat Fund which was intended to feed and clothe Belgian children and to whom the Belgian Soldiers Fund donated £17 6s 7d. Clarkson was a very shady customer, described by Manchester Police as an 'absolute rotter', and both his schemes were placed under administration by the Charity Commission in September 1916.[67] Despite having these dubious acquaintances there was never any direct evidence of wrongdoing against Carey and having looked through their audited accounts, which are on file at the National Archives, it is worth pointing out that there appears to be nothing obviously improper. Equally, the Fund *did* carry out some very worthwhile relief activities in Belgium and payments to staff do not seem excessive, at around 5 percent of income.[68] Nevertheless the Fund was not run as transparently as it might have been and if not actual, the potential for abuse of funds donated by the public existed. In addition to the character of Carey and her associates, there were three main concerns with the BSF. Firstly, it was run on extremely laissez faire principals. Despite dealing with substantial funds, £32,000 to August 1915, there was no formal committee, Carey being emphatic that she had a 'no committee policy.'[69] Secondly they were profligate as to whom they named as supporters. They did not have official recognition from the Belgian government and, after he had sent them a donation of two guineas, they named the Archbishop of Canterbury as a supporter in their literature, which he was forced to deny in a notice issued to the press. They also falsely claimed to have the support of the War Office and Admiralty. The third factor was the re-emergence of the enigmatic Blanchard. When the BSF started its 'million shilling appeal' a journalist from *Truth* visited its offices and asked who was responsible for the expenditure of the funds provided by the public. 'A gentleman present thereupon volunteered to explain the system. Asked for his name, he said it was Blanchard.'[70] It appeared that the Vigo Trading Company, 'one of the numerous companies which Mr Blanchard directs', made nearly all purchases for the Fund (for horses, field kitchens, boilers, water sterilisers etc). Reminding readers of Carey and Blanchard's previous history *Truth* summed up the entire enterprise:

> In reality, Miss Carey is merely a conduit by which the stream of gold flows through an unincorporated company of anonymous persons to the tradesmen who supply the goods, and in whose hands substantial balances are allowed to remain under the surveillance of an American citizen whose methods of finance are a bewildering puzzle.[71]

Though there was no hard evidence of outright fraud the authorities were determined to make an example of Carey and in November 1915 they had their opportunity. Scotland Yard put one of their most energetic and resourceful officers, Detective Inspector John Curry, onto the case.[72] Curry became the Yard's expert in bogus charities over the next three years and he soon had evidence against the BSF when one of the Fund's workers, Miss Millie Back, was arrested for unauthorised street collecting. The police and Home Office decided to take advantage of this case to make a more general statement about bogus charities and the unfortunate Miss Back found herself not only up before the Magistrates but with the press benches crowded with representatives of all the major national newspapers.[73] Treasury Solicitor Mr Muskett's message was very clear and connected only peripherally to Back's misdemeanour to which she was even pleading guilty. It was Back's employers that were in the dock rather than her. Muskett drew attention to two categories of swindlers: the small-scale, uneducated con artist who, though a menace, could be adequately dealt with through the existing law and large-scale schemes initiated by clever professionals into which category Carey was clearly placed.[74] Both Muskett and the court recognised that Miss Back had been acting in good faith and she was merely ordered to pay the cost of her summons, but the statement had the desired effect as it was widely reported in *The Times, Daily Telegraph, Daily Mail, Morning Post* and *Truth*. Although neither Muskett nor, in this article, *Truth* went as far as demanding new legislation, many already were.

'A CAST IRON METHOD'—THOMAS ALROY AND OTHER ROGUES

At the War Charities Committee hearings Inspector Curry described seven cases. The Committee included four of these in its final written report to which they added one further case from outside London. The first, the Belgian Soldiers Fund, has already been described. Both the Cripples Pension Society and the War Orphans Fund were straightforward frauds perpetrated by none-too-intelligent petty criminals. Alfred Worthington, alias Charles Swift, established the former in November 1915. He used the names of prominent MPs (including Will Anderson) to give legitimacy to his enterprise, calling them his 'Parliamentary representatives.' When they objected to their names being used he proposed to pay them a retainer of fifty guineas and three guineas for every question they asked in the House. Colonel Charles Yate (Conservative MP for Melton) responded that he considered this a gross insult but Worthington used the same tactic with his supposed chairman and vice-chairman, the Rev F.H. Gillingham, rector of Bermondsey, and the Rev A.J. Waldron, formerly vicar of Brixton. Worthington was clearly misguided in choosing patrons with such high moral principles. He advertised for disabled soldiers and 'smart ladies' to act as canvassers and one person at least parted with £100 which was immediately paid into Worthington's private account. It did not take long for the law to catch up with him. His feeble defence at Bow Street in August 1916 did not prevent a sentence of three months imprisonment.[75]

The War Orphans Fund was organised by a Frenchman, Jules Victor Ronnet, who was already a convicted swindler and whose first effort at dubious fund-raising was the British Belgian Association. He collected at least £235, all of which went in 'expenses'. The 'collectors employed were women, generally smartly dressed, and bedecked with red, white and blue ribbons.'[76] Ronnet was deported in January 1916 and, back in Paris, was soon arrested for fraud. At the time of the Committee's deliberations he was serving eight months in prison.

Heroes Poultry Farms was supposed to be an employment scheme for ex-soldiers that would provide eggs and poultry free of charge to military hospitals. Its promoter, Ritchie Gill (aka George Ritchie), a film renter from Twickenham, advertised the scheme in the press seeking subscribers. He was one of many to use the 'snowball' technique, thousands of small contributions that each individual would not miss. It seems that he set out with no intention of ever starting a real charity but intended to pocket the proceeds. He was, however, quickly unmasked. Although the Committee report suggests that 'he might easily have obtained a considerable sum of money', he seems to have collected less than £20.[77] He appeared at Bow Street Police Court charged with attempting to procure charitable contributions by fraud but after character witnesses described him as 'hopelessly optimistic' rather than a criminal he escaped a custodial sentence, instead being fined £25.[78]

The Counties Rest Home for British Soldiers was a slightly more ambitious project and its 'mastermind' seems to have been more plausible. Mr M.P. Shorrock had a history of financial irregularity. He had been bankrupted twice and was, at the time, undischarged from the second. He had been imprisoned for failing to pay his rates and had an outstanding verdict of £6,300 against him for fraud. He nevertheless 'succeeded in inducing three Earls and several Members of Parliament to become vice-presidents, and formed a committee of more than 80 ladies, most of whom were the wives of officers commanding regiments.'[79] He had succeeded in raising about £500, which again all appeared to have been swallowed up in expenses leaving the Fund with an adverse balance of £30. The embarrassment caused to Shorrock's patrons was a strong incentive for official action.

Another case was a far more blatant example of fraud but was not mentioned at the War Charities Committee. This may have been because the case was not handled by Inspector Curry but by his colleague, Divisional Detective Inspector Ashley. Ashley's tactics in bringing his man to book were particularly imaginative. The miscreant was sixty-year-old Thomas Alroy, alias Thomas, alias Johnson, a man who had 'given Police much trouble in connection with his exploits in various bogus charitable associations.'[80] Alroy invariably employed attractive female collectors and, since 1911, had operated the Christian and Temperance Mission and impersonated the, real, Fresh Air Fund. Though several of his collectors had been prosecuted, he had always managed to avoid conviction. Alroy's was an extensive network, operating fifty to sixty women at a time and he was also fairly well versed in the law as he gave each of his collectors a 'licence' to sell pamphlets and thus escape the Vagrancy Act. Inspector Ashley had his collectors followed and the surveillance reports indicated that Alroy 'occupies his time solely in visiting public houses' often in association with a woman, Miss Lucy Thornton, who seems to have been more of a business partner than a mistress though they had 'shown some intimacy' during surveillance and both 'exist solely on the money collected by these women [collectors].' Their income was estimated at £25 a week which, when one considers that an average wage was not much more than £1 to £2, was a very healthy sum. Alroy was also ruthless if anyone tried to swindle him. In February one of his collectors, Margaret Caddy, was sentenced to a month's hard labour for begging. The implication was that she had failed to give Alroy all her takings and that he had informed on her to the authorities. In April 1915 Alroy advertised in the *Daily Telegraph* for women collectors at a salary of 15s a week and Inspector Ashley saw his chance. He got both his own wife, Amy, and the wife of PC Saunders to reply to the ad and both were employed. Alroy clearly thought Amy Ashley was a cut above his usual applicants and quickly made her a 'district visitor' to supervise other collectors. The two undercover agents made several visits to Alroy and his associate with fake collections and, in addition, eight of the thirty-five others who answered the ad were followed. In receipt of the policemen and women's reports the Director of Public Prosecutions (DPP) authorised the issue of a warrant for the arrest of Alroy and Thornton. Though he was tipped off by his accountant, whom police had visited, Alroy was confident that he would again escape retribution and made no attempt to abscond. When arrested his first comment was that 'I have conducted this thing for years and we have a cast iron method.' He was wrong. Though Thornton was discharged, on 18 May 1915 Bow Street Magistrates sentenced Alroy to the maximum three months under the Vagrancy Act. Mrs Saunders was awarded 30s out of public funds for her invaluable assistance and Mr Muskett described Inspector Ashley's report as 'a model of its kind' and the Inspector himself as 'a detective Officer of exceptional intelligence and ability.' However, it was his wife's that was the crucial piece of evidence and her statement is beautifully written and a model of clarity.[81]

The other example not included by the Committee was perhaps left out as the case was going through the courts at the time. The war spawned a number of patriotic organisations that promoted the positive aspects of Britain and her empire but it also led to the creation of a smaller number that worked on the opposite principle, denigrating Germany and her culture. The Anti-German League was sprung upon the British public through a newspaper campaign in May 1915, coinciding with the sinking of the *Lusitania*. Its lengthy advertisement in *The Times*, headed 'An Appeal to the Nation', though clearly aimed at the 'better classes', resorted to the worst excesses of jingoistic hyperbole. The Founder and Director of the Anti-German league was E.J. Blasir Chatterton who, he regretted in his advertisement, was 'debarred from Military service owing to a slight physical disability' but who was, nonetheless, determined to do his bit for King and Country. He was seeking 'a Million Members . . . who will preach the Anti-German doctrine all over the Country.' The advertisement included a pledge to sign and return, with a one-shilling subscription, and concluded that 'it is the duty of every Englishman and every Englishwoman in the country to sign this pledge.' It is perhaps rather gratifying to relate that Chatterton was, in reality, no more patriotic than any of the other fraudsters and, despite some success in recruiting the 'great and the good' to his cause and 5,000 ordinary subscribers, his organisation lasted less than a year. In April 1916 he was declared bankrupt with liabilities of £1,278 and the following month was charged with fraud. The charge related to converting two sums donated to the League, one of £215 and another of £20, to his own use. He was tried and found guilty at the Old Bailey in July. It was then revealed that he had previous convictions for sending indecent literature through the post, a fact he failed to point out in his appeals, and he was sentenced to six months hard labour. Though Chatterton's exposure as a fraud and pornographer must have been something of a shock it did not prevent a number of his supporters from continuing their virulently xenophobic activities with other organisations.[82]

The case from outside London that the Committee included was of a very different nature though, again, linked with Belgian relief. Unlike Chatterton, Alroy, Shorrock and Carey, Dr Charles Sarolea was a prominent and highly distinguished citizen. In 1894 he was appointed to the newly founded Lectureship in French at Edinburgh University and in 1918 became the University's first Professor of French. He was a friend of George Bernard Shaw, Ernest Shackleton and Winston Churchill and his own authorship covered political, philosophical and literary subjects. Between 1912 and 1917 he was editor of the popular weekly journal *Everyman*. He and his wife were office holders of the Edinburgh Belgian Refugee Committee and he was for fifty years the Belgian Consul in Scotland. The criticism levelled at Sarolea was not of fraud but of bad management practice and hoarding of funds. He administered the *Everyman* Belgian Relief and Reconstruction Fund, which had raised around £50,000. It was claimed that though the Fund had a committee, in reality the entire administration of the Fund was in Sarolea's hands. The War Charities Committee castigated Sarolea in its report, though being careful not to mention him by name.[83] However, in this case, not all was what it seemed. The source of criticism against Sarolea came solely from the editor of the *Daily Chronicle*, Robert Donald. Donald gave evidence to the Committee on the lines outlined above and the *Chronicle* then repeated the claims being careful not to add that they stemmed from their own editor. Inspector Curry was asked for a report on the *Everyman* Fund but found no irregularities. He also made the point that the only evidence against Sarolea was that supplied by Donald. It would appear that Donald had a grudge against Sarolea. The latter had been a special war correspondent for the *Chronicle* and Donald had been a committee member of Sarolea's fund. The Committee took Donald's comments at face value but the circumstantial evidence suggests that he was pursuing a personal motive.

'A DISTINCTLY DOUBTFUL CHARACTER'— THE FRENCH RELIEF FUND

If Charles Sarolea was the most eminent individual to be accused of, at least, borderline fraud, the most prominent fund that came under suspicion was certainly the French Relief Fund (FRF). Promoting itself as the UK branch of the Secours National (the French equivalent of the NRF) to which it had gained affiliation in December 1914, its high-profile fund-raising activities included a concert by Clara Butt at Eton College, a matinee at Her Majesty's Theatre and, most prominent of all, a massive flag day held on Bastille Day, 14 July 1915. This involved fifteen to twenty thousand women selling millions of flags and it raised £60,000.[84] Even Megan Lloyd-George (daughter of the then Minister of Munitions) collected for the Fund, being highly successful in gaining donations in and around Downing Street. By this time the

FRF had recruited one of the most impressive patrons' lists of any wartime charity. French President Raymond Poincare and several other French Ministers gave their official support and were joined by even more distinguished British patrons including Lord Kitchener, Lloyd George, Bonar Law, Winston Churchill, Austen Chamberlain and, perhaps most embarrassingly, successive Home Secretaries Reginald McKenna and Sir John Simon. As late as November 1915 the *Daily Graphic* included it on their list of those charities it considered 'indispensable' and the work of which 'has been investigated and is recommended to the support of readers with confidence.'[85]

Inspector Curry's report says that the first suspicions were raised by the editor of the *Morning Post,* H.A. Gwynne, who went to Scotland Yard after he had been advised by the French consulate to have nothing to do with the Fund.[86] This visit was followed by two articles in *Truth* commenting adversely on the lack of a proper management committee.[87] At the time the committee comprised just four people: the General Secretary, Mr James Hargreaves Dickinson; the Joint Treasurer, Sir Thomas Brooke Hitching; and two Frenchmen, Paul Roth and Gustave Bernheim, who were later among those to withdraw their support. This criticism appeared to be partly allayed when a properly constituted committee was installed and Messrs Peat and Co appointed to audit the charity's accounts. Unusually *Truth* declared its full confidence and, by June 1915, the FRF was able to state that they had raised £48,000 from 12,000 subscribers.[88] However, it did not take long for a crisis to occur. In an open letter the Chair of the Fund's General Committee, T.H. Carson, said that the Secretary had placed advertisements in the press that the Committee had not approved. Shortly thereafter Carson, together with the Hon Treasurer Sir Thomas Barclay, Professor J.H. Longford and Sir Frederick Pollock resigned from the committee. In its 1 September edition *Truth* published a letter from Professor Longford giving the reasons for his resignation:

> Extravagant and unnecessary outlay on travelling expenses; excessive powers assumed by the Executive Committee, which latterly practically consisted of two persons; allocation of substantial grants from the funds on the recommendation of a member or of two members of the General Committee resident in Paris; retention of large balances in banks in London; and the unnecessary engagement of the services of a solicitor at the charge of the fund.[89]

In the light of the Professor's allegations the magazine felt that it had to backtrack on its previous expressions of confidence.[90] Dickinson refuted the accusations in detail in the following week's edition of *Truth* and he informed the paper that a new committee was being formed. However, November brought about the resignation of many of the FRF's most eminent patrons including Home Secretary Sir John Simon, Winston Churchill,

Lloyd George, Austen Chamberlain, McKenna and Kitchener. The whole matter was surrounded in some mystery as *The Times* reported under the heading 'The French Relief Fund—Curious Correspondence—Withdrawal of Ministers from Patronage.'[91] They published correspondence in which Dickinson appealed to Sir John to remain as 'your withdrawal would be a serious and might be a fatal blow to the fund.' *The Times* concluded that there was 'some organized opposition to [the] Fund which is operating . . . from Scotland Yard.'[92] There was indeed a 'warning off' process going on by the police. This was despite the fact that the accounts had been independently audited and no irregularities found. *Truth* published them and they showed a total income of £129,376. From this they had paid grants of £69,000 but administrative expenses of £18,139 had swallowed up 29 percent of income. *Truth* expressed themselves satisfied with the auditor's report. They commented, quite rightly, that the Fund had 'done big and useful work. . . . The plain fact [is] that in the course of the year this Fund contributed £110,000 towards the relief of acute distress in France.'[93] Scrutator went on to praise the openness of the Fund's Secretary, Mr Dickinson, comments the journalist no doubt regretted later, saying 'it is not his fault that he is young and inexperienced, or that he was when he started this Fund quite an unknown person to the public.' It was true that Dickinson's name was unknown to Scrutator and the public but it was not unknown to the police.

At the root of the police campaign was the fact that, despite the changes to the committee structure, the FRF was very much under the control of Dickinson and Hitching and it was their backgrounds and actions that led to suspicion. Dickinson's history did not become known until enquiries were made in his native Lancashire. It should be remembered that in the days before computerised police records it was often extremely difficult to tie information on individuals together so the fact that Dickinson could establish himself in the way he did is not altogether surprising. He was born in Colne in 1883, later moving with his parents to Blackpool, and early on in his career established a penchant for matters military and Gallic. His first brush with the police seems to have been in 1905 when he passed himself off as an army officer and was convicted of travelling without a ticket and giving a false name and address. In August 1908 he was made bankrupt with debts of £3,000 (he was discharged in 1912) and in 1909, claiming to be a representative of the French Aeroplane Company, he obtained premises that he did not pay for, subsequently being sued for a number of unpaid debts. The report on Dickinson by Detective Sergeant Leeson of Lancashire Police concluded that 'this man is, in my opinion, a distinctly doubtful character.'[94] It was not only Dickinson himself who was considered undesirable. Sergeant Leeson picked up local gossip that his sister was bragging that 'her brother is expecting to receive a Knighthood from H.M. King George and the Legion of Honour in connection with his work in the French Relief Fund.'[95] His father too was a bankrupt and had been summoned for assault in 1909 and the report concluded that 'the local reputation of the Dickinson family is extremely bad both socially and financially. Their sharp practices and doubtful transactions have brought them into notoriety throughout this district.'[96] Sir Thomas, though not a convicted crook, still had some questionable business dealings. A former Mayor of Marylebone and unsuccessful Conservative parliamentary candidate, in 1912 he was elected as a City of London Alderman but on petition was rejected as not being a 'fit and proper person to support the dignity and discharge the duties of the office.'[97] The reason for his ignominious rejection involved two cases of conflict of interest whilst in public office: the first in relation to the awarding of the contract for electric lighting in Marylebone and the second over the purchase of a property in St James's Street by the London County Council of which Sir Thomas was a member. In both cases Sir Thomas had financial interests he failed to declare.[98]

For a while after the publication of the FRF accounts things went quiet. It was not until September 1916, and a second flag day, that the activities of the Fund again came under scrutiny.[99] As the War Charities Act had now come into force, the Charity Commissioners decided to launch a full investigation into the FRF and the activities of Dickinson and Hitching whom fellow Trustees described as two men 'unequalled in artfulness and duplicity.'[100] The accusations against Dickinson and Hitching were threefold: firstly, that they had spent excessive sums on their own expenses, particularly on luxurious trips to France; secondly, that the FRF had paid excessive commission to Sir Thomas's son for the purchase of ambulances and thirdly, that there were doubts about a payment of £20,000 to an orphanage in France. There was also some suggestion (though no evidence) that in the early days of the Fund when Dickinson was running it as an employment agency for Frenchwomen that this was a cover for prostitution.

Letters started pouring in deprecating Sir Thomas and Dickinson's practices. It seems that Sir Thomas was in the habit of visiting France with a certain Mrs O'Reilly, described as a beauty specialist. Hitching and Dickinson had plans to open a hospital in France with O'Reilly employed as a nurse and Dickinson's wife as matron. They had even viewed a chateau, the Chateau Rimberlieu, with a view to purchasing it before they were thwarted by the investigations. Instead, just four days before the War Charities Act was passed (on 23 August 1916) they transferred £20,000 to the 'Edith Cavell Orphanage'. This was to be built by a M Paris who, as far as can be ascertained, was of good reputation. He ran the Maison de Pupilles and was a member of the Paris Municipal Council. The ambulances had been supplied by Blake Ltd of Liverpool, a company 'practically owned by [Hitching's] son.' The first consignment of fifty had to be replaced after being lost at sea when the *Caroni* was torpedoed and, overall, the commission appears to have been around £1,000. Not fraud perhaps but a useful bit of business. The Charity Commissioners were unable to deal with some of the charges, because they related to occurrences before the passing of the War Charities Act, but on 28 December 1916 they put the Fund under administration, its assets then standing at some £5,000. As a prosecution under the new Act was impossible, in 1917 the case papers were passed to Mr Austin Cantrell QC for an opinion as to whether a prosecution for breach of trust was possible. However, the evidence was not conclusive enough and both Hitching and Dickinson escaped justice for what were most certainly unethical and self-enriching practices.[101]

'CAPTAIN' ILLINGWORTH AND QUEEN ALEXANDRA

The case of the French Relief Fund was a very public scandal that was extensively quoted in the subsequent passing of the War Charities Act. However, another case was just as influential even though it was kept entirely from public gaze. Several of the charity fraudsters come through as out-and-out parasites (such as Alroy), others as clever but artful (Carey and Blanchard) and some as entirely reprehensible (Chatterton). William Henry Illingworth comes across as rather a likable, if distinctly unsuccessful, rogue. Illingworth had a long, and somewhat pathetic, history of crime though, again, he was not linked with his past for some time. He was born in 1850 and received his first prison sentence, twelve months hard labour for larceny, in 1876. This was followed by ten months for fraud in 1884, eight months in 1889, again for larceny, and six months in 1900 under the bankruptcy laws. By 1914 he was very down on his luck and, from 1913 to September 1915, was in receipt of poor relief; his local vicar had also helped out Illingworth and his wife on a number of occasions with gifts of food and money. If it had not been for his choice of fraud Illingworth would have been no match for his police opponent, Detective Inspector Curry.

It took Illingworth a little while to take advantage of the war but he was at least quite imaginative when he did. In August 1915 he managed to obtain a supply of material from the Parliamentary Recruiting Committee and applied for a street collection permit for the Army and Navy Recruiting Agency and Posting Office. He claimed that he wanted to collect money to establish a convalescent home at Little Tingewick, Bucks. Investigations in Tingewick revealed that he had indeed taken a house there on which he owed rent. He claimed the title of Captain from supposed service in the English Legion during the Franco-Prussian War and said he had fought at the Battle of Sedan. The police decided that he was not genuine and that 'his future movements will be observed.'[102] He used youngsters to collect for his various appeals and police traced and interviewed several of them. Illingworth left London in November 1915 after a suspicious fire and next popped up in Hastings seven months later. He placed advertisements (for which he failed to pay) in local papers on behalf of the White Cross Fund. He was appealing for £7,000 to restore and extend a house as a 'Home of

Rest and Convelescent' [sic]. Both this and his Tingewick appeal came with the supposed endorsement of Queen Alexandra's Field Force Fund and this was the root of the difficulties encountered in bringing him to justice. The Fund had been started in October 1914 by the King's mother. It was never huge (it raised around £80,000 by the end of the war) but it was very prestigious. Viscountess French, wife of the ex-C-in-C, was its President and the wives of four other generals, Ladies Allenby, Murray, Monro and Haig, were Vice Presidents.[103] In 1914 Illingworth had been allowed to collect on behalf of the Fund and though he had sent in a few articles of clothing no money appeared, even though he had made (unauthorised) press appeals. Illingworth had been in correspondence with Colonel Streatfield, Private Secretary to Queen Alexandra, from whom he received two letters. He 'doctored' these letters and invented a third to impress those he attempted to defraud; he told the owners of the Tingewick house that 'no doubt he would have Her Majesty down to see the place.' Police searched the house in Hastings in August and found several parcels from the *Evening News* campaign addressed to the 'Lonely Soldiers Guild'. Though the *Evening News* fund was not very tightly controlled and kept no records of its despatches, a postcard was found in Hastings to one donor in which Illingworth claimed he had just come out of hospital having been wounded at Ypres. In another, he pretended he was still at the front. Though unaware of Illingworth's criminal record Inspector Curry, hardly surprisingly, concluded that 'there can be no doubt that Illingworth is an impostor and a swindler.'[104]

In October 1916 Curry uncovered Illingworth's past and the papers on the case were sent to Mr Travers Humphrey KC 'who said that Illingworth had committed almost every kind of fraud possible.'[105] Though the case against him was cut-and-dried it did not come to court because 'a great objection was offered to Her Majesty's name being used in connection with the case.'[106] A frustrated Inspector Curry was instead despatched to 'warn him off'. Illingworth immediately 'admitted all the money he had collected for the QAFFF he had put into his own pocket . . . that he had been carrying on a series of frauds' and 'confessed that he had used this title [Captain] without any right whatever.'[107] In all he was totally cooperative, returning to Inspector Curry the two letters from Colonel Streatfield, and 'promised that he would lead an honest life in future and would not again make improper use of HM Queen Alexandra's name.'[108] A careful watch was put on the bogus Captain and it did not take an old lag like Illingworth long to get back to his old tricks. In February 1917 Inspector Curry ascertained that Illingworth, using the pseudonym William Henry of the Imperial Air Service, had attempted to obtain gramophone records by deception. Curry interviewed Columbia Records British Manager, Arthur Leidtke, who confirmed the suspicions and that Illingworth was still putting on military airs. 'Just outside my door I heard him giving military commands "Attention", "Quick March" and so on to one of my staff.'[109] Papers were again sent to the DPP who agreed to proceedings for attempting to obtain charitable contributions by fraud. A month went by but then, in April 1917, it was decided 'after full consideration' that no action could be taken 'as it was still feared that the name of HM Queen Alexandra would be dragged into proceedings at Court.'[110] A weary Inspector Curry turned his attention to other cases, William Illingworth probably turned to more petty crime and the honour of the Royal Family was preserved for another eighty years until the file was opened to the public.[111]

COMMITTEE RECOMMENDATIONS AND THE PASSING OF THE ACT

The most important stimulus to war charity legislation was the publicity surrounding these dubious or fraudulent organisations. Journalists, politicians and some prominent charities seized on these cases to urge government action to prevent abuses of public trust; but just how much evidence of fraud do they reveal? The evidence rests on the relatively small number of cases we have examined, nearly all of them London-based and investigated by the same person, DI Curry. Whilst Curry, in both his evidence to the War Charities Committee and his official reports to Scotland Yard, is commendably objective, some of the use to which his cases were put were far less fair and often drew conclusions that were not supported by the evidence. In addition most of the culprits were certainly 'up to no good' before the war and simply used it as a new cover for their activities. Where the cases potentially involved large sums (the Belgian Soldiers Fund and especially the French Relief Fund) there was no clear evidence of fraud. Where there certainly *was* fraud (the Cripples Pension Society, the War Orphans Fund and the activities of Thomas Alroy and 'Captain' Illingworth), the sums were minor. However, at this distance, it is very difficult to pontificate. It is easy to say that the cases were insignificant in relation to the totality of wartime charitable effort, but this is to ignore the impact of fraudulent activity on public opinion, especially in the circumstances pertaining at the time. As a modern report has suggested, 'the impact of fraud on individual charities and the sector as a whole can be devastating. It can damage reputations, lead to the loss of key employees, volunteers and donors, diminish financial reserves and limit the range and extent of charitable activities that can be undertaken.'[112]

Given only the *clear* instances of fraud and parasitic activity it is difficult to argue against the pressure for legislative change even if some supporters of legislation suggested that fraud was far more widespread than the evidence demonstrates. For example, the COS attacked two of the largest and most effective charities, the Salvation Army and YMCA, for wasteful administration which was simply a continuation of their campaign against what they saw as excessive administrative costs and was, like so many of their other ideas, entirely misplaced.[113] It is unfortunately still the case today that many very effective charities are criticised unfairly for high administrative costs without any reference to the nature of the work they actually do. It was difficult for critics in the COS to understand that effectiveness is not a function of low overheads and that those with the lowest were often the least effective. Nevertheless, when the Committee on War Charities submitted its report to Parliament on 19 June 1916, it was the concerns of the potential for fraud or misuse of funds and the reckless use of the names of prominent persons as patrons that underpinned their recommendations. They gave prominence to the witness statements, which asserted the unanimous opinion that 'in the public interest it was desirable that public appeals for funds on behalf of war charities should be placed under some system of control.'[114] The Committee pointed out that the majority of witnesses had wanted to go beyond this to regulate *all* charities but as this was beyond the Committee's remit, they declined to comment on its desirability. They were careful to say how far the legislation should go and that it would not, without undue cost, 'be practicable to attempt to stop waste arising from these causes.' Instead the aim of the legislation should be 'to prevent appeals being made by persons whose *bona fides* are not established and to secure that the control and distribution of charitable funds shall be in the hands of a responsible committee.'[115] They made the following key recommendations:

- Registration should be compulsory;
- Local authorities should be the main 'registering authority' and each local charity should register (i.e. not just their head office);
- The registration committee should contain people with charity experience and women as well as men;
- The Charity Commission should keep a central register compiled from throughout the country and should consider any appeals against refusal of registration;
- A charge of ten shillings should be made for registration (this was reduced to five shillings during drafting);
- Each charity should have a committee of no fewer than three;
- They must have a separate bank account and keep books of account, which should be audited, with an abstract published, and minutes;[116]
- The books should be open to inspection by the registering authority and Charity Commission; and
- Any public appeal by an unregistered charity would be a finable offence.

The committee had therefore answered two of the three key questions that were open for debate. They had decided on registration rather than closer control by licensing and were proposing Local Councils as the registering authority. What the report did not cover was the crucial definition of what constituted a 'war charity' and exactly what organisations would be exempted from registration, which was left to the parliamentary draftsmen. The question of exemption was included by the provision of the first clause of the Bill, which stated that it covered 'any appeal to the public'. Thus if an appeal was *not* made 'to the public' (i.e. was restricted to a defined group of people) an organisation could be exempt from registering. It was left to the registering authority to decide if the organisation was 'appealing to the public' or not. This only sidestepped the issue, as it did not define 'the public', and was interpreted differently in different parts of the country. The definition of what constituted a war charity was even more complex. Clause 10 eventually read:

> The expression 'war charity' means any fund, institution, or association (whether established before or after the commencement of this Act) having for its object or amongst its objects the relief of suffering or distress, the supply of needs or comforts, or any other charitable purpose connected with the present war, but shall not include any fund, institution or association established before the commencement of the present war where any such object as aforesaid is subsidiary only to the principal purposes of the charity, nor shall it include the Royal Patriotic Fund Corporation or the Statutory Committee or any local or district committee established under the Naval and Military War Pensions &c., Act, 1915.[117]

It left the ultimate decision as to whether a charity was a war charity or not to the interpretation of the Charity Commissioners, specifying the following key points:

- Unless an organisation had no more funds, the definition was retrospective. However, as the Act referred to 'appeals to the public', unless a charity was making further appeals to the public it need not register. This was something of an anomaly and was raised during the committee stage of the Bill.
- The definition was very wide and covered virtually all organisations formed since August 1914.
- Most charities in existence before August 1914 were exempt.

Whilst drafting was underway the Chief Charity Commissioner, H.W.T. Bowyear, threw things into some disorder by suggesting that the Commission could 'carry out the whole scheme by central registration only.'[118] Though initial reaction to this appears to have been favourable Sir Ernley Blackwell decided things by saying the Committee considered 'the Charity Commissioners were too old-fashioned a body to undertake this new work satisfactorily.'[119] As the Commission was entirely unused to dealing with collecting charities and given the local nature of the majority of schemes he was probably correct, even though this would have ensured consistency in applying the Act. The next fly in the ointment was none other than Sir Edward Ward. He wrote urgently to Henry Forster (still Financial Secretary at the War Office) saying he was alarmed that the requirement for all charities to register under the proposed Act would be seen as bureaucracy gone mad as all of the organisations affiliated to the DGVO would have to go through another registration process and this might 'result in disaster.'[120] He asked if those organisations already certified by him could be exempted from registration but the Home Office response was that this would be 'quite impossible ... without destroying the whole aim of the Bill.'[121] It would have been wrong to exclude DGVO organisations from registration under an Act that had been framed for a different purpose and here Ward was guilty of exactly the same confusion over his scheme as the newspapers had been, namely that it was emphatically *not* aimed at dealing with abuses and fraud. To be fair he was more worried that all his hard work might be undone if the new Act proved over-cumbersome but his fears were unjustified. There is no evidence that organisations under his auspices found registering under the new Act to be onerous or bureaucratic. What evidence there is from the records of local DGVO charities indicates that registration was straightforward and their work continued uninterrupted.[122]

On the day of Sir Edward's agitated letter the Bill received its second reading in the Commons. It was certainly not guaranteed an easy passage. Firstly, some still considered that government interference in the work of charities was unjustifiable state intervention. Then there were those who regarded the Bill as too weak to prevent abuses. However, critics of over-leniency had their fears somewhat allayed by action over flag days, though this had taken nearly a year to be extended from London to cover the whole country. The Police, Factories etc (Miscellaneous Provisions) Act, which gave local authorities the power to regulate street collections and so prevent the worst abuses of flag days, was something of a universal remedy covering everything from fraud to juvenile delinquency and what we now call 'chugging'. It was, however, a power that was widely adopted.[123] In introducing the Charities Bill, William Brace quickly tried to deal with both issues by saying, perhaps overoptimistically, that 'it will not only check but stop the exploitation of the public by unscrupulous people who do not hesitate to use the nation's sympathies for their own selfish end' and that 'the Bill is confined to war charities and I would ask the House to treat it as a war measure.'[124] Will Anderson was quick to respond. He again referred to his belief that fraud was widespread and accused the Cripples Pension Society of trying to bribe him, concluding that 'I regret that the Bill, which is so necessary and important, is too narrow in its scope, and think it ought to apply to all charities.'[125] Aneurin Williams, who had received the same 'flattering offer from the Cripples' Society', was of the opposite persuasion, worrying that 'from the point of view of the small local charities we must be careful or we may stop much good work that is being done.'[126] In commenting on extending the provisions of the Bill and the circumstances of smaller charities J.W. Wilson, a member of the Committee, supported this view and cautioned about the impact of the legislation on smaller charities who 'would find it very burdensome if the restrictions were made too onerous.'[127]

The Bill went to committee on 7 and 10 August. Among a number of, relatively minor, amendments accepted were the requirement to issue a certificate of registration or exemption and for prosecutions to be initiated by the Charity Commission rather than the Director of Public Prosecutions, which would have been taking a sledgehammer to crack a nut. On the Bill's return to the full House for report and third reading on 14 August the issue of extension to Ireland was tackled. Basil Peto (Unionist, Devizes) warned that 'all the people who want to have shady charities, with no supervision, will migrate to Ireland.'[128] He did have a point. Fraudsters probably did not migrate as far as Ireland but there was nothing to stop them setting up in an area where the Act was applied less scrupulously. However, the amendment proposing extension to Ireland was withdrawn and the Act finally included the provision of including Ireland by Order in Council. This provision was not greeted entirely favourably in the Lords when Lord Salisbury spoke for several with regard to the 'unconstitutional' nature of the provision, remarking that 'it appears to me that as the years go on Parliament is more and more divesting itself of the obligation of legislation on the details of measures, and handing it over to commissions, rules committees and orders in Council.' The provision was a further step in potential state control but in the event the Act was never extended to Ireland.[129] The Lords stages were most notable for the speech of Lord Hylton introducing the Bill. He asserted that the Committee had had 'a great number of bogus war charities brought to their notice.'[130] Hylton then summarised the five quoted in the report, namely the French Relief Fund, Dr Sarolea's refugee fund, Counties Rest Homes, the War Orphans Fund and Heroes Poultry Farms as being 'typical cases'. This was an exaggeration, as there were no more than ten cases of actual fraud brought to the Committee's attention and it is difficult to assert that the five quoted were 'typical'. Where Hylton *was* correct was in his assertion that 'without a Bill of this kind it is feared that genuine charities of all kinds may be involved in the cloud of suspicion that has been created owing to the exposure of these very gross and fraudulent cases.'[131] The Act was passed on the final day of the parliamentary session, 23 August. In the final analysis even if the frauds were unproven or petty, public opinion and the reputation of bona fide charities demanded some legislative action. In the circumstances the 1916 War Charities Act was about as good a piece of legislation as was possible.

THE OPERATION OF THE ACT AND CONTROL OF SCANDAL

On 28 August the Charity Commission issued the new regulations to local authorities. The Commissioners set up a subsidiary body of 'gentlemen of high business qualifications', the Central Trustees of Controlled War Charities, to supervise the affairs of problematic organisations.[132] There were inevitably some problems over the introduction and interpretation of the Act. A very small number of charities refused to register 'on principle'. There was some difficulty in the definition of what a bank was and what constituted an audit. The Commission took a narrow line on the former, which led to complaints from the Trustees Savings Bank and Post Office Savings Bank and, somewhat belatedly in 1918, to their recognition as such. Another problem of interpretation was over whether local branches of national charities had to register, where the Commission's sensible line was that if the local body had control over the dispersion of their own funds then they must register.

Defining what was a war charity and what constituted an appeal to the public caused greater inconsistency. For example, the London County Council (LCC) decided that the Ruhleben Prisoners Release Committee was *not* a war charity as it was purely a campaigning organisation to agitate for the prisoners' release and not for their 'needs or comforts' but refused exemption in virtually every other case.[133] Each local registration authority inevitably interpreted the Act in different ways. The LCC operated on the precedent principle, deciding on a case-by-case basis. An advertisement by the Merchant Taylor's School Old Boys Comfort Fund in the school magazine was considered a public appeal as it was not confined to old boys of the school. Likewise an appeal to 'officers and *friends*' [my emphasis] by the Grenadier and Scots Guards War Funds was also deemed a public appeal; it would not have been had it been solely to officers and so a very similar appeal on behalf of the Central Depot of the King's Royal Rifles Needlework Guild to 'officers and men' of the regiment did not require registration.[134] Non-public appeals were often those aimed at a defined work-force. Though collections at divine service did not require registration, appeals to congregations of churches that collected money outside services, such as the case of the Christ Church Fund for Soldiers and Sailors, were deemed a public appeal.[135] The case of church funds clearly demonstrates the inconsistency of interpretation. In Todmorden local church funds were exempted even if they raised funds away from the church or chapel. In practice, this probably did not cause too many problems, as registration was, for most, both straightforward and cheap.

A rather different and unexpected problem was caused by the public nature of the register. Some funds registered under the names and numbers of the military units for which they were raising funds, 1/4th Battalion Royal Berkshire Regiment Comfort Fund or 16th Battalion Rifle Brigade (St Pancras) Fund, for example. The Army Council objected to the publication of the numbers of military units as being liable to disclose information useful to the enemy. It is difficult to see exactly how this information might have assisted them but the Charity Commission removed such organisations from their published list and requested that organisations not use military titles in future.[136] Following these difficulties, the Home Office issued further advice on organisations that could be exempted from registration, adding two further categories:

1. Charities formed with the express approval of the commanding officer of a military unit or ship for the benefit of their men.
2. Charities formed under the direction of, and personally administered by, the proprietor, manager or editor of a newspaper for forces or prisoners of war.

The second had become an issue for newspapers who were unsure if their own appeals required registration and whether this was affected by who was to distribute the proceeds.

With regard to the reduction in fraud, in London, the centre of greatest concern, the Metropolitan Police Commissioner was quickly in touch with the LCC supplying details of those charities where there were grounds for suspicion.[137] Some of these were 'old friends' brought to attention before the passing of the Act but the list also included a few new organisations. The full list comprised the following:

1. Belgian Soldiers Fund;
2. French Relief Fund;
3. Counties Rest Home for British Soldiers;
4. Our Own Boys Day Fund;
5. Le Berceau Fund;
6. Workers Circle;
7. First British Field Hospital for Servia;
8. Mrs Honnold's Fund for Providing Artificial Limbs for Disabled Soldiers;
9. 'I Promise' Fund; and
10. Assistance aux Hospiteaux (sic) Allies.

To which the Albert Day Fund was quickly added. The first three have already been covered and all were quickly made the subject of administration orders by the Charity Commission, as were Our Own Boys Day Fund, Le Berceau Fund and the Workers Circle. Even when the more notorious funds were under administration, this was not always the end of the matter and the complexities of the French Relief Fund remained unresolved for some time. Winding up was only completed in 1919 when its remaining funds were paid over to the British Committee of the French Red Cross.[138]

Our Own Boys Day Fund had already been closed in November 1915. Ostensibly to provide disabled soldiers with jobs, all £500 it had raised had been used up in expenses by its Secretary, Mr H.C. Burke, and Treasurer, Sir John Taverner. Le Berceau Fund was run solely by its Secretary and Treasurer, Mlle Germaine Olivia Colas, and again all £600 it raised had gone in expenses, the majority to support its promoter's lifestyle as she lived at the Savoy Hotel. The Workers Circle raised a street collection on behalf of the Jewish Workers War Emergency Relief Fund and may, like the Jewish organisations mentioned later, have been included on the list because of their political sympathies. They initially refused to provide a balance sheet and were 'suspected of having diverted part at least of the money for the use of socialists in Russia.'[139] However, after investigation, they were cleared of suspicion and the Council upheld their appeal against refusal to register. The final four were sloppily run rather than being fraudulent. Of the First British Field Hospital for Servia and its Treasurer, Alex McConnell, the police 'suspected that there is considerable slackness of control over collectors.' Mrs Catherine Honnold of the Hyde Park Hotel 'collects money through appeals in the American Press, and manages the Fund without committee or other assistance.'[140] Both the 'I Promise' Fund and Assistance aux Hospiteaux Allies were rather more up-market. The former had been started by the prominent actors Ellaline Terris and Seymour Hicks to form a league against trading with Germany and assist disabled soldiers but operated with no executive committee, as did the latter whose promoter and sole manageress was the Countess de Morella.

The greatest problems with the Act were that it came with very little additional funding and, especially, the scope for interpretation by each local authority. In London, the LCC took a hard line. They scrupulously investigated every application and (with the single exception previously noted) rejected the idea of exemption, partly due to the zeal of their Chief Clerk, James (later Sir James) Bird, partly because they were better resourced and partly because they were very much in the public eye, especially that of the press. Further away from the capital local authorities were much more relaxed. In Todmorden, for example, over 70 percent of charities were granted exemption from the Act. The LCC were often over-bureaucratic, smaller authorities over-lax. For example, Bird was unhappy that the 17th Lancers Prisoners of War Fund did not have a properly functioning committee that met regularly.[141] Given that their Chairman was Sir Douglas Haig and most of the others were on active service the Secretary, Miss S.D. Whitton, wrote that 'the assembling of the members [is] quite impossible owing to their military duties.' Despite this, Bird still sought their full compliance with the Act. Perhaps he thought that Sir Douglas should break off the Third Battle of Ypres for a while to chair a committee meeting in London.[142] In the end, the Fund arranged for the Regimental Agency (which was registered) to take care of their PoWs. Some of the over-bureaucratic approach in London was class or racially based and led to error and abuse. Bird was indefatigable in investigating the bona fides of Jewish working class charities. Typical of these was the Koval, Ludmar, Lutsk and District Benevolent Society for the support of Jews in these areas of what is now the Ukraine and Bird went to great lengths to investigate them, obviously suspicious that they could be subversive. Every one of the thirty-seven members of the committee (including the Rabbi) was investigated through inquiry agents instructed by the LCC's solicitors. Several phrases in these reports have been marked; for instance with regard to Sam Goldsmith, 30 Frostic Mansions, Whitechapel, the report commented that 'the district *is a very poor one, principally inhabited by foreigners of Jewish extraction*' and on Israel Lewis, 47 Brick Lane, the report said he 'is not known to be a man of *any financial strength, nor does he appear to be regarded with much confidence.*' These are reports on their credit-worthiness rather than character but Bird obviously thought this very important. A report from the police said that the Chairman, Marks Goldstein, was a registered Russian and 'he is suspected of being a Receiver of stolen property, but there is no definite evidence on this point.'[143] Nothing was known about any of the other Committee members (other than their being registered Aliens). In his report to the Council Bird said that though 'we have no reason to suppose that this charity is not established in good faith for charitable purposes' he was not satisfied they would be properly administered, solely based on the fact that 'most of the officers and members of the Committee of the charity are Russian subjects in humble circumstances, and are not regarded as being of any financial standing.'[144] This was going well beyond what the Act intended and was, in effect, equivalent to the full-scale licensing so many had demanded. Unfortunately Bird only applied the Act in this way with regard to charities organised by the working class, especially if they were Jewish as well. The Act was not meant to be a credit check and Bird's class prejudices were being used to suppress what he thought of as 'dodgy foreigners'. There is no more correspondence from the charity so they obviously accepted this refusal. Further examples of Bird's misplaced zeal were the Tradesmen and Stallholders of Chapel Street and White Conduit Street Fund for Wounded Soldiers and the Jewish Workers War Emergency Relief Fund. No fewer than seventy confidential reports were obtained on the former for a charity whose income was only £156. The latter were initially refused registration due to unsubstantiated connections with the anarchist movement, though were registered on appeal.[145]

Bird was less scrupulous with charities not run by poor working class Jews and this double standard quickly backfired. At first, the British-American (Overseas) Field Hospital (BAOFH) appeared a very respectable case. Established in June 1917 for the relief of sick and wounded at the front they were registered on 25 June. The Chair was Lady Rosmead of Datchet (wife of one of Shackleton's expedition) and their Chief Patron the Duke of Atholl.[146] The Metropolitan Police were routinely asked if they had any observations to make about charities seeking registration but in the majority of cases expressed no view. However, just five days after registration the police report came in. This informed Bird that the Secretary, Henry Allen Ashton, had been involved with fraudulent share dealings in 1910. Ashton ran public competitions for worthless shares or sold them at inflated prices. Though civil court action had been taken, no criminal proceedings were.

When war broke out he turned his attention to publishing the *Recruiting Times* and organised the Voluntary Recruiting League (VRL), issuing a pamphlet entitled *One Clear Call*, with the usual list of influential patrons. In April 1915 Ashton organised a competition advertised in the *Daily Mirror* for people to make as many words as possible from the letters in 'One Clear Call'. Entries cost 1s 6d with prizes of £500 (£50 top prize). Ashton claimed to have made a loss on this enterprise. Then, in June 1915, he offered a bungalow on Hayling Island worth £700 as a competition prize in the *Daily Telegraph* for the person who collected the most money for the VRL. This competition 'fell through'. Though a file was sent to the DPP no proceedings were taken. When conscription came in Ashton promoted the War Organisation Committee, which was 'regarded by the Police with some suspicion', the report noted. He was interviewed by police in March 1916 and claimed to have spent £4,000 of his own money on the VRL and recruited 70,000 men through it. Another of Ashton's ventures, and the most extraordinary, was the Petronite Syndicate. Petronite was described as 'a scientific practical and effective invention for the destruction of submarines, Zeppelins, aeroplanes, and floating and submerged mines.'[147] All of these activities had been reported in *Truth,* which Bird obviously did not read. Having turned down a well-meaning, but Jewish, charity less than three weeks before, Bird had registered one of the most obvious fraudsters of the war. Mortified, Bird requested the Charity Commission and police keep Ashton's charity under 'close observation' and, somewhat belatedly, requested reports on its committee members from agents Perry and Stubbs. Things then got worse for him. On 24 July Bird received a letter from the Secretary of the Star and Garter Committee of the Red Cross asking if the BAOFH was bona fide. He could only reply that they were going to examine the accounts after three months. The Field Hospital itself attempted to become established in Belgium and then Italy. Acrimonious splits occurred in the committee and eventually Ashton was forced off. He made accusations against other committee members and these disputes gave the Charity Commission the opportunity to remove the charity from the register and apply a scheme for its administration. If only Bird had waited for the police report.

Just how successful was the Act in reducing fraud? In the House of Commons in 1930 it was claimed that 250 charities had been proceeded against or were either refused registration or removed from the register.[148] There is no evidence for this in the published figures from the Charity Commission. The actual number of abuses remained relatively insignificant (for example the total number of organisations refused registration up to 1919 was just forty-one) and in 1919 the Commissioners reported that 'proceedings were taken against 17 persons appealing to the public on behalf of unregistered War Charities' and that this had resulted in ten convictions. In nine cases the offenders were fined whilst one, Raymond Cecil Reeves of the Red Star Society, was imprisoned.[149] In London only seventeen organisations were refused registration during the war and of these six were allowed on appeal. There were just twenty-four cases represented by the Council to the Charity Commission under Section 7 of the Act, i.e. where there was suspicion of fraud. These included the eleven cases cited previously of which only six proved to be fraudulent. Of the additional thirteen, two, the Red Star Society and Tubs for Tommies, were proven frauds, and the police had strong suspicion against at least five others (though none appear to have been prosecuted) but the numbers were still small.[150] There was also a problem over the Romanian Flag Day held in London in November 1916. Though the organiser, Mr Smetham Lee, had obtained a licence, he utilised paid collectors (one was paid as much as £50) and the monies received were paid over to him rather than the charity.[151]

Of the post-1916 Act frauds the most notable were probably those of Tubs for Tommies and the Red Star Fund. The former was a charity money-raising scheme that went wrong. It started as a purely commercial idea between an American engineer's agent, G.L. Richards, and a British solicitor, Crawford Ely. It involved selling 6d puzzle-cards with four revolving discs each with the letters A to Z. Contestants had to spell out three words of four letters by manipulating the discs and the most original would receive a prize. As it was a game of skill it avoided the ban on lotteries. In late 1916, Richards had the idea of utilising the game as a charity fund-raiser and met with Mrs Burn of the Emergency Voluntary Aid Committee of the Empress Club (a prominent club for women) who were raising funds, most notably for providing heated baths for soldiers close to the front line.[152] The idea was that Mr Ely's interest would be bought out for £1,000 and the scheme would run with 50 percent of the proceeds devoted to prizes and expenses and 50 percent to the charity. In all it was not a dissimilar idea from today's lottery scratch cards and, had it worked, would have provided the charity with a profit of about £10,000. Unfortunately, things did not run smoothly and the charity was taking a big risk that the one million tickets they had printed would sell. The intention was that the cards would be sold over a three-day period but the charity was only able to get a permit to sell them on one day, 15 January 1917. Of the million tickets a mere 87,000 were sold, bringing in £2,166. After Ely had received his commission and expenses there was only £500 left for prizes, which was eventually paid out in June, leaving a balance of just £763. The prize fund was not handled with sufficient propriety (for some reason it was not deposited under the charity's name) and the whole scheme was too complex, the financial arrangement with the promoters too loose and there were too many fingers in the pie. The poor ladies of the Empress Club were out of their depth and both the Charity Commission and police were called in to investigate. Both were already extremely ill disposed towards schemes of this kind and flag days as a whole. During the last year, £286,830 had been collected in this way in London with overall expenses of £51,432. This was considered far too high a cost by the regulators, with Sir Edward Troup commenting that the percentage was 'utterly unjustifiable.'[153] Troup was also, rather gently, admonishing Henry for not having refused a licence for Tubs for Tommies and thus saving him a lot of bother. Henry responded by putting his best men onto the job and so the redoubtable Inspector Curry and his superior Superintendent McCarthy looked into the case. Their report cleared the Charity of any offence, other than naivety, but made three recommendations:

1. When articles are sold to aid charities the proportion of commission should be clear;
2. The registration authority should approve fund-raising schemes in advance; and
3. The press should not accept charity advertising unless the name of the charity appeared in the advertisement.[154]

The first two were forwarded to the Home Office for action whilst Sir Edward Henry wrote to newspaper editors regarding the third, his letter being published in *The Times* on 26 April 1918. Tightening of regulations for street collections of all kinds does appear to have reduced their numbers later in 1917 and in 1918 but they still remained relatively popular and effective methods of raising funds. Though Tubs for Tommies was a case of irresponsible management the general issue of fund-raising costs was poorly understood by its critics. Today the Institute of Fundraising recommends that FACE (fundraising and administration costs to total expenditure) ratios should lie somewhere within the range 20 to 30 percent, levels that would have horrified the likes of Troup and Henry.[155]

The Red Star Society was run by one of the most brazen, or foolhardy, fraudsters active during the war. Raymond Cecil Reeves had five previous convictions (under five different names in five different towns) for false pretences and had only been released from his last prison sentence of two years in May 1914.[156] This did not prevent him from obtaining a post in the Adjutant General's Department at the War Office immediately on the outbreak of war. He was dismissed in August 1915, but for insubordination and not because his record had been uncovered. He then worked for a 'well-known shipping firm' and later joined the Architectural Association Voluntary Aid Department.[157] This connection with charity clearly suggested a new source of income to Reeves and in March 1917 he founded his own charity, Westminster Entertainments for Wounded Soldiers (WEWS), with the apparently respectable Mrs Ferdinand Hodge (whose husband was a Captain and father-in-law a General) as Secretary. The laxness of the regulations even after the 1916 Act is perhaps demonstrated by the fact that Reeves registered the fund in July, signed up the Mayor of Westminster and several other prominent patrons and held two fund-raising entertainments at the Caxton Halls in April and June from which, Mrs Hodge later confirmed, 'Reeves took all the money.'[158] Reeves shared some of William Illingworth's characteristics in that he used an existing, highly respectable charity as a cover for his activities. He had joined the Red Cross as a volunteer and utilised their notepaper until they objected. If Reeves had also shared Illingworth's humbleness he may well have escaped retribution. However, he was of a very different temperament and was clearly annoyed by the Red Cross's quite justifiable response. In August he wrote to the Lord Mayor and all the other Mayors of London stating that he had tried to persuade the Red Cross 'to improve their air raid organization', that they had been disparaging his work and as a consequence he was starting a rival organisation, the Red Star Society, to assist air raid victims, wounded soldiers and orphans. Though this was no more than a rebadging of the WEWS, it required a further registration and, given the Red Cross concerns, the LCC asked the Metropolitan Police to run a check on Reeves.[159] Despite the problems of criminal records already noted Inspector Curry unearthed the truth. The Inspector had no idea, which, if any, of Reeves's aliases was his real name but there was no doubt at all that 'he is nothing but an arrant rogue.'[160] While Curry was carrying out his investigations Reeves was champing at the bit and complaining about the delay in registration. He began collecting money in September, falsely claiming the Red Star Society was registered, and planned to hold a meeting in Trafalgar Square in October which, the police said, might be difficult to prevent. Fortunately, Inspector Curry's report reached the Charity Commission at the end of September and, on 2 October, they placed the WEWS under administration. At the time it had a declared income of £150 and expenditure of £170 but there was 'grave suspicion' that these accounts had been falsified. Three days later Reeves was served with a summons under the War Charities Act. He was charged with appealing to the public on behalf of an unregistered charity, of which he was clearly guilty, but the main concern of the police was whether his criminal past could be proved so that the sentence passed would be exemplary. At first Reeves denied he had any convictions for fraud, at which point Mr Muskett (the Treasury Solicitor prosecuting) reminded him that 'there is such a thing as being charged with perjury.' The police had taken the precaution of bringing Sergeant Stuckey from Portsmouth Prison to identify him if necessary. Reeves still did not admit outright that he was the man being described, stating that even supposing it was true, 'he had wiped out his past, and had been working for the British Red Cross.' Mr Muskett said the Court had before it a 'rogue and a vagabond of the worst class—one of a type with which they were very familiar since the outbreak of the war, especially in charitable matters' and the Magistrate, Mr Chester Jones, agreed. He sentenced Reeves to the maximum three months imprisonment with hard labour and 'said the very purpose of the regulation [the War Charities Act] was to stop men like the defendant.'[161] At the end of the month Inspector Curry's colleague, Sergeant Burmby, discovered letters at Reeves's lodgings from his mother which revealed that his true name really *was* Raymond Cecil Reeves and that he had been born in 1873. The

Sergeant's conclusion was that 'there is no doubt that this conviction has put a check upon the activities of a clever and cheeky rogue.'[162] Superintendent Cantlef recommended both Sergeant Burmby and Inspector Curry for a reward for their work on the case and this might have been the end of the matter but for Reeves. He was clearly deluded that he had been persecuted unjustly and pursued an obsessive and self-destructive campaign to clear his name. In March 1918 he wrote to the Prime Minister accusing the Commissioners of Police of 'foul play' and saying that he was taking proceedings against the Charity Commission and calling for the repeal of the War Charities Act.[163] Lloyd-George was unimpressed but this did not stop Reeves bringing an action for malicious prosecution against the Commissioner, which failed. The following year Reeves brought an action for libel against the *Daily Mail* for saying in 1917 that he was 'one of the most impudent scoundrels in the country.' This case was heard before the Kings Bench Division of the High Court at the end of October. Reeves had no chance. Ranged against him was arguably the most able criminal barrister of the age, Sir Edward Marshall Hall, representing Associated Newspapers. The key was again Reeves's previous record, which he was unable to deny, and the jury, without even retiring, found for the defendants.[164] Reeves was made an example of because of who he was, because he was vilifying a 'pillar of the establishment' (the Red Cross), because of the authorities' embarrassment at such a crook being able to run events supported by such prominent individuals and because they could not prove fraud. Quite a few others did much what he did and did not get prosecuted. He should have pleaded ignorance but sealed his fate by continually pestering the Council and openly defying them. He then sued the richest newspaper in the land, confirming that either he was a fantasist of the highest order or was mentally unstable, so perhaps Herbert Muskett was right when he wrote, 'I myself think he is mad.'[165]

Despite the initial failure to prevent the activities of Raymond Reeves, the legislation does appear to have reduced the number of dubious charities. Equally there is very little evidence of the Act producing significant problems for legitimate charities or of over-regulation other than in a minority of cases in London. In 1917 the Charity Commissioners felt justified in reporting that the Act was working so well that it ought to be extended to all charities.[166] In this they continued to be supported by many of the major charities. However, there were also drawbacks to the legislation, not least of which was its uneven implementation. This was recognised in a report written in the 1920s when legislation on the supervision of charities was again being considered and, in 1927, the Cunliffe Committee also recognised that the Act was very unevenly administered.[167] They noted that, over the whole of the country, fifty-two charities had been refused registration and ninety-three had been removed from the register. Of these no fewer than twenty-six refusals and fifty-eight removals had occurred in London.

In other words, penal action was taken against 9 per cent of the total war charities registered in London, and against only just over 0.5 per cent in the rest of the country. We cannot bring ourselves to believe that this proportion—eighteen to one—is a true indication of the relative standard of the management of charities in and outside London respectively, and we are forced to the conclusion that the London County Council's administration of the War Charities Act was far more vigilant than that of the majority of other authorities.[168]

They did not say that this might also have been due to over-officious interpretation in London, of which we have seen some evidence, but their main point still holds true. This was always going to be a problem with a locally administered scheme and there was neither the will nor the funds to run it centrally. The Charity Commission was not sufficiently well regarded and it would have required a massive increase in resources.

LATER PRESSURE FOR LEGISLATION

Though British forces were still fighting in Russia and occupying Germany the majority of comforts and other funds closed down during 1919 and in April that year the office of the DGVO closed its doors for the last time. There was a suggestion that further legislation would help the disbursal of any surplus funds but a Home Office memo concluded that 'many charities are proceeding so rapidly that . . . by the time an Act became law we should nearly have finished our work. The Red Cross Charities, Voluntary Aid Detachment Hospitals, War Hospital Supply Depots, Prisoners of War Funds and Comfort Funds have been showering in upon us and are urgent in their desire to close down and deal with their surplus' but this did not mean that voluntary activities relating to the war had ended.[169] Many London-based charities ran into problems over the disposal of funds. They did not understand their obligations as charities in that they had to pass on remaining money to organisations with very similar objects. Even those run by prominent people had difficulties, including the Empire Union Clubs where Lieutenant General Sir Francis Lloyd, Commander of London District, 'illegally' distributed no less than £25,000.[170]

The largest number of schemes that remained in operation were for the victims of the conflict, including helping the devastated areas of France and Belgium, assisting disabled war veterans and commemorating the fallen. One response was for communities to adopt a town in France or Belgium as a twin and provide support. Sheffield adopted Serre and Wolverhampton Gommecourt, both of which had been destroyed during the Somme battles. Liverpool adopted Givenchy and even individuals continued to help the areas where they had fought. J.G. Colthart Moffat 'spent his military pension ensuring that the "aged and broken residents" of Guillemont, the village where he was wounded in 1916, never lacked food and fuel.'[171] Many relief workers also remained abroad working with the enormous numbers of refugees the conflict had created.[172] The war also led to the founding of a number of significant organisations that are still in existence today. St Dunstan's, founded by the blind newspaper magnate Sir Arthur Pearson, and the Women's Institute, an import from Canada, both started in 1915; the Royal Star and Garter Homes were established in the following year; the People's Dispensary for Sick Animals in 1917 and in 1919 Philip 'Tubby' Clayton began the Toc H, a continuation of his work with the YMCA during the war at Talbot House near Ypres.

As early as 1917 the Charity Commission was expressing its hope that some form of regulation of charities would be continued after the war. Their *64th Annual Report* commented that the operation of the War Charities Act 'has convinced us of the great value of some such control [being extended to all] Charities supported by voluntary contributions.'[173] In August 1920 the Blind Persons Act was passed, which extended the jurisdiction of the War Charities Act to charities for the blind, and immediately after the war the major charities and the Commission had supporters in Parliament who raised the issue on a number of occasions. No further action was taken however until the appointment of a Home Office Departmental Committee of Enquiry in 1925 under the chairmanship of Sir Herbert Cunliffe, whose investigation 'to consider and report whether any form of supervision is desirable over collecting charities' took two years to report.[174] Inevitably *Truth* contributed a file of evidence and a further twenty-five witnesses were questioned representing major charities, local authorities and the police. The Committee revisited many of the points considered by the War Charities Committee and raised many of the same problems. They were concerned at the scale of the issue, concluding that legislation would bring well over 80,000 charities within its remit, many of which were not in need of it. The level of checks required would make the task 'very large indeed and the existing resources of local authorities would be quite inadequate [and] the central direction of the scheme could not be carried out effectively without the creation of a new administrative body or the enlargement of some existing department.'[175] Unlike during the war the circumstances of the late 1920s did not lend themselves to favour action and the level of public and media pressure was nowhere near as great. The Committee noted that the number of proven frauds was very small and that witnesses kept mentioning the same cases, which was also true in 1916. However, they persuaded themselves that 'it is difficult to believe that any large number of undesirables can, over a long period of time, entirely hide themselves both from the police and from the Charity Organisation Society.'[176] The key phrase was 'over a long period'; during peacetime there was breathing space to uncover charity frauds, whereas in wartime there was not. The Committee therefore did not support 'the institution of any universal system of supervision over collecting charities.' They did however recommend that the Charity Commission should be given powers to investigate any collecting charity represented to it by a local authority as not being properly administered and given powers to wind up or remodel any where they found the allegations proven.[177] They also supported the licensing of all street collections and raising the minimum age of street collectors to eighteen. It was this last proposal that led to the failure of the Bill that was finally introduced in 1929. It proposed that each street collection would require a licence and the major charities estimated this would mean 200,000 cases a year and so opposed it. This opposition came as a surprise to the Home Office, who clearly had not done their homework, and the Bill fell before its third reading.[178]

Many of the issues that surrounded charity legislation in the First World War returned in 1939 but under very different circumstances. All parties were far more comfortable with the idea of state control in wartime and welfare provision for dependants was not an issue. With immediate conscription and vastly fewer troops abroad, troop comforts were less prominent. Nevertheless similar problems of a confusion of appeals arose and, in January 1940, a new Director General of Voluntary Organizations, Sir Alan Hutchings (who had been Ward's secretary), was appointed though he had a much narrower remit and a far less prominent role than his former boss.[179] A new War Charities Act was also passed in 1940, very similar to the 1916 Act (which it repealed) though it included Scotland from the outset. Geoffrey Finlayson summed up charitable activity in the Second World War by saying it

> Witnessed a great deal of charitable activity. Once again it brought the Servicemen's organizations, such as the Soldiers', Sailors', and—now—Airmen's Family Association, and the British Legion to the relief of war-related problems. But, *of course* [my emphasis], the Second World War gave greater scope for service among the civilian population at home than the First World War had done. Charitable organizations were active in helping with the process of evacuation, and in finding suitable accommodation in safe areas. Many voluntary organizations were also involved in the provision of social centres, recreational clubs for war workers, and family hostels.[180]

Whilst I do not dispute Finlayson's assertions regarding the level of activity in World War Two there is certainly no 'of course' about it. From the First World War one could substitute assistance for Belgian refugees for the evacuees and match the provision of social and welfare centres. On top of this there was the huge contribution of troop comforts and medical supplies that was significantly greater in the First World War: the army was far bigger, more of them were abroad for longer and by 1939 far more of these items were supplied by the state. Though I have not investigated charitable provision during the Second World War in great detail the indications are that the giving of both money and time was significantly greater in 1914–18. Finlayson is, however, correct in his conclusion that 'the Second World War, like the First . . . provided great spurs to philanthropic effort. War and want did, indeed, drive the state—but they also drove philanthropy.'[181] In the words of another writer 'the experience of the Great War . . . challenged the voluntary paradigm', altering its principles and its relationship to the state, but it proved to be more than up to the challenge.[182]

In 1948, William Beveridge published his influential book *Voluntary Action: A Report on Methods of Social Advance*, one of whose proposals was for a Royal Commission to review the doctrine of cy près. Accepting the suggestion, the government appointed a committee of inquiry under Lord Nathan in 1950. Reporting two years later the Nathan Committee not only supported the relaxation of cy près but also recommended a central register of all charities be established, despite the fact that they estimated the numbers to have now risen to about 110,000. The government again dragged its feet and it was not until 1960 that the Charities Act finally established the registration of all charities in the UK. The eventual registration of all charities thus finally came about when it was recognised that the increasing partnership between the state and the voluntary sector required greater government control and, not least, when the issue ceased to be politically controversial.[183] Even then the 1940 Act remained in force and as late as 1977 there were still 2,250 war charities registered (some of which did not qualify as charities under the 1960 Act). It was agreed that to repeal the War Charities Act might stir up more problems than retaining it and it was left on the statute book.[184] It was finally repealed by the Charities Act of 1992, which mainly dealt with the control of fund-raising and charitable collections.

In the view of the Home Office in the 1920s, the War Charities Act was passed to do two things:

- Prevent appeals being made to the public by persons whose bona fides were not established; and
- To ensure that funds were in the hands of a responsible committee.[185]

In this it was probably as successful as it was able to be. Charity fraud and scandal is impossible to eliminate, even under the far stricter conditions prevailing today. A 2008 report found that 18 percent of charities reported being the victim of fraud at least once in the previous two years, costing the sector an estimated £680 million a year.[186] Given these figures legislators still demand more action against charity fraudsters. In August 2000 the Public Accounts Committee 'demanded an explanation' from the Charity Commissioners after an investigation by the *Independent* into 'a string of cases' and in 2010 Conservative MP Tracey Crouch tabled a motion calling on the government to ensure that local police authorities tackled criminal gangs responsible for bogus charity clothing collections.[187] It is also remarkable how little the nature of these crimes have changed. For example, in 2002 police investigated the Dream Foundation, a charity to make sick and dying children's wishes come true, after an anonymous tip that up to £300,000 had gone missing. The Fund was backed by a host of celebrities from television and sport, including footballer Alan Shearer, and was run by a retired police officer, David Foley. Foley, his wife and the founder, David Mulcahy, were given prison sentences.[188] Within days of the Haiti earthquake, in January 2010, scam e-mails and websites proliferated.[189] It is simply not defendable to allow the activities of charity fraudsters to go unchecked and the legislators of 1916 realised this. As Richard Hurley from Cifas, the UK's fraud prevention service, said in relation to the Haiti scams, charity fraudsters prey 'on your feelings for those innocent victims and your desire to help them. . . . It's making use of human suffering and the best in human nature at the same time simply for commercial profit.'[190] The donors of 1914–18 were just as caring, and just as vulnerable. Cahalan's summary is therefore eminently fair when he says:

> Several old bugbears . . . were stamped out, the Commissioners cracked down on flag days, and poorly-managed charities were compulsorily reorganised. . . . On the whole [the Act] succeeded in eliminating the worst cases of fraud and in forcing some duplicate charities to merge. The War Refugees Committee and other large organisations were satisfied and the Act silenced the volume of criticism of the eighteen months before its enactment. But small organisations continued to flourish and proliferate.[191]

Case Study 5
'Nothing Like a Book'—The Camps Library

On the outbreak of war Lord Kitchener asked Sir Edward Ward if he would look after the welfare of the many soldiers from overseas who were arriving to support Britain's war effort. One idea Ward had was to ensure a supply of books and magazines for the camps and billets where the soldiers were stationed. At the end of 1914 he placed an appeal in the press for donations of literature and the Camps Library was born. The enterprise quickly outgrew its initial premises in Great Smith Street which had despatched 40,000 volumes to camps on Salisbury Plain and elsewhere. It eventually found larger and permanent premises at 45 Horseferry Road, provided courtesy of the Belgian Army. The warehouse had previously been occupied by Broadwood's, the piano makers, and its reinforced floors were essential for the mountain of books that poured in from all sources, quickly reaching 75,000 a week. The Queen was an enthusiastic supporter as were many prominent authors including Rudyard Kipling, George Meredith, Arthur Conan Doyle, Marie Corelli, Hall Cain and John Galsworthy.[1] The success of the enterprise meant that its activities were soon extended to encompass all British troops, both at home and abroad and, later still, prisoners of war in not only Germany but Austria, Bulgaria and Turkey as well as internees in Holland. Probably every camp, canteen and rest hut on the Western Front had its supply of Camps Library material. The war's most famous cartoonist, Bruce Bairnsfather, produced advertisements for the Library and every parcel of books sent out contained postcards for the recipients to send home to friends and relatives to encourage further donations. Given his contacts, it is not surprising that Ward received support at the highest possible level. To keep distribution costs down he negotiated free postage for all donations with Herbert Samuel, at that time the Postmaster General; the Boy Scouts, Girl Guides and Church Lads' Brigade helped in collection and distribution.

The Library had strong support from senior army commanders, though sometimes not from their subordinates. In late 1915 the QMG, General Maxwell, questioned whether the expense to the army of the Camps Library, £60 per week, was worthwhile. The C-in-C, Sir John French, replied that 'all Commanders were unanimous and he concurred in recommending the expenditure.'[2] Sir Douglas Haig, shortly to succeed French, lent his personal support by writing:

> Those who have not visited our Armies in the field can scarcely realise what books have meant during two years of war to the men in the trenches. . . . Any movement to increase the circulation of books has my whole-hearted support.[3]

In all, by the end of March 1919 when the Library closed, it had distributed the astounding total of sixteen million books. Some of these donations were not entirely welcome (old telephone directories or copies of *Bradshaw* for example) but the majority seemed to match what the troops desired. 'What the men chiefly wanted were stories—good stories, love stories, detective stories, sentimental stories', commented one officer.[4] One donation initially seemed misguided but eventually proved otherwise:

> Books of every language were sent in: French, German, Chinese, Japanese, Greek, Hindustani, Maori and Gaelic found their way to the Library, and once, in grave and anxious days at the beginning of the war, someone sent in a *Guide to Germany*. It was first suggested that this should be thrown away, but a far-seeing optimist rescued it from destruction and set it in a prominent place to be kept for the day when it should be useful to guide our army into the land of our enemies. On the day the Armistice was signed that book went over to France.[5]

The work of the Camps Library, and its sister organisations the War Library and the British Prisoners of War Book Scheme, are perhaps easy to underestimate. The First World War was uniquely literary and books and magazines played much the same role as iPods and computer games play with today's troops and their aid to morale and in alleviating boredom must have been immense. Perhaps it was going too far when one adjutant of a front-line battalion wrote that 'in the trenches I think books are even more appreciated than tobacco,' but the views of another officer probably got close to reality when he said 'cramped in a crumbling dug-out, time passes slowly, and the monotony is greatly relieved by a few "mags" from the old folks at home.'[6] Another letter from France came with the message that 'the last parcel of your books came just as we had been relieved after the gas attack, and there is nothing like a book for taking one's mind off what one has seen and gone thru.'[7] If it were thought that Australian troops might be less inclined to literary pursuits these comments from the Australian Infantry Base Depot at Havre should dispel those illusions:

> Your parcel came today, just as a crowd of our men were leaving for the front. I wish you could have seen their faces as I was able to relieve the tedium of a 36-hour journey, and then the books would be passed

on to the men in the firing line. I do thank you on their behalf, and like Oliver 'ask for more.'[8]

Obviously as Ward's wartime responsibilities increased, he was less able to take an active part in the running of the Library and so the key role in its success was played by its Honorary Director, Eva Anstruther. Anstruther was born Eva Hanbury-Tracy, in 1869, the eldest child of the 4th Lord Sudeley. She was herself a writer and the estranged wife of Liberal Unionist politician Henry Torrens Anstruther. She and Ward's relationship became more than professional during the war and he was 'sometimes to be seen emerging from [Anstruther's] house in the afternoons.' He also visited her regularly at her country home though 'how long the affair lasted is not recorded.'[9] At the end of the war, on Ward's recommendation, Anstruther was created DBE and her daughter continued her literary tradition; as Jan Struther she was the author of the popular World War Two novel *Mrs Miniver*.

7   The Extent and Impact of Wartime Charitable Giving

We have already seen the extent of some of the charitable and voluntary activity that took place after 1914 in, for example, the amounts raised for the National Relief Fund. Though this was one of the largest schemes there were dozens of others whose fund-raising or value of goods and services contributed provided substantial sums.[1] The single largest charity operating between 1914 and 1918 was, not surprisingly, the British Red Cross Society. Their total wartime income was an enormous £22 million of which the majority came via *The Times* appeal.[2] As troop comforts became a major part of the voluntary effort on the home front it was estimated that 'during the first year of the war alone some £5 million of comforts were supplied to the army and navy.'[3] There were also the numerous charities, many connected with the Church, operating in theatres of war. The Church Army established more than 800 canteens and recreation rooms on the Western Front and in Italy. The YMCA had ten in the Ypres Salient alone, turning over 260,000 francs (about £13,000) by March 1918.[4] The YMCA's overall contribution was impressive, as Michael Snape has demonstrated: 'although [the YMCA] defrayed a substantial amount of its costs through the sale of refreshments and merchandise, the net cost of its work during the First World War was eventually estimated at a staggering £8,000,000.'[5] Charities collecting in aid of disabled veterans were also highly successful and we have noted the connection between the Girls' Patriotic Union and the Star and Garter Home. The Star and Garter campaign was also supported by the British Women's Hospital Committee for whom the famous actress May Whitty supervised hundreds of charity theatricals, benefit performances and appeal concerts. In their first month they raised £20,000, within eleven months £150,000 and within a year and a half £225,000.[6] Another significant philanthropist for the disabled was the theatre owner Sir Oswald Stoll. In 1919 the *Daily Telegraph* estimated Stoll's war charity work had raised £260,993.[7] These, however, are individual examples; just how many organisations were there and how much, overall, did they raise?

Figure 7.1 Poster for the Coachbuilding and Motor Trade Fund for Entertaining Wounded Soldiers; note the smoking competition (top right picture) (courtesy of the City of London, London Metropolitan Archives).

NUMBERS OF CHARITIES AND HOW MUCH THEY RAISED

The first problem is that it is quite difficult to agree on a definition of a wartime charity. Do you include just *new* organisations, omitting those that pre-existed but turned their efforts to war-related causes, like the Red Cross? As we saw, the legislators drawing up the War Charities Act in 1916 were faced with exactly the same problem. The only precise statistics are the published figures of the Charity Commission recording those who registered officially following the passing of the 1916 Act. Even after the war ended new 'war charities' were being created (for example to build war memorials or support disabled servicemen) so the date also affects the figures. There were some who, whist clearly connected with the war, were deemed not to be 'war charities' in the definition of the Act.[8] Then one needs to consider both those who operated only before the 1916 Act and any who were simply too fleeting or unofficial to show up in statistics. Thus the number of organisations in the war charities register must be considered a minimum number. If we take 1920 as the cut-off date, the

Figure 7.2 Poster for charity football match in aid of the London General Omnibus Company (Dalston Garage) Charity (courtesy of the City of London, London
Metropolitan Archives).

Table 7.1   Number of Registered War Charities, 1920

Registered 1916–1920	11,407
Exempted from registration	6,492
Refused registration	42

Source: PP 68th Report of the Charity Commissioners of England and Wales, 1921, ix, Cmd. 1198.

total number of war charities was, as shown in Table 7.1, 17,899.[9] This is a huge number, especially when compared with the number of charities operating before the war, 36,865 in 1913, as it represents an increase of nearly 50 percent.[10]

If the number of organisations operating is difficult to calculate accurately the amounts they raised is even more problematic as no official figures were compiled.[11] However, there are a number of indirect methods one can adopt. The first can be inferred from figures given by contemporary commentators. The earliest national estimate would seem to have been calculated by the journalist and social commentator W.E. Dowding. Dowding's calculations came from careful research of what organisations had raised and his results were publicised by the Liberal politician and head of the British War Propaganda Bureau, Charles Masterman, in an article in the *Contemporary Review* in July 1915.[12] Referring to Dowding's calculation, Masterman said that in the opening ten months of the war some £25 million, in money or in kind, had been donated.[13] Masterman reported that Dowding was working on a book that would cover 'every description of fund from the largest to the smallest.'[14] Unfortunately Dowding did not publish a book; instead, in November 1915, he published an article, also in the *Contemporary Review.*[15] His conclusion at this stage of the war was that 'in money and in kind the United Kingdom has given nearly thirty millions.'[16] A similar figure to Dowding's (minus the 'in kind') was given in a parliamentary debate on 8 December 1915 when Will Anderson raised the issue of government control over wartime charities.[17] His source was a statement at Marlborough Street police court in the last week of November where the sum of £20 million was given as an official estimate of the money collected for war charities since the commencement of the war.[18] Around the same date another semi-official Home Office estimate was that £27 million had been raised.[19] In February 1916 the *Daily Chronicle* reported that 'it is estimated in the past 18 months £29,000,000 have been subscribed by the British people to benevolent objects at home and abroad connected with the war.'[20]

What veracity can be placed on these figures? There are two ways they can be partially verified. The first is the audited figure we have from the NRF, which had realised £5 million by April 1915. This would mean that for Dowding's figures to be correct all the other funds combined would have had to be worth approximately four times more. This is not an unreasonable assumption given, for example, that *The Times* Fund had raised £3.4 million by February 1916. Another way of confirming his figure is to look at an 'average' charity. If there were 10,000 charities operating at any one time then the average raised by each would need to be £125 a month. Even if only just over 6,000 were up and running during the early part of the war then that would be an average of £200 a month. The Croydon War Supplies Clearing House was raising over £400 a month in cash during this period. Admittedly, CWSCH may have been above average but it was not primarily a money-raising organisation, being more concerned with donations of goods. From these figures contemporary estimates do not appear over-excessive. In fact, it may well have been an underestimate if Croydon and Todmorden's fund-raising was typical of the rest of the country. In these towns, they had raised well *over* four times the amount collected for the NRF for other causes by mid-1915.[21]

The next question is, if £20–£27 million had been raised by the end of November 1915 how much had been raised by the end of the war? Again we can only theorise but a straightforward rounding-up would not be inaccurate. Some have argued that donor fatigue set in or that the sums raised by charities remained steady throughout the war, meaning that when inflation is taken into account they fell in real terms. For example, the conclusion of Trevor Wilson, usually a most reliable and meticulous researcher is that:

> As the war went on, these forms of gift in cash and kind diminished, and increasingly the state was looked to as the proper supporter of the war's victims. This was evidence of the scale of the problem but also the way in which the conflict was diminishing the incomes of the charitably inclined.[22]

By the charitably inclined Wilson was speaking of the upper and middle classes, especially those on fixed incomes, whose spending power decreased as wartime inflation hit them hard. My own researches have however found no evidence to back up the assertion that charitable donations declined, either in gross or real terms. Certainly, the state took over in many areas, such as dependant allowances and pensions, but charity moved from these into new areas. As the war continued, a number of high-impact new funds such as those devoted to disabled ex-servicemen and war memorials also helped compensate for any losses. There was also another compensatory reason why charitable income did not decline, as many working class people saw a real increase in their incomes and 'income gains were greatest, both absolutely and relatively, among the poorest paid and least skilled of the labouring population.'[23] In contrast to Wilson's assertion modern research clearly indicates that poorer people contribute proportionally *more* of their income to charity. One study (in 2001) found that those earning under

£10,000 a year contributed around double the percentage of their income than did those earning above £20,000 and in 2010–11 the poorest 20 percent of donors in the UK gave 3.2 percent of their gross monthly income to charity, compared with only 0.9 percent donated by the richest 20 percent.[24] In his study 'Financing Public Goods by Means of Lotteries', John Morgan comments on the 'regressivity' of both lotteries and voluntary charitable contributions.[25] His findings are consistent with both lotteries and charitable donations being regressive in their impact, i.e. of poorer people contributing a significantly higher proportion of their incomes in both cases. Though there are no equivalent systematic statistics stretching back to the period of the First World War there is plenty of circumstantial evidence and research that backs up this trend. 'Poor-to-poor' (or, at least, working class to working class) charity was recognised as being highly significant by many social commentators of the period. In *The Condition of the Working Class* Engels, no lover of bourgeois philanthropy, noted that 'although the workers cannot really afford to give charity on the same scale as the middle class, they are nevertheless more charitable in every way.'[26] Frank Prochaska has backed this assertion, noting that 'a survey of rather more prosperous working-class families in the 1890s showed that half of them contributed funds to charity each week' and, for example, that 'well over half the income of several hospitals in the North of England came from "workmen" [and] the Methodist Missionary Society raised millions of pounds from humble subscribers in the nineteenth century, largely through its sophisticated network of local associations.' Prochaska points out that, not surprisingly, 'the respectable working class, often identified with church and chapel, was particularly noticeable in its charitable activity' and that this motivation was not solely altruistic but also, as with middle and upper class philanthropy, carried implications of self-interest. This was especially the case 'when they cooperated with their wealthier neighbours, as in hospital provision, education, or foreign missions.'[27] This 'dual motivation' has been commented on in charitable activity up to the present day. In the light of this evidence it is probable that, as middle class donations to charity fell, donations from workers, whose pay was at least keeping pace with inflation, increased to compensate.

What other evidence is there of at least a steady state of donation? One set of indicators are the sums raised by street collections in London later in the war and the year after victory.[28] These are shown in Table 7.2 and confirm a rise that more than compensated for inflation.

An even more reliable indicator that donor fatigue was not significant is the income of the largest of all wartime fund-raising efforts, *The Times* Fund. Started on 1 September 1914 the full income figures for the fund are shown in Table 7.3.

The remarkable thing about these figures is that, adjusted for inflation, the income remained so constant throughout the war. If this is thought to be evidence with an urban, or London, bias then Armstrong's research on

Table 7.2   Amounts Raised from London Street Collections

Year	Number of Collections	Amount Raised (£)	Adjusted for Inflation (£)
1916–17	263	268,736	268,736
1918	261	391,864	281,916
1919	287	416,640	285,370

Source: TNA, HO 45/11217.

Table 7.3   Income per Year to *The Times* Fund

Income	Yearly Total (£)	Yearly Total Adjusted for Inflation (£)
To August 1915	1,655,807	1,655,807
Sept 1915–August 1916	2,652,300	2,244,676
Sept 1916–August 1917	2,944,107	2,058,863
Sept 1917–August 1918	4,203,299	2,555,273
Sept 1918–August 1919	4,666,426	2,676,493

Source: The Times, 1915–1919 passim.

rural Kentish charities is relevant. He found that 'these charitable efforts do not appear to have flagged as the war continued.'[29]

As a final confirmation of at least a steady state of donation one straightforward statistic is the date of formation of charities registered under the War Charities Act. Clearly this does not cover those that had ceased operation by 1916 or did not register and, it might be argued, takes no account of the scale of the organisation; however, it gives some sort of guide. Taking one example, of the 150 charities registered in Blackburn: 15 percent were formed in 1914, 7 percent in 1915, 10 percent in 1916, 29 percent in 1917 and 39 percent in 1918. Not conclusive, but certainly not an indicator of declining interest. Assuming this steady state theory then the total value of funds raised for wartime charities based on Dowding's and other contemporary estimates was not less than £75 million.

Another method of calculating a national figure is to multiply up from reliable local statistics. Though many local histories of the Great War were produced, only a handful of them attempted a comprehensive listing of amounts raised. Seven of those that did, plus Glasgow whose figures are estimated in an alternative way, are listed in Table 7.4 together with a calculation of amounts raised per head of population.[30]

How likely are these figures to be typical across the entire country? The first point is the consistency of the per-head totals with the exception of the

Table 7.4   Amounts Raised in Local Communities

Town	Amount Raised(£)	Population (1911)	Amount Raised per Head (£)
Bradford	190,061[i]	288,458	1.63
Bristol	586,026[ii]	357,144	1.64
Hartlepool	93,969	63,923	1.47
Leicester	350,000	227,222	1.54
Preston	230,454	117,088	1.97
Todmorden[iii]	38,377	25,404	1.51
Crieff (Scotland)	17,735	5,500	3.22
Glasgow	3,500,000	784,000	4.46

i In twenty-one months, total estimated up to £470,627.
ii Excludes income from flag days.
iii This is definitely an underestimate as the figures exclude many events associated with local charities such as fund-raising by the, extremely influential, Todmorden Cricket Club. See Freda, Malcolm and Keith Heywood, In a League of Their Own: Cricket and Leisure in 20th Century Todmorden (Todmorden: Upper Calder Valley Publications, 2011), 44.

two Scottish examples. Crieff is perhaps not surprising in that smaller communities might well have raised more per head than larger ones, but how can one explain the apparent anomaly of Glasgow?[31] This is, perhaps, the most significant of all the statistics as it was the only place, as far as I have been able to ascertain, that collected comprehensive, systematic information on wartime charitable giving. These were accurately audited at least until the end of 1915 and later presented before the War Charities Committee and in a detailed newspaper report at the end of the war.[32] The higher figure could perhaps be partly explained by the fact that Glaswegians contributed relatively little to national, London-based appeals. For example, opposition to the NRF led to a Glasgow-based version being started. Alternatively, perhaps it reflected the city's historical generosity. It was the first city in the UK to utilise flag days for wartime charities and, by April 1915, £50,000 had been raised at twelve such days.[33] However the likeliest explanation is that giving from working class donors rose with their incomes, coupled with Glasgow being more systematic at recording donations from this source. In fact Glasgow contributed disproportionately in virtually *every* aspect of support for the war. Recruitment figures were higher in Glasgow with one Glaswegian in the army for every twenty-three Englishmen, twice the English enlistment rate. The city also contributed out of proportion to supporting war bonds. In 'Tank Week' in January 1918 Glasgow raised £14 million, breaking all records.[34] Yet this was in a city considered by some, both at the time and since, as a hotbed of industrial unrest.[35] The explanation again lies in the relative prosperity of many working class Glaswegians, as the city became a hub of wartime production.

The places in Table 7.4 are reasonably different (in size and geography) and cannot be considered over-prosperous or impoverished. They cover both highly urbanised and rural areas where networks of giving may have differed significantly. The sums raised do not contain any donations made by people in these places directly to UK national charities, *The Times* appeal for example, and so must be an underestimate. If the median figure per head (£2.32) were multiplied up over the entire country, you get a total of £107 million, significantly above the former estimate of £75 million.[36] If the overall average (£2.90) is used which, given the greater precision of the Glasgow figure, may be more accurate, it would yield a national total of £133 million.[37] If the Glasgow figure were repeated nationally, the total would be over £200 million. More research and more examples are needed to confirm the validity of these findings but they may be more accurate than those of Dowding and his contemporaries.

To these cash figures we need to add the value of goods donated or produced for troop comforts and hospitals and contributions that came directly from officers and regimental associations for the comfort of their troops. Especially in the early years of the war, prior to the establishment of the DGVO, 'it was extremely common for officers to use their own money to buy gifts for their men.'[38] Such gifts were not only welcomed but also helped in the officer/man bond with soldiers having 'affection for officers who took pains to attend to the needs of individual men.'[39] What figure can be put on these in-kind gifts? Here we have Frederick D'Aeth's estimate that the figure was equivalent to £5 million in the first year of the war and the Glasgow figure of £240,000 after two years. From studies of a range of organisations, these are not an overestimate, and this would add a further £20 to £30 million to the total figures.[40] In addition, other hidden figures might be added. One example was the money that came through the exhibition of the most popular official film made during the war, *The Battle of the Somme*. E.S. Turner notes that 40 percent of the takings for the film (probably representing the film distributor's percentage) were donated to charity.[41] As more than twenty million people saw the film in its first two months of release this would have raised around £100,000 given that an average ticket cost about 3d.

Overall then the total fund-raising effort for the war was certainly not less than £100 million, was more likely to have reached £125 to £150 million and may well have been significantly greater than that. This meant that for every man of the six million who served in the forces during the war (however briefly) around £20 was contributed to his support and to other causes, worth about £1,000 today. At the time of the war the total value of *all* charity investments was £34 million and annual charitable income was just £14 million.[42] Therefore, war causes more than doubled pre-war charitable income. With regard to fund-raising for domestic purposes the increase is even more dramatic, as 40 percent of pre-war charity income went to overseas missionary activity. The amount was also greater than the total annual government expenditure in every year up to the Boer War.[43] At the 'median' modern purchasing value of the wartime pound £100 million would be the equivalent of £5 billion today, or rather more than £1 billion a year. This is roughly equivalent to the total sum raised for 'good causes' by the UK National Lottery. In relation to the value of giving, the 'cost' to the giver, the figure would be closer to £30 billion today. One might also compare it to fund-raising figures for World War Two. Probably the largest philanthropic fund was the U.S. National War Fund, 'the most ambitious venture in united fund-raising the United States had yet seen.'[44] This raised a total of $750 million, worth around £187.5 million in 1940–45, or £131 million at 1916 values. So this massive effort in the U.S., a far richer country than the UK twenty-five years earlier, probably achieved no greater response.

EFFECTS ON EXISTING CHARITIES

There is a further question that should be asked before leaving this subject and that is what the impact was on existing charities and existing charitable giving. Was some of the income of war charities simply displaced from existing causes? There is some evidence of a detrimental effect on charitable giving in the early war years. Between 1913 and 1916 both the number of endowed charities registered and the value of new endowments went down. However, the figures from the Charity Commission for the *entire* war period, shown in Table 7.5, demonstrate that there was certainly no obvious adverse effect on endowed charities.

Figures for London charities for the period are also available from two different sources and these specifically exclude both war-related charities and those whose work shifted to wartime causes. The number of charities surveyed by Howe went down from 897 in 1912–13 to 885 in 1917–18 (a decline of just 1.3 percent) but two of the years (1913–14 and 1917–18)

Table 7.5   Income of Endowed Charities, 1913–18

Year	New Endowments (£)	Total Investments (£)	Income from Investments (£)	Number of Charities
1913	890,127	32,509,761	934,533	36,865
1914	509,884	33,622,526	961,569	36,302
1915	275,445	34,167,136	1,026,057	32,395
1916	388,610	35,545,274	1,073,478	30,551
1917	559,765	37,098,272	1,147,085	33,989
1918	1,166,712	40,930,233	1,264,360	29,637

Source: Charity Commissioners for England and Wales Annual Reports.

Table 7.6   Income of London Non-War-Related Charities, 1912–18

1912–13	1913–14	1914–15	1915–16	1916–17	1917–18
£8,088,778	£8,705,980	£8,443,131	£8,590,484	£8,335,620	£9,098,997

Source: *Howe's Classified Directory to the Metropolitan Charities*, 39th to 44th editions.

Table 7.7   Charitable Contributions to, and Overall Income of, Metropolitan Charities

Year	Charitable Contributions (£)	Total income (£)
1912	3,800,153	8,672,980
1913	3,534,105	8,307,573
1914	3,523,405	8,920,711
1915	3,318,025	7,660,449
1916	3,800,919	8,437,467
1917	3,805,307	8,195,427
1918	4,618,387	9,884,415
1919	5,348,742	10,880,441
1920	5,434,235	13,606,666

Source: Annual Charities Register and Digest, 22nd to 31st editions, 1913–1922.

actually show slight rises in numbers. Again, the pre-war trend had already been downwards (from 933 in 1910–11 or a 4 percent drop by 1912–13). The income of these charities (Table 7.6) actually shows an *increase* in income of over £1 million a year during the period.

These figures include, of course, investment income as well as donations and do not take inflation into account. Those from the *Annual Charities Register and Digest* (Table 7.7) are very similar but also include figures for direct charitable contributions and point to immediate post-war trends.

Finally, there is the view of contemporary commentators. W.E. Dowding was clear that the massive contributions to war causes had been achieved 'without any diminution . . . in support of the permanent charities.'[45] What can reasonably be concluded is that the dramatic increase in charitable effort and giving to war-related causes had no catastrophic effect on existing charities. Indeed the significant post-war increase in charitable income tentatively suggests that the stimulus to charitable activity during the war may have continued into peacetime, with people now donating at a higher rate to existing causes, at least while higher wages and full employment continued. Finlayson confirms that war-related charities did not have a negative impact on existing causes even after the war, saying that 'contrary to expectations, therefore, World War One did not destroy the contributory principle—nor did it deplete the finances of organisations in the mutual-aid side of the voluntary sector.[46] Overall, if you looked at the figures for the income of existing charities without knowing their historical setting, it would be difficult to realise that such a cataclysmic event as the First World War had even taken place.

HOW MANY PEOPLE WERE INVOLVED?

The evidence suggests that the value of wartime charitable activity was significantly greater than has previously been realised. One might also ask how many people were involved in this effort. Though not having a direct monetary value it was again highly significant. This is an even more elusive question as it requires a definition of what constituted a contribution and therefore what to count. To take just a few examples: in the first year of the war more than 20,000 new workers entered the field of personal case work for the Soldiers' and Sailors' Family Association; by May 1915 over 60,000 volunteers were assisting the British Red Cross and in Birmingham 'in the distribution of relief over 2,000 persons are working voluntarily; 3,000 assisted in the street collection, and 3,500 took part in the house-to-house collection.'[47] There were 53,000 subscribers to the Active Service League, an early attempt led by the sister of Field-Marshal French to coordinate charity volunteering prior to the DGVO.[48] Of course, many people could only spare an hour or two a week but thousands spent their entire time on war charity work, many of them members of the leisured middle and upper classes who otherwise would probably never have done any 'real' work in their entire lives. Virtually every schoolchild was involved in at least one of the national campaigns whether it was collecting eggs for the wounded or horse chestnuts for explosives, and seven million children contributed £35,000 to the Jack Cornwell VC Memorial Fund to commemorate the boy hero of the Battle of Jutland.[49] If we try to confine the question to just those who regularly and consistently gave a significant amount of their time to charitable work there is again some indirect evidence. Inevitably the fact that, by definition, these people had to have time to give meant that certain sectors of the population were overrepresented: women more than men; older people more than the young; the better off rather than the working class, but not as disproportionately as some have claimed.[50]

Local histories again provide some help as they sometimes list the numbers engaged in wartime voluntary work. In Stamford, Lincolnshire, 176 women were awarded the Voluntary War Workers badge issued by the DGVO for regular helpers.[51] In Stamford in 1911 there were 3,590 women aged fifteen to seventy so this represents 5 percent of the female population and is probably an underestimate as it only includes those whose work was eligible and who bothered to apply for the badge. In Bradford the numbers engaged in regular war charity work was put at 2,000 men and 5,000 women from an adult population (excluding those in the services) of about 100,000, 4 percent of men and 10 percent of women. In nearby Leeds with a population of 445,000 there were 10,000 women involved in voluntary activity by the spring of 1915.[52] All of these examples represent a huge increase on the pre-war numbers involved in voluntary action. For example, in 1911, the number of volunteers for the entire Guild of Help network, the largest social welfare organisation at the time, was 8,000 and they were considered 'uniquely successful in enrolling citizens for charitable work.'[53] These local figures indicate that nationally something like 400,000 men and 1.2 million women were regularly engaged in working for wartime charities. They can be partially substantiated by reference to the total number of people (mainly women) who applied for and received the DGVO badge. In his final report, Sir Edward Ward gave the number of badge holders as 400,000. To qualify for the badge a volunteer had to work on a regular basis for a period of at least three months for one of the charities registered with the DGVO. These numbered 2,983 or approximately one-sixth of the total number of wartime charities. If the badge holders also represented one-sixth of all regular charity workers then this would give an overall number of 2.4 million, a figure that would compare favourably with the 2.6 million men who volunteered for the armed forces. It is also highly significant in relation to the numbers of women who were employed on other activities during the war. There were 57,000 WAACs, 60,000 female VADs and 260,000 in the Women's Land Army. There were 950,000 'munitionettes', still fewer than the likely numbers who were regularly working for charities.

Gender and Class Analysis of Office Holders of Wartime Charities

Was charity work as middle class an activity as is usually suggested? Croydon's War Supplies Clearing House certainly had a preponderance of middle class volunteers, but how typical was it? Examining contemporary local histories is bound to give a distorted view as they tend to concentrate on the dignitaries who fronted the major charities rather than on those who worked for them or who ran smaller organisations. Instead, the detailed records from the original central register of charities were analysed.[54] Evidence from two contrasting areas reveals a more complex picture. In Croydon, the Mayor, Howard Houlder, chaired six of the thirty-eight registered charities and his wife, Mary, chaired two more. The town clerk, John Newnham, the Borough Treasurer, William Gunner, and the Borough Accountant, James McCall, served on a total of twelve committees. Overall, the impression is very much of a top-down process: a small number of larger charities run by experienced, middle and upper-middle class office holders. The picture in Blackburn was entirely different. Here smaller charities based on a workplace or church/chapel were more characteristic. Of the 148 Blackburn charities, 41 percent were workplace based and 39 percent based on a church or chapel.

Figures 7.3–7.7   Posters and leaflets of the Croydon War Supplies Clearing House (by permission of Croydon Local Studies Library and Archives Service; posters from Record of Advertisements AR140/4).

The figures in Croydon were only 5 percent in each category. This resulted in a remarkable geographical concentration of charity workers. For example at 93 Queen's Road lived William Jones, Secretary of the Audley Range Congregational Church Charity. The Treasurer, William Oldham, lived at number 147 and another Committee member, Jones's brother Frank, lived at

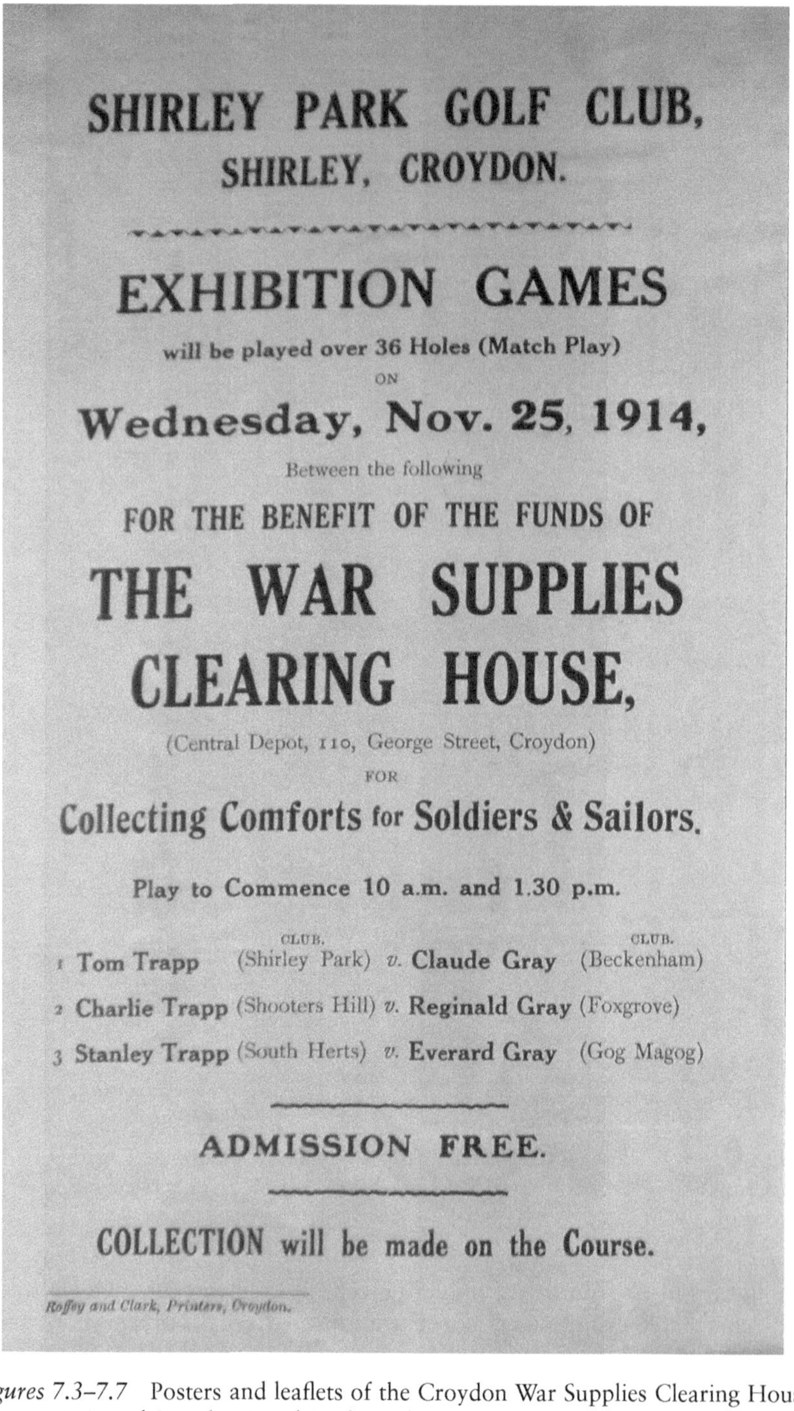

SHIRLEY PARK GOLF CLUB,
SHIRLEY, CROYDON.

EXHIBITION GAMES

will be played over 36 Holes (Match Play)
ON
Wednesday, Nov. 25, 1914,
Between the following

FOR THE BENEFIT OF THE FUNDS OF

THE WAR SUPPLIES
CLEARING HOUSE,

(Central Depot, 110, George Street, Croydon)
FOR
Collecting Comforts for Soldiers & Sailors.

Play to Commence 10 a.m. and 1.30 p.m.

		CLUB.			CLUB.
1	Tom Trapp	(Shirley Park)	*v.* Claude Gray	(Beckenham)
2	Charlie Trapp	(Shooters Hill)	*v.* Reginald Gray	(Foxgrove)
3	Stanley Trapp	(South Herts)	*v.* Everard Gray	(Gog Magog)

ADMISSION FREE.

COLLECTION will be made on the Course.

Roffey and Clark, Printers, Croydon.

Figures 7.3–7.7   Posters and leaflets of the Croydon War Supplies Clearing House (by permission of Croydon Local Studies Library and Archives Service; posters from Record of Advertisements AR140/4).

WAR SUPPLIES CLEARING HOUSE.

Head Depot: 110, George St., Croydon.

Shopping for the **WOUNDED**
Week

(3rd - 9th December.)

URGENT NEEDS

of our WOUNDED MEN

See our Special Display

ONE WEEK ONLY.

Please Call. Select. Pay.

Leave Name & Address on Label.

We Send to Head Depot.

GOODS DESPATCHED FREE.

Figures 7.3–7.7 Posters and leaflets of the Croydon War Supplies Clearing House (by permission of Croydon Local Studies Library and Archives Service; posters from Record of Advertisements AR140/4).

Figures 7.3–7.7   Posters and leaflets of the Croydon War Supplies Clearing House (by permission of Croydon Local Studies Library and Archives Service; posters from Record of Advertisements AR140/4).

Figures 7.3–7.7 Posters and leaflets of the Croydon War Supplies Clearing House (by permission of Croydon Local Studies Library and Archives Service; posters from Record of Advertisements AR140/4).

number 127. Between them, at number 107, was the Chairman of the Blackburn Parkside Manufacturing Co Soldiers Comforts Fund, George Burke, whilst a few doors down at number 31 resided William Howorth, committee member of the Chapel Street School Soldiers and Sailors Comfort Fund. At number 20 was Ellen Carr, chair of Daisyfield Co-Operative Society Women's Guild Soldiers and Sailors Comfort Fund; at 149, William Harrop, chair of the Furthergate Congregational Church and School Soldiers and Sailors Comfort Fund; at 63, Joseph Broughton, Secretary of Oxford Street Primitive Methodist Church Charity and at 105, its Chairman Nathaniel Brown; at 111, Joseph Smyth, Chairman of St Jude's Blackburn Soldiers Comforts Fund; at 89, Charles Gregson, committee member of St Matthew's Blackburn Soldiers Comforts Fund and at 103, its Treasurer, John Swarbrick; no fewer than twelve charity officers in a quarter-mile long street. In two of the streets parallel to Queen's Road, Pringle Street and Audley Range, lived another nineteen charity officials, an astonishing concentration and a pattern very much indicative of a bottom-up approach.

To determine how typical these preliminary findings were I undertook a more detailed examination of these and three other areas with regard to the gender and class of charity office holders: North Kent, Todmorden and Coventry. Todmorden has detailed records of unregistered charities and, as detailed records of exempted charities in Croydon (and the rest of Surrey) are not available, I included unregistered charities in metropolitan Kent. As a comparison, registered charities in Coventry were also examined. This was an area of specialist high-technology industry, cycles and Britain's nascent car and aircraft industries. It also experienced significant social unrest during the strikes of 1918. For registered charities the occupation of the Chairman and two further committee members, and often those of the Secretary and Treasurer as well, are recorded. The occupations of those persons applying for exemption are sometimes recorded but rarely what positions in the organisations they held. I attempted to discover the occupations of remaining office holders through searches of the 1901 and 1911 Censuses. This is an imprecise exercise, especially as only some could be traced in this way and people may have changed jobs. However, as mobility was not as great in this period the data is probably reasonably robust. Those women listed as 'married women' or 'spinster' have, where possible, been classified by their husbands' or fathers' occupations.

The social class classification adopted is modified from that of T.H.C. Stevenson, the medical statistician in the General Register Office. The classes are usually described as in Table 7.8. This classification was found more useful as it avoids artificially separating skilled manual workers employed in the textile industry (a very large category in Todmorden and Blackburn) from other categories of skilled manual workers such as those employed in the engineering, cycle and aero works in Coventry. More recently devised systems were rejected as being both over-complex and too difficult to relate to contemporary statistics.

Table 7.8   Social Class Classifications Used in the Study of Charity Office Holders

I	Professional etc occupations (including living on unearned income)
II	Managerial and technical occupations
III (N)	Skilled occupations (non-manual)
III (M)	Skilled occupations (manual)
IV	Partly skilled occupations
V	Unskilled occupations

Table 7.9   Gender of Officials in Wartime Charities

	Percentage Male	Percentage Female
Croydon (Registered) (n = 189)	74	26
North Kent (Exempted) (n = 46)	70	30
Coventry (Registered) (n = 82)	99	1
Blackburn (Registered) (n = 733)	69	31
Todmorden (Exempted) (n = 181)	70	30

Firstly, Table 7.9 analyses the gender of charity officials.

The interesting feature here is the consistency of the figures with the exception of Coventry. This may be explained by the nature of the social structure of the town and its industries, resulting in the fact that women made up only 26 percent of the workforce compared to 35 percent in Croydon (the largest number being domestic servants) and 45 percent in Blackburn (the majority as weavers). As a comparison a survey of twenty-five forces-related charities in 2010 showed that 75 percent of their trustees were men, so the figures appear to have changed little in 100 years.[55]

Table 7.10 indicates the proportion of women holding named office (Chair, Secretary and Treasurer). It is only possible to consider the registered organisations as it was not a requirement to indicate these for exempted bodies (though it was sometimes done the numbers are too small to consider).

Table 7.10   Percentage of Women in Named Offices in Charities

	Chair	Treasurer	Secretary
Croydon	19	5	39
Coventry	0	0	6
Blackburn	11	28	32

Table 7.11   Social Class of Office Holders of Charities by Percentage

	I	II	III (N)	III (M)	IV	V
Croydon (n = 135)	53	24	15	6	1	1
North Kent (n = 33)	52	30	15	0	0	3
Coventry (n = 63)	10	25	13	43	10	0
Blackburn (n = 552)	19	20	7	25	28	1
Todmorden (n = 79)	6	14	10	24	35	10

These figures indicate that women were relatively underrepresented in the most prestigious office of Chair. Chair*man* was certainly the rule and this is no surprise. It is also not surprising that women were underrepresented as Treasurers, a role often filled by a bookkeeper, accountant or bank manager, almost exclusively male preserves. The higher representation of women Secretaries would lend support to the contention that men were more likely to act as the figureheads of charities but that women often did the majority of the day-to-day work. The other feature is the significantly larger number of women Treasurers in Blackburn. This result needs to be considered in conjunction with the results on social class (below) and may be a reflection of the social structure of the mill towns of Lancashire.

The next analysis (Table 7.11) is that of the social class of office holders based on the considerations, selections and assumptions noted above.

These results can then be compared with the occupational make-up of each area. The figures in Table 7.12 are taken from the 1911 Census. As Todmorden was not separately identified the statistics for Blackburn were used in both comparisons. This analysis has to be treated with some caution as I have allocated the occupational classifications from the Census to the class categories utilised here. In the Census tables it is impossible to separate the semi-skilled from the more skilled textile workers. Somewhat arbitrarily I have placed all the textile workers in Class IV and therefore the Class III (M) and IV figures might better be looked at as a combined total. In some categories a somewhat arbitrary split has had to be made between those in authority and others. This has been done with local and national government workers (split 1:4 between classes I and III (N)) and those in the armed forces (split 1:19 between classes I and III (M) which was approximately the proportion of officers to other ranks). As there are clear occupational differences between men and women separate results are provided for each sex as well as one for the combined totals in each area.

For comparison Table 7.13 shows the national divisions by class in 1911.

To compare the class of charity office holders to the class make-up of the district the results were matched against the combined figures from Table 7.12 to produce the figures in Table 7.14 that indicate whether each class

Table 7.12 Social Class Percentages (1911) in Croydon, Coventry and Blackburn Based on Occupational Categories

	I	II	III (N)	III (M)	IV	V
Croydon – Males (n = 48,746)	3	12	26	33	7	20
Croydon – Females (n = 25,714)	11	7	17	14	3	49
Croydon – Combined	6	10	23	26	5	30
Coventry – Males (n = 37,364)	1	6	11	70	4	9
Coventry – Females (n = 13,435)	4	7	17	47	4	21
Coventry – Combined	2	6	12	64	4	12
Blackburn – Males (n = 44,110)	1	9	11	25	42	12
Blackburn – Females (n = 35,499)	1	4	4	8	75	8
Blackburn – Combined	1	7	8	18	57	10

Source: *Census of England and Wales, 1911, X: 'Occupations and Industries Part II Occupations (Condensed List) of Males and Females at Ages in Administrative Counties, Country Boroughs etc'* (London: HMSO, 1913), 557–59, 596–98 and 668–70.

Table 7.13 Percentage Proportion of Population by Class (1911)

Class I	7
Class II	7
Class III (N)	11
Class III (M)	31
Class IV	34
Class V	10

Source: Adapted from Robert Price and George Sayers Bain, 'The Labour Force', in British Social Trends since 1900, 2nd ed., ed. A.H. Halsey (Basingstoke and London: Macmillan, 1988), 163; and A.H. Halsey, Change in British Society: From 1900 to the Present Day, pbk ed. (Oxford: Oxford University Press, 1978), 35.

group was under- or overrepresented on the charity committees. Positive figures (+) show an overrepresentation by that ratio, negative figures (–) an underrepresentation, an exact correlation is indicated thus (=) and '0' indicates there were no representatives of that class on a committee.

These figures indicate that in every area Class Group I was, not surprisingly, significantly overrepresented (charities today show the same tendency) but that this was less marked in Coventry and, especially, with the exempted charities in Todmorden. The overrepresentation of Class Group II was fairly even with the exception of Coventry where this may have evened up the relatively smaller proportion of Class I representatives. Skilled non-manual workers were the group whose proportion on committees most

Table 7.14   Ratio of Over/Underrepresentation of Class Groups on Charity Committees

	I	II	III (N)	III (M)	IV	V
Croydon	+ 8.8	+ 2.4	– 1.5	– 4.3	– 5.0	– 30.0
Coventry	+ 5.0	+ 4.2	=	– 1.5	– 2.5	0
Blackburn (registered)	+ 19.0	+ 2.9	– 0.9	+ 1.4	– 2.0	– 10.0
With 3M and 4 merged				– 1.4		
Todmorden (exempted)						
(Blackburn/Todmorden)	+ 6.0	+ 2.0	+ 1.3	+ 1.3	– 1.6	=
With 3M and 4 merged				– 1.3		

closely matched that in the general population. Manual workers of all kinds were underrepresented but this underrepresentation was significantly more marked in Croydon than in the other towns. The overrepresentation of Class III (M) and underrepresentation of Class IV in Blackburn and Todmorden probably has more to do with the categorisation problem mentioned above.

This analysis can be further explored by looking at the overall class composition of charity committees. How many were *entirely* composed of upper and middle class members, how many of *only* working class members and how many of members of both or all classes? These are shown in Table 7.15.

These figures reinforce the findings from the analysis of individual class. In the South 60 percent or more of the charities operated without *any* committee representation from the working classes whereas only about 12 to 13 percent did so in the Midlands and North. Equally, virtually no charities

Table 7.15   Class Composition of Charity Committees

	Percentage with All Members from Class I	Percentage with All Members from Classes I & II	Percentage with No Members from Classes I & II	Percentage with at Least One Member from Classes I & II and One from Classes III to V
Croydon (n = 37)	38	22	3	38
North Kent (n = 13)	15	46	0	38
Coventry (n = 17)	0	12	29	59
Blackburn (n = 148)	1	12	32	54
Todmorden (n = 50)	2	10	76	12

in the South were entirely run by working class members (the single exception was the Croydon branch of the National Federation of Discharged and Demobilised Sailors and Soldiers). In Coventry and Blackburn, the figures demonstrate the greatest social mix on committees with over 50 percent having members of both upper/middle and working classes. In the smaller Todmorden charities, an overwhelming 76 percent of organisations operated with *no* input from upper or middle class representatives.

What these tables demonstrate is that there are clearly significant differences in the make-up of charity committees in the suburban locations of the South and those in the industrial Midlands and the North. This can be partially explained by the class structure of the areas in question and, perhaps, by the differing views on class in these communities. Despite these factors, it is clear that working class people were far more likely to be involved in the organisation and running of wartime charities in the Midlands and North than in the suburban South. There is little difference in the social class of officials in the registered and exempted charities in the South, whereas there are between the registered charities in Blackburn and the exempted ones in Todmorden. More research needs to be carried out to confirm these findings and other areas need to be analysed but the above results give further credibility to the argument that the working classes contributed a far greater degree of support to wartime charitable activity than previously considered and that this strengthened as the war went on, most notably after the introduction of conscription when the majority of the smaller charities were formed.

ALIENATION OR SOLIDARITY—THE REACTION TO CHARITY

How was the outpouring of charitable and voluntary effort received by the fighting forces? As the largest proportion was directed towards their aid, both in the trenches and if they were wounded or taken prisoner, this is a critical question. Were soldiers resentful of this charity, seeing it as the reaction of an out-of-touch and overpatriotic civilian population? Did some react negatively because they believed that the state should be providing for their needs? Alternatively, did the majority react favourably, gratefully receiving the gifts and assistance and generously thanking their givers? These questions are important from the perspective of the thesis of social capital. To what extent was there a united response to 'charitable' works? If reaction were split, with a negative response by servicemen, this would seriously undermine the view that voluntary support led to the accumulation of social capital which, in turn, assisted Britain's war-winning effort.

Much received wisdom says that there was significant resentment, or at least cynicism, on the part of the troops towards philanthropic efforts and the home front in general. This view is one of the many myths that have become accepted about the war, which Martin Stephen has suggested includes the views that:

> The soldiers sympathized with their opposite numbers in the German trenches, and felt bonded to them by a universal horror of experience. The men hated the top brass, who were seen as malevolent and murderous incompetents. All women at home handed out white feathers to any man not in uniform, and parents cheerfully sent their sons out to die.[56]

The proposition certainly has some validity in relation to the relief of distress early in the war among servicemen's families. We have seen the resentment that was caused by the enquiries of the SSFA's volunteers which one left-wing commentator summed up as 'the charity-mongering excesses of unemployed members of the upper and middle classes.'[57] But what about the greater proportion of work carried out after the initial efforts of the NRF?

It is certainly true that a large number of soldiers expressed feelings of *difference* from the home front, that civilians simply could not understand, or soldiers could not explain what trench conditions were really like. There is probably no war in which soldiers have *not* expressed such feelings.[58] In the First World War the close contact between the Western Front and home provided perhaps the only opportunity in modern war where soldiers could stay so closely in touch with what was being said at home. When one could leave a front-line trench in the middle of a major battle and be sitting at home or in a London restaurant within a few hours such feelings of unreality are hardly surprising. This close communication meant that soldiers' alienation was made far more manifest and was more likely to be expressed. But the extreme form of this alienation, outright hostility or resentment, was highly selective. It was alienation from certain individuals, particularly those seen as slackers (including striking workers and conscientious objectors) and, especially, those elements of the press whom soldiers felt were distorting the facts.[59] However, as Nicholas Hiley has suggested, 'we should not assume that . . . their feelings of alienation extended to the whole of the press. The soldiers of the BEF were simply discovering that peculiar mixture of involvement and ironic detachment that we now associate with all popular culture in the twentieth century.'[60]

On the other hand are there examples of positive reactions from soldiers to the home front and, if so, are they representative? The first evidence is from those who worked on the home front at the time. It was clearly the view of Millicent Garrett Fawcett that the work of war charities provided a positive bond with soldiers that helped to win the war.[61] Masterman backed up her views. His summary of the 'temper of the people' in July 1915 was that, to whatever part of the country he travelled, everyone was determined to 'endure to the end, however great that sacrifice, however bitterly that end may be delayed.'⁶² Dowding expressed a similar view suggesting that voluntary action was building social capital when he wrote:

> We preserve our own calm determination, and we forge constant links between the men out there and the people here at home. The woman who knits mittens is doing more than knitting mittens. She is knitting tokens of love, and admiration, and confidence, and gratitude that will hearten the fighting men, and keep her own spirits up. Thus, there is a rich psychological value in the voluntary work of a nation in such days as these.⁶³

Dowding got to the crux of the issue when he concluded elsewhere that the British 'welded that innate comradeship which is the main driving force of a nation at war. . . . To put it positively, the voluntary making, or buying, or giving, or doing of something is one of the many ways in which the *morale* of the nation is preserved.'⁶⁴ Some might argue that the views of Fawcett, Dowding and Masterman are tainted as they are the very civilians detested by the troops (especially Masterman, given his role as an official propagandist) but there is significant support for their conclusions from recent scholarship.

An eloquent exposition of servicemen's responses to the public and their philanthropic efforts is presented by Deborah Cohen. Even though she is specifically referring to responses by disabled ex-servicemen, her findings still hold true; indeed one might have expected those who had been disabled by the war to have greater resentment than others. She says that 'the literary lights of the 1920s and 1930s took as an article of faith the ex-serviceman's hostility to his fellow citizens, but it is doubtful this sentiment, which so aptly expressed modernism's disdain for the public, was broadly shared.'⁶⁵ In other words some writers simply transposed their own, postwar, views retrospectively, the same process that is at work in so much later writing on the First World War. Cohen suggests this view was then taken up in more academic circles. However, she concludes:

> In the course of my research, I found very little evidence, whether published or unpublished, to support the idea that disabled ex-servicemen were hostile toward the public. From secondary sources as well as the literature of the time, I had expected bitterness, anger, or at the very least grousing. Yet in the thousands of letters from disabled veterans that I read in philanthropic and state archives, I found almost nothing of the sort. For example, in the more than 600 letters of application to the War Seal Mansions, only one man referred to the public's obligation with any sort of ire.⁶⁶

Adrian Gregory supports Cohen's conclusions, adding that 'the idea that civilians were indifferent to the suffering of the soldiers is manifestly absurd.'[67] I would entirely concur with Cohen's view, which is fully supported by my own research.

Representative of comments about charity workers is this from Trooper George Jameson of the 1/1 Battalion, Northumberland Hussars:

> I'd give full marks to the Salvation Army. They had one place I used to drop into often. And it was a most uncomfortable spot to be in. . . . The Germans reckoned that transport used it at night, so they would keep strafing it the whole time. But tucked into the side of the hill was the Salvation Army. And they used to have tea and whatever going all hours of the day. How they survived there I don't know. Wonderful people.[68]

All of the major religious charities worked in close proximity to the fighting. In 1917 the YMCA was opening centres close to dressing stations and casualty clearing stations on the Western Front and this policy exposed many of the voluntary workers to danger of death and injury from shellfire and capture by the enemy.[69] In the wake of the German offensive in spring 1918, the Church Army lost at least fifty-five huts and the YMCA a similar number. At the same date perhaps the best-known recreation centre, Talbot House, also refused to retreat when ordered. A senior staff officer who recognised that its closure would be harmful to the morale of the troops endorsed this defiance.[70] Michael Snape considers it significant that 'the French army had no equivalent of this ubiquitous network of practical support, an important consideration given the mass mutinies it suffered in 1917.'[71] The activities of Talbot House and its fellow organisations were a great bolster to morale, which accounts for the fact that they were still hugely appreciated long after the war as Snape discovered from a Mass Observation survey during World War Two.[72]

Critics might discount comments like these as they were about those charity workers who were sharing the troops' dangers, but soldiers were just as appreciative and supportive of those who remained in comparative safety at home. For example, supplies to prisoners of war could be life-savers, as the following letter from Sergeant C. Lowman of the Hampshire Regiment to his local prisoners of war support organisation, written in February 1919, demonstrates:

> I have just returned from Turkey where I have been a prisoner for the last three years. . . . Owing to the hardships we endured in the siege and the terrible way we were treated after falling into the hands of the Turks my constitution was completely wrecked. I now feel it my duty to write and thank you for your kindness in sending us parcels and medical comforts which I am sure saved the lives of many prisoners in Turkey. . . . Many thanks for all you have done.[73]

Even the gift of a simple scarf picked up from the stores produced a generous letter when the recipient, Frank Fielder of the Royal Field Artillery, found the address of the young girl who had knitted it, Lucy Bateson of Preston. He wrote that 'I will keep it forever, and take it to my home in London, when I go home for good, as a souvenir from you, although I have never seen you, I appreciate it very much indeed.'[74] Another prisoner of war, the author and poet F.W. Harvey, expressed the importance of contact with home saying that 'the most valued letters of all were those written in rich Gloucestershire dialect to tell me, with eagerness contemptuous of all stops, the news of my dear little village. . . . These letters did more to alleviate the lot of prisoners than ever their kind writer could know.'[75]

One of the largest repositories of servicemen's comments lies in a remarkable collection of letters from the villagers of Great Chart, near Ashford, in Kent. The archive is that of the Great Chart Sailor's and Soldier's War Fund and runs to no fewer than twenty-two volumes. These are just a sample that demonstrate the great importance of an attachment to a locality for the servicemen:

From Pte G. Barnes, 1st Royal West Kents, 5th Division, 3 April 1915:

> My dear friends I can't explain to you how thankful I was to receive your parcel which I tell you it could not have come at a more convenient time as it was a very wet day and we all came off duty that morning and not happen to be on any fatigue duties so we all sat down in our tents and smoked your health and had a few sweets.[76]

From Sgt William Brunger, 1/5th Buffs, Kamptee, India, 8 July 1915:

> Dear Friends of Great Chart, I consider it the highest honour of my career to address my letter thus. . . . What a great amount of thought and trouble must be taken in the arranging and dispatching of them all. For myself it will always be one of my most cherished possessions and I shall attach the greatest importance to its preservation.[77]

From Pte William Harding, E Coy, 1/5th Buffs, Kamptee, 5 August 1915:

> It gives us all great pleasure to know that so many friends have taken our welfare to heart, and although we are so many miles away we are still respected by all our dear Friends at home. . . . It is with great pride that I read of all brave men who have given their services in time of need. More especially do I look with pride upon the role of honour from my own little village, and although our little village is small, we all hope its deeds will bear out its name *Great* Chart.[78]

Despite the caveats you need to put on the content of letters (for example, censorship and the desire not to upset those at home) it takes little

Figure 7.8   The YMCA Huts outside Kings Cross Station (© Imperial War Museums, Q 28739).

imagination to understand how such tokens helped in establishing and maintaining a soldier's morale. The importance of such local contacts in maintaining morale and connections with the home front is expressed in Keith Grieves's collection relating to Sussex and the letters to the Ashurst Wood Comforts Fund.[79] Both his study and Helen McCartney's examination of the Liverpool Territorials have, in the view of Jessica Meyer, 'highlighted the ways in which the fighting front and the home front were consistently entwined throughout the war, challenging the argument that the community of fighting men formed a distinctive culture of their own that was both alien to and alienated from civilians on the home front.'[80] Peter Simkins too has recognised the value of voluntary action and its role in developing and maintaining social capital when he wrote:

> British military historians are in broad agreement that the nature of British society in 1914–18 provided a bedrock of social cohesion which prevented the BEF from total collapse, even during the crisis of March and April 1918. There may be some truth in the view that the huge network of welfare facilities—including canteens and YMCA and Church Army huts—as well as provision of concert parties and organized sports, offered the British soldier comfortably familiar recreational and cultural outlets which were not enjoyed to the same extent by men of other armies.[81]

Figure 7.9   Interior of a YMCA London Station Hut (© Imperial War Museums, Q 80148).

This is a view shared by many other writers who have studied the full extent of opinion during the war. Jay Winter has added a huge amount to our knowledge of the social and demographic history of the period and reached a perceptive conclusion regarding the immense contribution voluntary action played in strengthening social capital in Britain. He suggests that a decentralised state with strong voluntary institutions gave Britain 'an essential resource in wartime' that enabled its people to see the war through to victory. Far from there being a division between the civilians and the troops there was a 'commonality of purpose [which] fused home and battle front.'[82]

It is clear that cynicism towards the public at home is, at best, an exaggeration. It is based on a misunderstanding of the nature of the gap between front-line and home front experience, a natural divide in all wars, and on a small number of high-profile literary examples which, even then, are an exaggeration of the attitudes of the writers quoted. The weight of evidence is that the troops' response to philanthropy and voluntary efforts was overwhelmingly positive.

Case Study 6
'The Biggest Communal Arts Project Ever Attempted'—War Memorials

The most visible example, as the title notes,[1] of charitable fund-raising efforts after the war came in the form of the thousands of war memorials that were constructed. Of close to 6,000 memorial unveilings that took place to commemorate the war over 5,000 had occurred by 1920.[2] The subject of memory and the place within it of physical memorials has recently received much coverage; here I wish only to concentrate on the role of voluntary action in this process and how it was similar or different from activities during the war itself.[3] Most war memorials in Britain, in whatever format, were an expression of local community feelings of indebtedness to the dead. Unlike the war cemeteries overseas they were not planned on a national basis and the government did not prescribe what form they took, hence the 'traditional' physical monument was not always adopted. Many took a more utilitarian form, such as a memorial hall, hospital extension or playing field and the choice between the two could sometimes lead to heated local debate.[4]

Makeshift shrines began appearing in the streets during the war itself but the need for some kind of physical memorial was, above all, rooted in the decision not to repatriate the war dead.[5] Partly this was a logistical decision, given the numbers, and was confirmed as official policy by the War Office in 1915. This led to the creation of the Imperial War Graves Commission (IWGC) and the hundreds of war cemeteries that dot the French and Belgian countryside (as well as many other more far-flung locations). This decision has engendered highly contrasting views as to its interpretation. One version has suggested that 'when the British government used regulations to wipe the home front clean of corpses, they unwittingly wiped away something else: the British soldier's sense of home. The fracture between combatant experience and civilian perception of the war ensured a combatant alienation so profound that the idea of homecoming became impossible.'[6] This interpretation confuses two separate things. The criticism of the repatriation policy came not from soldiers but from their relatives at home. I am not aware that the troops reacted strongly either way; from the number who wrote about the bodies of their dead comrades or raised temporary memorials to them on the battlefields the evidence would appear to be that they probably favoured the government line. However, the obvious fallacy of the argument is its linkage to the alienation theory. It seems to be a 'corpse-centric' approach, crediting the dead with having their views confirmed by the method of disposal of their bodies. It might just be feasible to suggest that non-repatriation made the relatives more alienated from the troops, but not the other way round. Though one can certainly criticise the policy this needs to be done from the perspective of the living. The principal reasoning behind it was an ideological one, the 'concept of unity of sacrifice ... and that the cemeteries were not for use simply in the present, but for all time.'[7] Given this, it is fair to apply hindsight to the decision. Would the scale of loss of the war be as clear, and its memory as deep, if the war cemeteries did not exist and the graves were instead scattered throughout the Commonwealth? I think the answer is an emphatic 'no'. To that extent at least, Sir Fabian Ware, first Director General of the IWGC was astute as to how posterity would view the decision. Having made many visits to them, I am also struck by how they can challenge visitors' perceptions through the uniformity of the headstones. Many are surprised that officers and men are commemorated in the same way and their graves mingled together; it does not quite tally with some notions of the class nature of the war. Unlike the French war graves, they are also 'religiously neutral'. Mark Connelly has commented that there was great controversy over the adoption of headstones rather than crosses.[8] This too was partly a utilitarian choice. The headstone shape deflects rainwater and allows much more space for an inscription than would a cross.

In Britain, local memorials could also act as a unifying symbol though there were some interesting contrasts with wartime activities. The funding and choice of most memorials usually fell to local committees intended to be representative of the community as a whole. Writers who have investigated these in some detail note, however, that 'although public interest at a local level was usually quite strong, those who became involved in the actual decisions about commemorative forms were usually a small minority drawn from the established social and political elites.'[9] Though supporting this point Catherine Moriarty is careful to note that the committee 'was rarely free to act in complete autonomy, remaining answerable to the general public whose support ... was vital for both funding and the memorial's meaning.'[10] If the public did not agree with the committee, arguments could be protracted such as in Saddleworth, in Lancashire, where the debate over whether to erect a cenotaph or a hospital went on for a decade.[11] It is certainly true that even in those areas where ordinary working people played a major role in running charities during the war, the war memorial committee was often a return to the principles of the great and the good taking the lead, an example of pre-war values reasserting themselves.[12] Nevertheless it was still important for the whole community to be seen to have contributed, no more so than when the memorial was unveiled or opened, when 'every facet of the community was represented: schoolchildren, choirs, ex-servicemen, the bereaved and the general public were all allocated their places.'[13] Sometimes a widow or a child might perform the actual ceremony itself though it was more usual for this to be done by a local dignitary or a national figure with local connections. Whichever form of memorial was chosen, the names of those who had died were invariably inscribed in some way. This remains an extremely important issue even today with many individuals and organisations campaigning to ensure that any missing names are added to their local memorial.[14] It is not easy to estimate what additional funds were raised specifically for war memorials as no national figures exist (again) and there is no such thing as a typical memorial. Probably the largest, in all senses, was Freemasons' Hall in London which eventually raised over £1 million.[15] However, the evidence from a range of funds outlined in contemporary local histories and other sources suggest that a figure of £500 each would be a reasonable estimate. If this were multiplied up, just the physical memorials unveiled would give a figure of £3 million; if the 38,000 memorials of all types were included (at perhaps a more modest average cost of £300) this would be over £11 million.

8   Conclusions

THE ENCROACHMENT OF STATE CONTROL

If there is one point on which all writers about the First World War agree it is with regard to the huge increase of state control over every aspect of life in Britain. In the words of John Stevenson, 'state intervention was to become not merely an argument in the hands of progressive thinkers, but part of the habit and assumptions of government.'[1] There were no fewer than 409 official commissions, committees and agencies set up to deal with questions arising out of the war from the 'Abrasives and Polishing Powders Research Committee' to the 'Zinc and Copper Research Inquiry Committee.'[2] To cope with the requirements of total war some of these, such as the Ministries of Munitions, Pensions or Food employed tens of thousands (millions in the case of Munitions). Others were tiny but in many of these areas government was intervening for the first time in people's lives.

What is more contested is to what extent this intervention was entirely new. Though Britain was one of the least centralised and regulated societies in Europe in 1914, it was by no means the laissez faire canvas it had been in the mid-nineteenth century. Between 1870 and 1914 government employment had increased fourfold and central and local public expenditure tenfold and 'a continuous stream of new specialist administrative departments', including the Local Government Board, Board of Trade and Board of Education, had been formed.[3] The reforming Liberal administration had accelerated this process and in Britain, along with much of the rest of the Western world, state intervention was already increasing in the years prior to 1914.[4] Rex Pope's summary is therefore a fair one when he concluded that 'increasing intervention in people's lives was not a process begun by war; the introduction of collectivist social policies had been very much a feature of the quarter century or so preceding the War. The demands of war, though, enhanced sharply the state's role in relation to the individual.'[5]

When war came, near universal state intervention was not the government's planned intention. In discussing the establishment of the Ministry of Munitions, Marwick quotes their official historian as saying that the state-owned factories 'owed their inception not to any definite plan or policy of State monopoly but to the immediate stress of practical necessity' but that 'once any measure of control had been undertaken the forces pressing for complete control became stronger and were ultimately irresistible.'[6] DeGroot agrees that 'when the government intervened, it first asked for voluntary compliance with stated goals, then gently cajoled and only regulated as a last resort.'[7] This is the pattern already observed in relation to voluntary action and charities. There is perhaps a tendency by some writers to overexaggerate moves towards state intervention as being inexorable in every field when there were limitations on both the pace and nature of state control, not least because the prevailing attitude of the civil service was still strongly laissez faire.[8] John Bourne has shrewdly noted that governments are rarely willing to proceed at a pace faster than they believe public opinion will tolerate and this is more critical in wartime where, in a democracy, public support is even more necessary. Therefore, even under the more interventionist Lloyd George coalition, property rights were respected and cooperation with business encouraged in the name of efficiency but, for example, neither the railways nor the mines were nationalised.[9] At the other end of the spectrum:

> Libertarian resistance to compulsion in all its forms never died away in Britain during the war. The Labour movement fought tooth and nail against the "conscription of labour" with a great measure of success. But compulsion and interference gained ground as the war progressed and people lost faith in the ability of purely voluntary measures.[10]

Nevertheless, there certainly was a strong tendency for the voluntary principle to be replaced by more planned state centralisation as the war went on. Adrian Gregory has accurately characterised one crucial reason for the loss of faith in the voluntary approach as being 'based on an ever-increasing fear that there were many who, for selfish reasons, remained uncommitted, leaving those who took voluntary action shouldering an unfair burden. . . . Almost everyone came to feel that the state should compel support for the war effort in the name of "equity."'[11] The most obvious example of this principle in action was the case of conscription but it was also apparent even in the moves towards state intervention in voluntary activity. Despite some reservations about the over-deterministic flavour of some of the characterisations of increasing government intervention, it is nevertheless hard to argue against its reality. George Robb sums up the process, astutely commenting that 'during the war an increasingly familiar pattern developed, whereby early reliance on market forces gradually gave way to half-hearted state regulation and eventual state control. This pattern manifested itself in military recruitment, munitions production, labour supply, food distribution, and even propaganda.'[12] He might have added philanthropy to this list.

In identifying a clear move towards greater state control during the war, many writers have also attempted to divide the conflict into different phases. The earliest phase was cemented in the public mind by the pronouncement on 4 August 1914 by Lloyd George, then Chancellor of the Exchequer, that the government would 'enable the traders of this country to carry on business as usual.' This famous phrase was more of an attempt not to panic the markets rather than set out the government's overall intentions as the deeply interventionist Defence of the Realm Act was passed just four days later. It does though have some validity as characterising the early period of the war, not least in relation to the voluntary activities described in Chapter 3. A stimulus for change is often sought and various crises in the course of the war are seen as watersheds in the development of state control. Inevitably July 1916 and the commencement of the Battle of the Somme is often cited as a turning point and Marwick chooses this when suggesting that 'as nearly as such things can be calendared, the summer of 1916 was the time when, as far as intelligent opinion is concerned, the tide of collectivism was definitely in flood.'[13] However, in terms of social impact, it was the introduction of conscription that March that was a clearer and more decisive step. If it is always rather dangerous to generalise over such individually decisive turning points it is perhaps more defendable in discussing one specific area such as voluntary action. Here it is possible to identify three clear phases, the transitions between them each marked by a key event as illustrated in Figure 8.1.

A key element of these phases is their link with the varying involvement of capital and labour. In society as a whole, it has been suggested, the war 'widened labour's institutional horizon. Fundamental to this was

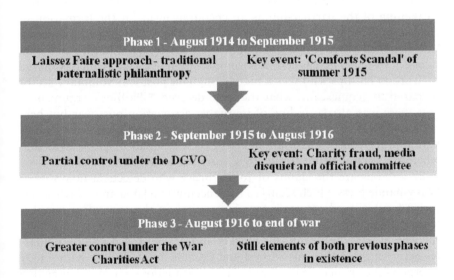

Figure 8.1 Phases of state control.

the importance of the working class to the war effort: the government needed channels through which to maintain the commitment of the working class.'[14] This process of inclusion operated at both local and national levels. Local trade unionists and other representatives of labour, including women, joined 'a variety of statutory, official, semi-official and voluntary bodies: exemption tribunals under the Derby scheme, relief of Distress Fund Committees, local Pensions Committees, Food Control Committees and so on.'[15] In most cases the cooperation of labour was secured by allowing trades union representation in these new agencies and nationally many committees of enquiry included working class members for the first time.[16] Pro-war Labour MPs joined the government and some union leaders found themselves holding high political office, including membership of the War Cabinet itself.[17] This was mirrored in the increasing importance of ordinary working people in the governance and operation of wartime charities.

A REPOSITIONING OF PHILANTHROPY

The idea of a partnership between the state and charity was certainly not one that was new during the war.[18] Most writers are clear that the relationship between the state and philanthropy changed during the war, with the former encroaching more decisively on the territory of the latter. The question is what was the impact of this change? One approach views it as placing philanthropy in a far less significant role than previously. Alan Kidd, for example, suggests that 'the real transition to a "new philanthropy" came during and after the First World War, when charity found itself more clearly subordinated to rather than a partner of the state.' He sees this weakening of the partnership as an encouragement for the formation of the National Council of Social Service (NCSS) in 1919, bringing together 'the disparate parts of an emerging "voluntary sector"', to give charity a stronger voice.[19] There is certainly some truth in this view, which is shared by Gordon Phillips who sees a more compliant post-war voluntary sector prepared to acquiesce in what the state decreed.[20] Phillips's argument is that there was also a decline of mutualist association post-war but here he is on far shakier ground as he bases his view partly on a decline of paramilitary youth organisations, most of which had religious links and where the decline could be due to a lessening of religious influence. Even more dubious are the claims of John Turner who detects 'a new sort of heavy-handedness which seems to have been war related and which seems to have substituted the state for civil society in the control of people's lives.'[21] Though he is perfectly correct that the role of the state grew during the war in relation both to the market and to civil society and boundaries between these elements shifted and became more blurred, he wrongly interprets the changes.[22] He sees the rise of state dominance as happening mainly during the war, seriously underestimating its encroachment into the social sphere during the late Victorian and Edwardian periods. Far more seriously, he totally misrepresents charitable activity during the war and which elements of it were most critical. Firstly, he concentrates entirely on the early, paternalistic, period without noticing the major changes brought about by the creation of the DGVO and smaller, mutualist charities. Secondly, like many others, he is entirely blinkered by the activities of the COS which he sees as being representative of voluntary action as a whole during the war when it was totally the opposite. Though the COS was one of the dominant charitable bodies in the pre-war years and was often given a leading role by government during wartime, its approach was increasingly marginalised by the more direct, practical and reactive stance of many smaller bodies and by those under the control of the DGVO. Turner believes the patriarchal approach lasted throughout the war and afterwards and bases his view on three examples: the operation of separation allowances, increases in welfare activities designed to reduce infant mortality and the crackdown on the use of alcohol. In choosing these areas, he notes that 'there was often very little change in personnel and methods' with 'the same middle-class women' of the COS at the helm.[23] These are very partial examples chosen to support his argument. If he had instead selected troop comforts, industrial tribunals and food controls he would have been forced to different conclusions.

A much more carefully argued approach, though still supporting the 'increased subordination' view, is put forward by Keith Laybourn.[24] He sees the first ten years of the twentieth century as being the crucial period of change in the 'balance of power' between philanthropy and the state. His thesis is that increased state intervention in the social sphere was due to a 'failure of philanthropy' to deal with the rising social problems faced by the British working class. Laybourn bases many of his conclusions on his study of the Guild of Help that superseded the COS as the largest voluntary body in England during this decade. The war, in Laybourn's view, speeded up the transition and 'swallowed up voluntary help, which became a mere adjunct to, rather than a partner with, state social welfare.'[25] He gets this analysis partly right, as the state did, over the period leading up to and including the war, become by far the leading provider of social welfare. However, I would not consider that this was due to a failure of philanthropy to meet the problem. It was clear far earlier than the commencement of the twentieth century that philanthropy could not possibly deal with the problems of a modern industrial society; however, it took some time, and a more sympathetic administration between 1905 and 1914, for the *state* to fully recognise this fact. Laybourn makes it sound as if philanthropy declined over the period in question when it actually expanded in financial terms. He bases his views too narrowly on the philosophy of the COS and Guild rather than the wider philanthropic community and on one field, the relief of poverty. These two bodies, the 'leading lights' of pre-war philanthropy, were clearly devastated by the war, both becoming redundant in the new alignment between voluntarism and the state. The Guild ceased to be an independent force, subsumed within the new NCSS, and the COS, in Robert Humphreys's phrase, 'became a social leper, largely shunned by other charities and by government agencies.'[26] Philanthropy was about far more than this, and the war widened its horizons further. In some major fields, such as the provision of hospitals, the state did not assume the lead role for many years after the First World War. The motivations for increased state provision were complex and various: the recognition that philanthropy could no longer provide the answer and pressure for reform from below by trades unions, the Labour Party and others as well as a broad enough consensus that pensions, secondary education, health care and other provisions should be a right and not a privilege. When Laybourn summarises the war period as ensuring 'that the state became dominant and the voluntary sector a subsidiary force' he is, therefore, wrong. This fact, in terms of the provision of social welfare, had been determined some time before; the war simply made it clearer.[27] Interestingly in his earlier book on the Guild of Help, Laybourn recognised that the war had a transforming effect on charitable bodies and his conclusions were far more positive. He noted that the Guild had been forced to change, to work more cooperatively, and that this 'ultimately led to its absorption into the wider voluntary movement.'[28]

Both Finlayson and Lowe's views are more accurate. Lowe agrees that 'during the emergency of war, the relationship between government and traditional relief agencies . . . permanently changed.' He sees this change not just as a realignment of the boundaries of state intervention but in the outlook reflected in the nature of the main charity umbrella bodies of the pre- and post-war eras, 'the fiercely independent Charity Organisation Society and the more accommodating National Council of Social Service.'[29] Finlayson argues that philanthropy was *not* totally submerged by state intervention but remained a vibrant, though significantly different, entity.[30]

The decline of voluntarism is another war myth. It has been cultivated by an over-concentration on the comments of those who decried the declining influence of philanthropy on certain welfare problems and by the fact that the dominant voices of the inter-war and immediate post-Second World War period saw a declining role for charity if not its total demise.[31] Philanthropy fills the gaps that the state does not provide for. With little state provision of basic welfare services prior to the later nineteenth century, philanthropy provided a good deal of support for the poor or destitute. As society accepted that people had a right to a minimum income (or it became politically unacceptable to believe they had not, for example at times of unemployment), then the state took over from philanthropy. Equally, as access to education (late nineteenth and early twentieth centuries) and basic health care (mid-twentieth century) were accepted as a right so the state increasingly intervened. Where this was not accepted, for example the provision of higher education in the U.S., then philanthropy continued to play a prominent role. The point at which a social provision becomes a right is where pressure for change from below (political campaigns by interest groups or their democratic representatives) coincides with agreement for change from above. Such changes do not, however, mean that philanthropy has failed. Philanthropy can never provide anything like the resources of a modern state, so once an area of social provision becomes accepted as a right, philanthropy's role will inevitably decline in these areas. What happens then is not a contraction of philanthropy but a refocussing onto other areas. One example is that many people believed in the early to mid-twentieth century that poverty in Britain would be eliminated. Their error was to believe that poverty was an absolute rather than a relative concept. As the affluence of society has increased so our view of what constitutes poverty has changed. The only areas where philanthropy can accurately be said to have failed is where an area of concern becomes regarded as no longer relevant, such as the move away from proselytising missionary work in the twentieth century. There is no doubt that in two specific areas, its response to poverty and its links to religion, philanthropy in 1918 was very different to the pre-war period. With regard to the latter, Prochaska has commented that 'most dramatically, the First World War offered fresh fields for voluntary social action. It contributed to a loss of faith and disrupted parish charity, but it enlarged the need for personal service and national effort.'[32] Prochaska is correct in his view that the new concerns of charity moved away from many of the traditional religious causes, most notably support for overseas missions. In relation to poverty, there is some agreement that 'after 1914 poverty meant deprivation rather than destitution' and this inevitably meant that philanthropy had to adapt its attitude to the poor.[33]

The war actually provided a new impetus to voluntarism based upon the principle of mutual aid. There was a profusion of small, local organisations providing support for the troops of their town, village or workplace. Other examples were the significant rises in trades union membership and the emergence of veterans' bodies. Eventually all of these independently formed mutual aid organisations moved into some form of closer cooperation with the state whether through the coordination of the DGVO, formal political partnerships or amalgamation into the British Legion. One can perhaps suggest that at first, the two strands of philanthropy and mutual aid were relatively distinct but that, during the First World War, they came into greater alignment. Post-war, though they drew apart to some extent, they remained far more closely linked than before 1914.

Overall, I would agree with Finlayson that 'war . . . provided a focus for a profusion of philanthropic giving and effort. It may have weakened traditional charitable occupations; but it provided opportunity for new ones.'[34] The most important new organisation to emerge after the war was the NCSS, now the National Council for Voluntary Organisations (NCVO). The NCSS had its roots in the 1915 Westminster Conference of major voluntary bodies at which D'Aeth had suggested the formation of such a body. The new organisation was created in 1919 with a legacy of

£1,000 left by a young soldier and pre-war philanthropist, Edward Vivian Birchall. Its aims were 'to reduce overlapping and duplication, and to work in cooperation with the developing statutory services.'[35] In an Annual Report, the NCSS commented:

> The council was born out of the experience of these four years. . . . A huge army of voluntary workers had been enlisted and in the relief of civilian distress and the care of soldiers and their families public authorities and voluntary agencies had learnt to work as partners. It was natural that this new sense of unity should find public expression.[36]

Though unremarked in any of the histories of the NCSS it seems quite possible that it was significantly influenced by the management structure of the DGVO.[37]

Another conclusion is that the First World War contributed towards an increased professionalization of the charity sector. Only after the war were social workers regularly paid and turned from amateurs into professionals.[38] Many modern fund-raising techniques were invented or expanded, including payroll giving, direct mail, charity-related gifts to purchase for friends or relatives, flag days and charity merchandising. The War Charities Act tried to ensure that even the smallest charities were run on professional lines with elected committees, books of accounts and minutes. I have said that voluntary action was particularly effective during the war and it is possible to adduce at least three key mission-related criteria being demonstrated which helped account for this effectiveness. Firstly, there was a direct feedback mechanism from the beneficiaries of most charities, especially the troops. The fact that, contrary to the myth, there was a close connection between the Western Front and those at home ensured that any problems were quickly noticed, as with the 'comforts scandal' in 1915, and could be rectified. The very close local links with troop comfort and prisoner of war funds ensured this feedback mechanism operated at both the macro (DGVO) and micro (local fund) levels. Secondly, there were clear performance measures that were shared and understood—were soldiers, prisoners of war, hospitals etc getting what they needed? If they were not supplies could be adjusted, especially through the DGVO mechanism. Thirdly, all of these charities had very specific aims that were, in the most part, fulfilled through links to state provision. There was no 'mission drift' during the war and there were official support bodies created to assist their missions.

SOCIAL CAPITAL AND ITS CONTRIBUTION TO WINNING THE WAR

Most writers suggest that social capital has three basic components: a network (without which there could be no social element), a cluster of norms comprising values and expectations that are shared by group members and sanctions—punishments and rewards—that help to maintain the norms and network. Could the voluntary organisations of the First World War be defined as having networks, norms and sanctions? Certainly, in their most organised form, through the DGVO, this is easy to agree. The various bodies formed a cohesive network where they were all part of larger whole contributing their part to the war effort. There were both formal and informal norms of behaviour adopted by the different bodies and there were rewards (thanks from the troops, badges of service) and sanctions (the withholding of thanks or striking off the approved list) in place. Even between the less organised bodies, the same elements were certainly present, though not perhaps in such a clear form.

One of the key writers on social capital, Robert Putnam, determined that there are three distinct levels within social capital: bonding, bridging and linking. Bonding social capital refers to relations amongst relatively homogenous groups such as family members and close friends, church groups or sports clubs. Bridging social capital refers to relations with more distant friends, colleagues and associates who share a common aim or principle, so this includes political organisations or trade unions. Finally, linking social capital refers to relations between individuals and groups in different social strata in a hierarchy and so provides cohesion at a national level, especially in times of crisis or war. It is important to have a balance between these levels because an excess of one can have negative outcomes. For example, an excess of bonding social capital without sufficient bridging social capital being present can lead to extreme divisions within a society, as for example has been the case with the various sectarian communities in Northern Ireland.[39]

Table 8.1 Matrix of Social Capital for Wartime Voluntary Bodies

	Bonding	*Bridging*	*Linking*
Networks	Small-scale local organisations (workplace or street based etc)	Larger voluntary sector bodies (YMCA, Red Cross etc)	National-scale bodies (DGVO, War Refugees Committee)
Norms	Local, denominational or trade links etc	Shared values, often class based	Common purpose in wartime to support the country, cutting across class boundaries
Sanctions	Esteem or opprobrium of friends and colleagues	Prestige of 'being a member', rules etc	Official recognition and 'rules'

One can combine the two dimensions of social capital (its components and levels) into a relatively simple model of social capital as it operated during the First World War (Table 8.1).

There of course exists a counter-argument that denies the strength of social capital during the war. From the late 1920s onwards a group of writers have suggested that an irrevocable split was present between soldiers and civilians. Initially these were mainly middle class war poets including Robert Graves and Siegfried Sassoon. They were later supported in the academic writings of Paul Fussell and others. Eric Leed is prominent amongst them and goes as far as arguing that this ensured that social capital was significantly damaged in the process. He contends that 'the war had divorced [soldiers] from civil society . . . radically [severing] the soldier from his society and [producing] in him a profound sense of injustice.'[40] We have already seen some evidence that this split was illusory and the contemporary evidence is strongly to the contrary. Soldiers' letters regularly report their feelings of linkage with those back home and some went much further. Sheffield comments:

> During the war years, there was much talk among civilians about the positive effects of war service on social cohesion. In 1916 the Bishop of London spoke of a "brotherhood" being "forged of blood and iron" in the trenches, which should be maintained into peacetime, thus ending the class war between "Hoxton" and "Belgravia" and the psychoanalyst Wilfred Trotter was effusive in his belief that the war had created significantly greater social cohesion in Britain.[41]

Another contemporary example of social capital at work was the success of the campaigns to raise war loans. In Britain, these continued to bring in huge sums in the latter part of the war and the campaigns were boosted by a number of innovatory marketing techniques. *Businessman's Week* (March 1918) provided examples of what communities or business people could raise. For example, the £80 required to buy a machine gun might be raised by a group of thirty-five people, whereas a tank costing £5,000 was aimed at a population of 2,000. During the week, London raised over £75 million in war bonds and war loans.[42] The idea for Tanks Week came from a member of the public, William Milligan from Tynemouth, and as a result some 'worn-out and battered' tanks toured the country during December 1917 acting as giant moneyboxes. The visit to Bristol was typical; 'each investor was presented with a souvenir flag. . . . Boy Scouts were found to be very useful for odd jobs and messages. . . . Military Bands enlivened the proceedings throughout the week and many speeches [were] given from the Tank.'[43]

The Feed the Guns Campaign went to even greater lengths with displays of artillery in Trafalgar Square in October 1918 followed by Liverpool, Sheffield, Birmingham and Edinburgh. The Square itself was turned into a replica of a French village complete with ruined houses and this brought in

£29 million in just eight days.[44] The sums raised for war bonds were spectacular. In the six months from November 1917, forty towns in England and Wales each raised over a million pounds with the largest contributions in Liverpool (over £25 million), Manchester (over £17 million) and Birmingham (just under £15 million).[45] Overall Britain raised over £1 billion in war bonds between October 1917 and September 1918.[46] Though these were investments rather than gifts the continuing flow of money was an indication that the public still believed in and supported the war. All of these campaigns were promoted by the National War Savings Committee who relied on 120,000 war savings workers, yet another mighty band of volunteer labour. One can contrast this success with the failure of the later issues of German war bonds and the fact that the Germans were so worried about the success of British war loans that they produced propaganda in an, unsuccessful, attempt to dissuade the British public from contributing.[47] In contrast 'the fourth German loan in March 1916 attracted 5.2 million savers, but the fifth in September 1916 attracted only 3.8 million and the ninth was undersubscribed by 39 percent.'[48]

The idea of 'soldier separatism', as David Englander terms it, relies on the assumption that those who fought in the war thought of their service as something entirely separate from their previous lives as civilians.[49] There is now overwhelming evidence that this idea of 'the discontinuous character of war service' is entirely false. The outstanding contribution to this debate has been by John Bourne who demonstrated that the bond between soldiers and civilians remained because the soldiers still thought of themselves primarily as civilians. This is a theme that comes through exceptionally strongly in Helen McCartney's detailed study of the Liverpool Territorials. She emphasises the strength of local pre-war class and social groupings that were maintained when the men donned their uniforms. 'Each individual held a separate set of allegiances, dictated by his ethnic origin, occupation and religion, and was defined by membership of various institutions and organizations.'[50] Her conclusions match those of Bourne in that the men 'arrived back in their home communities with their civilian identities intact, ready to pick up their lives where they had left off. They were by no means unscathed by their ordeal, but, collectively, they had not become the obedient, passive victims of popular myth. They had remained civilians in uniform for the duration of the war.'[51] As Bourne suggests, 'the bulk of Britain's urban working-class army did not find the courage to stick it out by accepting and internalizing the values of the pre-war Regular Army. Their values and their inspiration remained obstinately civilian.'[52] Bourne's conclusion, one now shared by many other writers, is that 'the British working-class was well adapted to the challenge of war. Working-class culture provided the army with a bedrock of social cohesion and community on which its capacity for endurance rested.'[53] Bourne recognises that morale was boosted by 'the huge network of welfare facilities, including YMCA canteens, concert parties and organized sport', with many of the activities supplied by voluntary organisations or charitable contributions.[54] From his extensive examination of contemporary written sources, Peter Liddle links voluntary support for the troops, amongst women in particular, to 'the strong sense of national and local identity' shared by civilians and soldiers. This 'called for concern and care for others and it required that one did one's best to keep cheerful because times for all were harsh.' His conclusion is that far from there being a division between soldiers and civilians 'there was . . . a considerable unity of purpose throughout British society during the First World War.'[55] He is strongly supported by Adam Seipp's study of Manchester during the latter part of the war. Seipp concludes that the war

> Created wartime communities in unlikely places like factories, hospitals, schools and families. These communities were cross-cutting, complementary, and widely varied, but they served the same function. They integrated the home front and the front lines and gave ordinary people a stake in the final victory. They catalyzed the self-mobilization of combatant societies and proved, in some cases, far more durable than anyone imagined at the time.[56]

W.E. Dowding's contemporary analysis is linked directly to philanthropy and is quite complex in its understanding of the operation of social capital. He suggested that some of the effects of wartime philanthropy were more a 'matter for the psychologist than the statistician' and that 'the voluntary making, or buying, or giving, or doing of something is one of the many ways in which the *morale* of the nation is preserved', recognising a key operation of social capital with gift-giving cementing the bridging element between civilians and troops.[57] Alan Kidd supports this view, though from a different theoretical perspective, suggesting that there are three views of philanthropy:

- Philanthropy as altruistic, broadly the view of both Harrison and Prochaska.[58]
- Philanthropy as a social control mechanism.[59]
- Philanthropy as social exchange, the argument Kidd puts forward.[60]

Both the first and second are one-way transactions. In the first, assuming altruism in its purest form, it is only the recipient who benefits; in the second, only the donor. Neither can therefore be producers of social capital. It is only the third interpretation that involves an *exchange* of benefit. There were certainly elements of all three versions of philanthropy existing before 1914 but it was the third that became overwhelmingly prominent in the war giving of the British public.

If a final piece of evidence is required, it is worth quoting from a detailed study of an individual community in wartime. This is Aberdare in South Wales, a mining community dubbed by *The Times* in 1916 as 'the industrial storm centre of Britain' and yet Anthony Mor-O'Brien found it was 'fundamentally patriotic and in favour of victory in the field.'[61] However it is his comments on philanthropy that are most pertinent as they support several of the propositions in this study:

> With the First World War . . . philanthropy became the responsibility of everyone, not just the social leaders, and was inextricably bound up with patriotism. A fundamental change both in the nature of philanthropy and in the role of the state seems to have taken place specifically because of the war. . . . For the first time in British history, philanthropy experienced an unguided change which involved the whole of society over an extended period and under the emotional stimulus of wartime, developing from the preserve of the well-to-do and religious leaders, as had traditionally been the case, into a mass voluntary activity with patriotic connotations.[62]

In all there is extremely compelling evidence that voluntary charitable activities during the war significantly reinforced social capital in Britain.

COMPARISONS WITH GERMANY

If voluntary activity and its skilled management made a significant contribution to social capital in Britain did it also make a similar contribution in Germany? The evidence suggests that, at first, the similarities were greater than the differences but, towards the end of the war, the situation in Britain remained stable whereas in Germany social capital significantly weakened.

In the pre-war period there is strong evidence that Germany exhibited the same dense network of local voluntary associations, youth organisations and women's groups that existed in Britain.[63] Likewise the war 'spawned an unprecedented volunteerism in support of the troops' and 'opened vast new challenges to women's charitable organisations [which] began to oversee all manner of services, including hospitals, soup kitchens, child-care centres, classes in running a frugal household, and agencies for collecting old clothing and shoes.'[64] However, this situation masked some significant differences between the underlying structures of the two societies. Notwithstanding Germany's universal manhood suffrage, Pat Thane has depicted pre-war Germany as 'a highly autocratic and bureaucratic state with exiguous national democratic institutions and few effective parliamentary and other sources of Liberal opposition.'[65] Germany thus began the war with a far greater degree of state intervention in welfare provision than Britain and this increased significantly as the war went on, reaching its climax in the 'command economy' under Hindenburg and Ludendorff. Many historians have suggested that Imperial Germany began with the military having a massive influence on the working of the state and ended as a virtual military dictatorship.[66] Though some have questioned this interpretation, Roger Chickering has suggested that 'military accents seeped into the activities of Social Democratic voluntary associations', a very different situation from Britain where even in the Army Council-inspired DGVO programme it was voluntarism that predominated.[67] Consequent upon this militarisation was the problem that, unlike in Britain, 'opposition groups could not be institutionalized and integrated into the political system' as, for example, elements of the more militant trades union movement were in Britain, 'but were denounced as "enemies of the Reich."'[68] Even the fact that there were fewer strikes in Germany than in Britain could be seen, paradoxically, as a sign of the far greater degree of control exercised over labour by the German state. Unlike Britain, trades union membership in Germany declined during the war.[69]

What happened in Germany was that trust in state institutions broke down, which loosened the bonds of social cohesion and negatively affected linking social capital. The situation was exacerbated by food shortages, 'the failure of rationing and the growth of the black market [which] undermined the legitimacy of the German state.'[70] Winter and Robert contrast the situation in Germany with that in France and Britain suggesting that 'in Berlin, a different order of priorities existed. The military came first, and the economy created to service it completely distorted the delicate economic system at home.'[71] This decision to prioritise the military was doubly misguided. Firstly, as Bill Philpott has argued, 'mass armies were vital, resilient things, able to absorb a great deal of punishment before collapse. . . . But the societies which sustained them were more fragile.'[72] Secondly, and paradoxically, favouring the military over civilians undermined *troop* morale more than that of the home front. Knowing that their families were facing severe deprivations not far short of outright starvation led soldiers to react by, for example, writing home to ask their friends not to subscribe to war loans, or even to what Deist has termed a 'covert military strike' with between 750,000 and one million men faking illness.[73] Jane Retallack's conclusion is that 'during the First World War, the ideal of social cohesion was tested and found wanting; Germans' recognition that they shared a common fate could not invest the "people's community" with meaning.' In total contrast to Britain 'the nation was more divided than ever when peace broke out in 1918.'[74] Philpott is even more revealing when he states that the situation towards the end of the war in Germany was one in which the state did not trust the people.[75] Without trust social cohesion breaks down and total war becomes impossible to sustain.[76]

Given the rigidity with which the German state attempted to control voluntary efforts and the failure of trust within German society it followed that German voluntary organisations were inevitably straitjacketed into rigid organisational forms in contrast to their British counterparts whose organisational flexibility both contributed to and fed off enhanced trust in voluntary organisations and increased levels of social capital. Adam

Seipp recognises this contrast in his comparison between Manchester and Munich. In the former strong 'wartime communities' emerged and were maintained. In the latter:

> A very different dynamic emerged in which local structures were subsumed into a larger Bavarian/Imperial war effort that left far less room for responsiveness on the part of local and regional officials. The harder the state worked to assure its citizenry that it and it alone had the answers to the problems of wartime society, the more self-evidently false those claims became.[77]

THE LEGACY OF THE WAR

In much the same way as many commentators have assumed a decline in voluntary charitable activity *during* the First World War there is also 'something of an historiographical consensus [which holds] that the inter-war period marked an era of associational decline.'[78] This view is, again, mistaken. I have already noted the great similarities between the organisation of the office of the DGVO and the nascent NCVO and there is no doubt that in the post-war decades many charities and voluntary organisations took on a more 'professional' character. Part of the reason for this error may come from the fact that the closer working relationship between state and voluntary sectors that occurred during the war continued and intensified after it. Bernard Harris, among others, has noted that there was 'a growing trend in the financial relationship between the state and the voluntary sector' and that the two sectors worked increasingly more closely together in the inter-war period.[79] Helen McCarthy has elucidated the way in which 'associational voluntarism was closely identified with the values of democratic citizenship between the wars' and goes on to discuss whether voluntarism supported or challenged the divisions in society.[80] Her conclusions are that the evidence speaks against the 'social control' model and that though religious divisions, gender differences and class inequalities did not disappear from associational life between the wars 'there was a growing recognition ... of the legitimate claim of all social groups—including those previously marginalised or excluded—to democratic citizenship and to an equal share in the development of their local communities.'[81]

One telling example of this change was in the sphere of support for war veterans and it provides some contrasts with what happened in post-war Germany. In Britain after the war the same rather piecemeal intervention of the state into areas previously occupied by charitable or voluntary support continued. Whereas war pensions became a state responsibility care of disabled ex-servicemen did not and 'the reintegration of disabled veterans proceeded primarily through voluntary and philanthropic efforts.'[82]

This has led some writers to conclude that war veterans, especially the disabled, were alienated from post-war society, a carryover of divisions from the trenches to peacetime. Eric Leed is prominent among them stating that veterans groups organised themselves out of a sense of hostility towards civil society as well as a desire to replicate the 'comradeship of the trenches.'[83] There were certainly some good reasons for discontent by veterans, not least the initial unfairness of demobilisation that favoured those with jobs to go to over those who did not, usually because they had spent more time in khaki. There were also some isolated outbreaks of violent protest but these were the result of specific local grievances, the Folkestone 'mutiny' in 1918 and Luton riots in July 1919, for example, or they occurred at demonstrations against government policy exacerbated by poor policing, such as the disturbances in Hyde Park in May 1919. They were not expressions of more general discontent and they were often not instigated by veterans at all.[84] As one writer has commented, 'soldiers were more interested in getting into civilian clothes, returning to their jobs and even to their traditional [political] parties. They did not want to alter the face of England.'[85] Cohen entirely rejects the idea of ex-servicemen being alienated from the British *public*. Hers is a more subtle argument that the failure of the state to provide for disabled veterans may have led to disillusion with regard to *politicians* but it actually bound them more closely to the rest of society where:

> British philanthropists brokered a lasting peace between a public eager to prove its gratitude to soldiers and a conservative ex-service movement looking for signs that the country cared. Shoddy treatment at the hands of the state did not shake disabled veterans' belief that the public had appreciated their sacrifices. . . . Voluntarism shielded the British state from the consequences of its unpopular policies, binding veterans closer to their society.[86]

British veterans were not treated at all well by the British government in comparison to their counterparts on the Continent and in the Dominions, yet despite this there was very little civil unrest initiated by veterans.[87] The major confrontations with the state that occurred in the 1920s were very much a continuation of pre-war clashes between capital and labour exacerbated by worsening economic conditions. In the mediation of veterans' discontent and their reintegration into society, Britain was conspicuously more successful than other countries despite the lack of concern shown by successive governments. There really is only one possible explanation for this apparent paradox as Cohen has pointed out:

> States and powerful interest groups alone could not ensure post-war stabilization. The attainment and maintenance of social peace depended ultimately on the institutions of civil society—on the dense layer of

voluntary organizations that mediated between the individual and the state. . . . British philanthropists [meaning all philanthropists, not just wealthy ones] reconciled the disabled with those for whom they had suffered. The gratitude of the public shielded the state from veterans' anger. In Germany, by contrast, the state regulation of charity isolated the disabled from their fellow citizens.[88]

Cohen's view is strongly supported by Helen McCarthy who demonstrates that voluntary associations did not become dominated by ideological class-based politics but instead educated and socialised the new mass electorate into the workings of the liberal democratic system.[89] It was therefore the very strength of British voluntary action that ensured the country reintegrated its veterans better than others. Those who seek to suggest otherwise look only at the superficial evidence and usually lack this comparison.[90] If Cohen's argument is credible it also suggests that not over-regulating charities during the war was a strength rather than a weakness and supported civil society in Britain.

There was a further movement towards democratisation in the post-war voluntary sector as well as moves into new areas and greater use of business principles. These changes were clearly influenced by what had happened during the war itself and continued the trends I have examined in relation to these activities. The strong elements of bonding social capital noted as being present during the war continued into the post-war period and beyond. In addition there was an increasing influence exercised by the working class continuing beyond the Second World War, when 'the voluntary sector was . . . shaped by a working-class culture, even at the height of the welfare state, with the provision of services generating engagement rather than apathy.'[91]

Afterword

One of the results of this study has been to explore and challenge some of the enduring myths surrounding the First World War. Contrary to what most British people believe 'the war itself was overwhelmingly popular, and the nation came together to a remarkable degree despite critical differences that reflected the nature of divisions in English society.'[1] Or as Trevor Wilson puts it, 'the war had proved a striking vindication of the British way of life . . . it had converted millions of untrained civilians into capable soldiers [and] its community generally had summoned forth great reserves of endurance.'[2] These social characteristics were converted into a strength of social capital that enabled both soldiers and civilians to endure over four years of terrible conflict. In this, they were immeasurably helped by the activities of a myriad of non-uniformed voluntary organisations.

Though the war did not, perhaps, usher in a deluge of social change there were some advances, especially psychological change in the consciousness of many ordinary women who assumed positions of responsibility in wartime charities. One of the dangers of playing down the impacts of the war on social change and considering it an aberration of history is the acceptance of the disillusion and alienation myths. In the 1930s these myths supported the idea that 'it must never happen again' and the appeasement of Nazism. However, as the *Independent* more recently claimed, in the eyes of the British public 'Joan Littlewood has the best tunes still. The [First World] war is remembered as a conflict based on class, an episode in which ordinary people were sent to their death in hecatombs because this was not, in the way the Second World War was, a democratic and popular conflict.'[3] Yet there are more similarities between the First and the Second World Wars than is generally acknowledged. It is accepted that World War Two was fought as a defensive war to prevent a takeover of Europe by a militarist dictatorship but very much the same could be said about the First. As Michael Howard suggests 'the First World War was just as much an ideological and moral conflict as was the Second, and with just as much reason.'[4] Perhaps this similarity makes it easier to understand the motivations of the volunteers (in the widest sense) of the First World War but, ultimately, many of these remain extremely difficult for a person living in the early twenty-first century to grasp.

Millions of ordinary men and women played their roles in supporting Britain's commitment to total war, not by putting on a uniform but through voluntary action. The organisations they joined also underwent a transformation. In 1914, the main coordinating force was the COS, with its outdated concept of poverty and the state. The sector that emerged from the war had an entirely different view. Led by the new National Council of Social Service they were far more open to both cooperation with government and the adoption of modern management principles. In undergoing this transformation, voluntary organisations had contributed in no small part to Britain's ultimate victory. Lloyd George recognised this when he wrote that 'the home front . . . is always underrated by the Generals in the field. And yet that is where the Great War was won and lost. The Russian, Bulgarian, Austrian and German home fronts fell to pieces before their armies collapsed.'[5] However, he was wrong in that Britain's army, from privates to generals, did appreciate the importance of the home front and this bond ensured victory in what was truly a people's war.[6]

Notes

NOTES TO THE ACKNOWLEDGMENTS

1. The latest to do so are Timothy Bowman and Mark Connelly in the otherwise excellent *The Edwardian Army: Recruiting, Training, and Deploying the British Army, 1902–1914* (Oxford: Oxford University Press, 2012), 140.

NOTES TO CHAPTER 1

1. *The Labour Year Book 1916* (London: Co-operative Press, 1915), 37.
2. Jay Winter has pointed out that Webb's voice was the most influential on the programme of the WNC. Jay Winter, *Socialism and the Challenge of War: Ideas and Politics in Britain 1912–18* (London: Routledge and Kegan Paul, 1974); Jay Winter and Antoine Prost, *The Great War in History: Debates and Controversies 1914 to the Present* (Cambridge: Cambridge University Press, 2005), 136–37.
3. They originally numbered one to thirteen but for some reason there is no number five.
4. The only ones that had not were number nine, which was not war-related, and twelve, which was a post-war demand.
5. The term 'voluntary organisations' is used throughout to denote all those bodies run by volunteers, whereas 'charities' is a narrower term denoting only those voluntary bodies falling within the definition of the 1601 Statute of Charitable Uses. Likewise, I adopt the term 'voluntary action' to mean activity which is undertaken 'without coercion or compulsion that is deployed through voluntary organisations in the provision of welfare services'.
6. Mrs C.S. Peel, *How We Lived Then 1914–1918* (London: Bodley Head, 1929), 26.
7. These include Arthur Marwick, *The Deluge: British Society and the First World War* (Boston: Little Brown, 1965); Gerard DeGroot, *Blighty: British Society in the Era of the Great War* (London: Longman, 1996); Jay Winter and Jean-Louis Robert (eds.), *Capital Cities at War: Paris, London, Berlin 1914–1919* (Cambridge: Cambridge University Press, 1997); Trevor Wilson, *The Myriad Faces of War: Britain and the Great War, 1914–1918* (Cambridge: Polity Press, 1986).
8. Adrian Gregory, *The Last Great War: British Society and the First World War* (Cambridge: Cambridge University Press, 2008), 5.
9. E.S. Turner, *Dear Old Blighty* (London: Michael Joseph), 1980, 31.

10. DeGroot, *Blighty*, 31; Samuel Hynes, *A War Imagined: The First World War and English Culture* (London: Pimlico, 1992), 91–93.
11. Alan G.V. Simmons, *Britain and World War One* (Oxford: Routledge, 2012), 131.
12. Arthur Marwick, *Women at War 1914–1918* (London: Fontana, 1977), 35.
13. Marwick, *Women at War*. See for example page 35 on the uselessness of 'sock knitting', page 12 on the lack of impact of charitable work and pages 142–43 for rather patronising remarks about charitable organisations and the Women's Institutes (which first came to Britain, from Canada, in 1915).
14. Frank Prochaska, 'Philanthropy', in *The Cambridge Social History of Britain 1750–1950, Vol. 3: Social Agencies and Institutions*, ed. F.M.L. Thompson (Cambridge: Cambridge University Press, 1990), 359.
15. 'The Last Romantic War: The First Modern War and the Genesis of Modern Wartime Humanitarian Relief in the Crimean War 1854–6', 2007, http://www.philanthropy.iupui.edu/Education/last_romantic_war.doc, accessed 7/4/10. Confirmed by Mark Bostridge, *Florence Nightingale: The Making of an Icon* (New York: Farrar, Straus, and Giroux, 2008); Marjie Bloy, 'Florence Nightingale (1820–1910)', http://www.victorianweb.org/history/crimea/florrie.html, accessed 6/3/12.
16. *Crimean War – Loyal Addresses and Contributions to the Patriotic Fund from Australian Colonies*, Australian Archives, Canberra, A5954/1, 1195/4.
17. Melanie Oppenheimer, 'Home Front Largesse: Colonial Patriotic Funds and the Boer War', in *The Boer War: Army, Nation and Empire*, conference papers, http://www.army.gov.au/ahu/books_articles/ConferencePapers/The_Boer_WarOppenheimer.htm, accessed 7/4/10.
18. Will Bennett, *Absent-Minded Beggars: Volunteers in the Boer War* (Barnsley: Leo Cooper, 1999).
19. The New Labyrinth of East London Lore, http://www.eastlondon-labyrinth.com/history/boer-war-04.jsp, accessed 6/4/10. Mansion House Funds were a regular philanthropic response by Lord Mayors to disasters of all kinds and others in this period included those for the relief of distress in Ireland (1880), victims of the Trafalgar Square riots (1886), survivors of the Titanic and as a memorial to Captain Scott which raised £75,000 (both 1912).
20. L.M. Field, *The Forgotten War: Australian Involvement in the South African Conflict of 1899–1902* (Melbourne: Melbourne University Press, 1979), 177.
21. Simon Fowler, 'The Absent-Minded Beggar: An Introduction', http://www.sfowler.force9.co.uk/page_10.htm, accessed 7/4/10.
22. Soldiers, Sailors, Airmen and Families Association History Fact Sheet, http://www.ssafa.org.uk, accessed 7/4/10.
23. Fowler, 'The Absent-Minded Beggar'.
24. Andrew Thompson, 'Publicity, Philanthropy and Commemoration: British Society and the War', in *The Impact of the South African War*, eds. David Omissi and Andrew S. Thompson (Basingstoke: Palgrave, 2002), 107.
25. Thompson, 'Publicity, Philanthropy and Commemoration', 112.
26. Adrian Gregory, *The Silence of Memory: Armistice Day 1919–1946* (Oxford: Berg, 1994), 95.

NOTES TO CHAPTER 2

1. Notably Frank Prochaska, *The Voluntary Impulse: Philanthropy in Modern Britain* (London: Faber and Faber, 1988); Justin Davis Smith, 'The Voluntary Tradition: Philanthropy and Self-help in Britain 1500–1945', in *An*

Introduction to the Voluntary Sector, eds. Justin Davis Smith, Colin Rochester and Rodney Hedley (London and New York: Routledge, 1995).

2. For the debate over the nature of Victorian philanthropy see Bernard Harris, *The Origins of the British Welfare State: Social Welfare in England and Wales 1800–1945* (Basingstoke: Palgrave Macmillan, 2004), Chapter 7.

3. The figures exclude self-help or mutual charities such as friendly societies.

4. David Owen, *English Philanthropy 1660–1960* (Cambridge: Cambridge University Press, 1964), 478.

5. Alan Kidd, *State, Society and the Poor in Nineteenth Century England* (London and Basingstoke: Macmillan, 1999), 65.

6. John Stevenson, *British Society 1914–45* (London: Penguin Books, 1984), 47–48.

7. Quoted in Justin Davis Smith and Melanie Oppenheimer, 'The Labour Movement and Voluntary Action in the UK and Australia: A Comparative Perspective', *Labour History*, No. 88 (May 2005).

8. Cathryn Cornes and John Hughes-Wilson, *Blindfold and Alone: British Military Executions in the Great War* (London: Cassell, 2001), 27–28.

9. Brian Harrison, *Peaceable Kingdom* (Oxford: Clarendon Press, 1982), 178. The statistics come from the *15th Abstract of Labour Statistics*, Parliamentary Papers PP, Cd. 6228, cvii, 254.

10. Most famously by Paul Fussell in *The Great War and Modern Memory* (Oxford: Oxford University Press, 1975).

11. Jonathan Rose, *The Intellectual Life of the British Working Classes* (New Haven, CT: Yale University Press, 2001), 78–83.

12. Prochaska, 'Philanthropy', 29.

13. T.W. Laqueur, *Religion and Respectability: Sunday Schools and Working Class Culture* (New Haven, CT: Yale University Press, 1976).

14. Richard Holt, *Sport and the British: A Modern History* (Oxford: Clarendon Press, 1989), 136.

15. Peter J. Beck, 'Leisure and Sport in Britain, 1900–1939', in *A Companion to Early Twentieth-Century Britain* (Blackwell Companions to British History), ed. Christopher John Wrigley (Oxford: Blackwell Publishers, 2003), 461.

16. Gary Sheffield, *Leadership in the Trenches: Officer-man Relations, Morale and Discipline in the British Army in the Era of the First World War* (Basingstoke: Macmillan, 1999), 69.

17. Ian Beckett, 'The Nation in Arms 1914–1918', in *A Nation in Arms: A Social Study of the British Army in the First World War*, eds. Ian F.W. Beckett and Keith Simpson (Manchester: Manchester University Press, 1985), 5.

18. DeGroot, *Blighty*, 37.

19. Albert Marrin, *The Last Crusade: The Church of England in the First World War* (Durham, NC: Duke University Press, 1974), 187.

20. John Springhall, *Youth, Empire and Society: British Youth Movements, 1883–1940* (London: Croom Helm, 1977), 16. Cyril Pearce supports Springhall's thesis viewing the rational recreation movement as being 'imposed' and Working Men's Clubs as being a reaction against this; *Comrades of Conscience: The Story of an English Community's Opposition to the Great War* (London: Francis Boutle, 2001), 40–41.

21. Springhall, *Youth, Empire and Society*, 40.

22. Springhall, *Youth, Empire and Society*, 126.

23. Springhall, *Youth, Empire and Society*, 125; Allen Warren, 'Sir Robert Baden-Powell, the Scout Movement and Citizen Training in Great Britain 1900–1920', *English Historical Review*, Vol. 101, No. 399 (1986): 376–98; Allen Warren, 'Citizens of the Empire', in *Imperialism and Popular Culture*, ed. John M. Mackenzie (Manchester: Manchester University Press, 1986).

24. See for example the comments of working class people in Salford in Robert Roberts, *The Classic Slum: Salford Life in the First Quarter of the Century* (Manchester: University of Manchester Press, 1971), 145.
25. Tim Jeal, *Baden-Powell: Founder of the Boy Scouts* (London: Century Hutchinson, 1989).
26. See for example DeGroot, *Blighty*, 40.
27. R.J. Morris, 'Clubs, Societies and Associations', in Thompson, *Cambridge Social History*, 418.
28. Prochaska, *Philanthropy*, 74. His source is Angela Burdett-Coutts (ed.), *Women's Mission* (London: 1893), 361–66.
29. Jacqueline de Vries, 'Women's Voluntary Organizations in World War 1', introductory essays to the microfilm collection *A Change in Attitude: Women, War and Society, 1914–1918*, ed. Susan Grayzel (Woodbridge, CT: Thomson Gale, 2005).
30. As Waites has observed, 'the wives of labourers were relatively untouched by social institutions such as the Cooperative Society and Women's Cooperative Guild which were so significant for artisan families.' Bernard Waites, 'The Effect of the First World War on Class and Status in England, 1910–20', *Journal of Contemporary History*, Vol. 11, No. 1 (January 1976): 32–33.
31. Davis Smith, 'Voluntary Tradition', 15, my emphasis.
32. John Bourne, 'The British Working Man in Arms', in *Facing Armageddon: The First World War Experienced*, eds. Hugh Cecil and Peter H. Liddle (London: Leo Cooper, 1996), 346.
33. Judith Fido, 'The COS and Social Casework', in *Social Control in Nineteenth Century Britain*, ed. A.P. Donajgrodski (London: Croom Helm, 1977), 208; Harris, *Origins of the British Welfare State*, 74–75.
34. See for example Owen, *English Philanthropy*, Chapter 8, '"Scientific Charity" the Charity Organisation Society', 215–47.
35. Davis Smith, 'Voluntary Tradition', 19.
36. Jacqueline de Vries, 'Women's Voluntary Organizations in World War 1'.
37. Margaret Vining and Barton C. Hacker, 'From Camp Follower to Lady in Uniform: Women, Social Class and Military Institutions before 1920', *Contemporary European History*, No. 10 (2001): 353.

NOTES TO CASE STUDY 1

1. J.M. McEwen, 'The National Press during the First World War: Ownership and Circulation', *Journal of Contemporary History*, Vol. 17 (1982): 468 and 471.
2. J.M. McEwen, 'Brass-Hats and the British Press during the First World War', *Canadian Journal of History*, Vol. 18 (1983): 44.
3. Simon Fowler, 'War Charity Begins at Home', *History Today*, Vol. 49 (September 1999): 19.
4. *Evening Standard*, 1 March 1915.
5. Keith Grieves (ed.), *Sussex in the First World War* (Lewes: Sussex Record Society, Vol. 84, 2004), xxix.
6. W.E. Dowding, 'The Romance of Voluntary Effort: Part VI – How the Press Has Helped', *TP's Journal of Great Deeds of the Great War*, Vol. 3, No. 36 (19 June 1915): 260.
7. London Metropolitan Archives (LMA), LCC/MIN 8350 (Vol. 16), Case 15.
8. *Daily Express*, July 1915; and Imperial War Museum (IWM), Women's Work Collection (WWC), B.O. 2 51/11.
9. The National Archives (Kew) (TNA), FO 383/19, letter from Lt A.J. Brown RAMC to his mother, 17 February 1915.

10. Dowding, 'How the Press Helped', 260.
11. Dowding, 'How the Press Helped', 259.
12. Fowler 'War Charity', 19.
13. IWM, WWC, BO 38/2, letter from F.J. Wall, FA Secretary to Agnes Conway, 28 February 1919.
14. Ali Melling, 'Wartime Opportunities: Ladies' Football and the First World War Factories', in *Militarism, Sport, Europe: War without Weapons*, ed. James A. Mangan (London: Frank Cass, 2003), 120–137. For the assistance of sport in raising funds for war charities see also Tony Mason and Eliza Riedi, *Sport and the Military: The British Armed Forces 1880–1960* (Cambridge: Cambridge University Press, 2010), 84–85 and 151.

NOTES TO CHAPTER 3

1. Marwick, *Deluge*, 34.
2. Wilson, *The Myriad Faces of War*, 149.
3. *Report of the Special Work of the Local Government Board Arising out of the War (up to 31st December 1914)*, PP, Cd. 7763, xxv, 299.
4. John A. Lee, *Todmorden and the Great War 1914–1918: A Local Record* (Todmorden: Waddington and Sons, 1922), 133.
5. *Report of the Special Work of the Local Government Board*, 299.
6. Edith Abbott, 'The War and Women's Work in England', *Journal of Political Economy*, Vol. 25, No. 7 (July 1917): 656.
7. Containing three members of the Cabinet, the Committee was chaired from October 1914 by Sir George Murray.
8. Extracted from the *Final Accounts of the National Relief Fund in Final Report of the National Relief Fund*, March 1921, PP, Cmd. 1272 (London: HMSO, 1921).
9. Their independence is demonstrated in the report of the Fund in Scotland, *Report by the Scottish Advisory Committee on the Administration of the National Relief Fund in Scotland up to 31st March 1915*, PP, Cd. 8129, 5.
10. Lee, *Todmorden*, 56.
11. Lee, *Todmorden*, 56–57.
12. Frederick D'Aeth, 'War Relief Agencies and the Guild of Help Movement', *Progress: Civic, Social, Industrial*, No. 10 (October 1915): 140–47; Jane Lewis, 'The Boundary between Voluntary and Statutory Social Service in the Late Nineteenth and Early Twentieth Centuries', *Historical Journal*, Vol. 39, No. 1 (March 1996): 175.
13. Millicent Garrett Fawcett, 'War Relief and War Service', *Quarterly Review*, Vol. 225, No. 446 (January 1916): 117.
14. Elizabeth Macadam, *The New Philanthropy: A Study of the Relations between the Statutory and Voluntary Social Services* (London: George Allen and Unwin, 1934), 56.
15. D'Aeth, 'War Relief Agencies', 147.
16. Marwick, *Deluge*, 43.
17. George Robb, *British Culture and the First World War* (Basingstoke: Palgrave, 2002), 79.
18. These were recurring issues at the major conference for members of the SSFA, Guilds of Help, COS and others held at Westminster Hall between 10 and 12 June 1915, documented as *Proceedings* (London: Longman Green and Co, 1915).
19. Letter from Harold Baker MP to the WNC, December 1914; *War Emergency Workers National Committee, Publications, Reports and Executive Committee Minutes* (London: Co-operative Press, 1914–1916).

20. WNC Executive Committee minutes, *WNC Publications*, 7 December 1914.
21. *Daily Herald*, 10 August 1914.
22. Caroline E. Playne, *Society at War 1914–16* (London: George Allen and Unwin, 1931), 94.
23. *The Times*, 13 April 1915, 5.
24. *The Times*, 21 April 1915, 5.
25. Sir George Murray in his address to the 1915 Conference on War Relief and Personal Service; *Proceedings*, 61.
26. The WNC again protested in two resolutions, the latter invoking both the name of the Prince of Wales and long-established charity law. WNC Executive Committee minutes, *WNC Publications*, 3 February 1916.
27. Deborah Thom, *Nice Girls and Rude Girls: Women Workers in World War 1* (London: I.B. Tauris, 1998), 147; Robb, *British Culture*, 79.
28. *Final Report of the National Relief Fund.*
29. Susan Pedersen, 'Gender, Welfare and Citizenship in Britain during the Great War', *American Historical Review*, Vol. 95 (1990): 983–1006.
30. Marwick, *Deluge*, 43.
31. Helen Fraser, *Women and War Work* (New York: G. Arnold Shaw, 1918), 44.
32. Simon Fowler and Keith Gregson, 'Bloody Belgians!', *Ancestors*, May 2005: 43–49.
33. Fowler and Gregson, 'Bloody Belgians!' For more detail on the formation of the WRC see Katherine Storr, *Excluded from the Record: Women, Refugees and Relief 1914–1929* (Bern: Peter Lang, 2010), 17–20, 43–44 and 52–62.
34. Tony Kushner, 'Local Heroes: Belgian Refugees in Britain during the First World War', *Immigrants and Minorities*, Vol. 18, No. 1 (1999): 1–28.
35. *First Report of the Departmental Committee Appointed by the President of the Local Government Board to Consider and Report on Questions Arising in Connection with the Reception and Employment of the Belgian Refugees in this Country*, PP, 1914, Cd. 7750, vii, 473.
36. Peter Cahalan, *Belgian Refugee Relief in England during the Great War* (New York and London: Garland, 1982), 42–43.
37. Turner, *Dear Old Blighty*, 77.
38. Cahalan, *Belgian Refugee Relief*, 82. Kushner notes that relations between the WRC and the LGB were 'often strained'; 'Local Heroes', 5.
39. *Report of the Work Undertaken by the British Government in the Reception and Care of the Belgian Refugees* (London: HMSO, 1920).
40. Storr, *Excluded from the Record*, 5–6.
41. Cahalan, *Belgian Refugee Relief*, 17.
42. Cahalan, *Belgian Refugee Relief*, 174–75.
43. Minutes of the Croydon War Refugee Committee (compiled by the Hon. Sec. Miss Muriel Scarff), Croydon Local Studies Library.
44. Lee, *Todmorden*, 73.
45. K.W. Mitchinson, *Saddleworth 1914–1919: The Experience of a Pennine Community during the Great War* (Manchester: Saddleworth Historical Society, 1995), 44.
46. Mitchinson, *Saddleworth*, 44.
47. Quoted in Richard Van Emden and Steve Humphries, *All Quiet on the Home Front: An Oral History of Life in Britain during the First World War* (London: Hodder Headline, 2003), 225–26.
48. Rev Lawrence P. Field, *The Souvenir Book of Eye: Being Some Records of the Great War 1914–1919: From the Parish of Eye, in the Soke of Peterborough and in the County of Northampton* (Eye, Northamptonshire: Eye Patriotic Association, 1920).

49. Mitchinson, *Saddleworth*, 45.
50. Lee, *Todmorden*, 74.
51. W.D. Bavin, *Swindon's War Record* (Swindon: Drew, 1922), 39.
52. George I. Gay, *The Commission for Relief in Belgium, Statistical Review of Relief Operations: Five Years November 1, 1914 to August 31, 1919* (Stanford, CA: Stanford University Press, 1925).
53. Gay, *Commission for Relief*, 129, 52–53.
54. *Daily Chronicle*, 16 February 1916.
55. *45th Annual Report of the Local Government Board*, PP, Cd. 8331 (London: HMSO, 1916).

NOTES TO CASE STUDY 2

1. Ronald F. Roxburgh, *The Prisoners of War Information Bureau in London: A Study* (London: Longman, 1915).
2. The Blue Cross, whose President was Lady Smith-Dorrien, later also served the Italian Army whilst the Purple Cross maintained three hospitals for horses at Vesoul, Foulain and Bordeaux, T.N. Kelynack (ed.), *Pro Patria: A Guide to Public and Personal Service in War Time* (London: John Bale, 1916), 56 and 116. However, these later closed through lack of funds and the charity was refused registration by the London County Council. LMA, MIN 8335 (Vol. 1), Case 40.
3. W.E. Dowding, 'The Romance of Voluntary Effort: Part V – Mindful of His Beast', *TP's Journal*, Vol. 3, No. 34 (5 June 1915): 204.
4. Charles Messenger, *Call to Arms; The British Army 1914–18* (London: Weidenfeld and Nicholson, 2005), 435, gives the Boer War wastage rate as an appalling 93 percent.
5. IWM, WWC, BO 2 57/6, 'Our Soldiers' Love for Dogs', NCDL Press Advertisement.
6. Winnie was the mascot of the Canadian 2nd Infantry Brigade.
7. Edward G. Fairholme and Wellesley Pain, *A Century of Work for Animals: The History of the RSPCA 1824–1924* (London: John Murray, 1924), 220.
8. Fairholme and Pain, *A Century of Work for Animals*, 218.
9. IWM, WWC, BO 3 14/9.
10. *Daily Chronicle*, 26 June 1915.

NOTES TO CHAPTER 4

1. Mrs Humphry (Mary) Ward, *England's Effort: Six Letters to an American Friend* (London: Smith, Elder and Co, 1916), 159.
2. Ward, *England's Effort*, 160; *Reports by the Joint War Committee and the Joint War Finance Committee of the British Red Cross Society and the Order of St John of Jerusalem in England on Voluntary Aid Rendered to the Sick and Wounded at Home and Abroad and to British Prisoners of War 1914–1919* (London: HMSO, 1921), 643–55. Henceforth *Red Cross Reports*.
3. Michael Snape, *God and the British Soldier: Religion and the British Army in the First and Second World Wars* (London and New York: Routledge, 2005), 211.
4. Snape, *God and the British Soldier*, 208; Sir Arthur K. Yapp, *The Romance of the Red Triangle: The Story of the Coming of the Red Triangle and the Service Rendered by the YMCA to the Sailors and Soldiers of the British Empire* (London: Hodder and Stoughton, 1919).

5. Fraser, *Women and War Work*, 21.
6. Kelynack, Pro Patria, 81.
7. *Queen Mary's Needlework Guild: Its Work during the Great War* (London: St James's Palace, 1919). It should be noted that prior to the First World War direct Royal involvement in charities was not common. It was the activities of King George, Queen Mary and their family that established this tradition.
8. *Queen Mary's Needlework Guild: Its Work during the Great War.*
9. Anonymous comment quoted on BBC Schools World War One website, http://www.bbc.co.uk/schools/worldwarone/observer/nf_needlebook.shtml, accessed 20/9/06.
10. Abbott, 'The War and Women's Work', 647.
11. Winter, *Socialism and the Challenge of War*, 193.
12. Abbott, 'The War and Women's Work', 647–48.
13. *Labour Year Book 1916*, 80.
14. Abbott, 'The War and Women's Work', 651.
15. Abbott, 'The War and Women's Work', 652.
16. Susan Bruley, *Women in Britain since 1900* (Basingstoke: Palgrave Macmillan, 1999), 39.
17. John Brophy and Eric Partridge, *Songs and Slang of the British Soldier, 1914–1918* (London: Eric Partridge, 1931), 86.
18. IWM, WWC, BO 2 19/3, 'Report of Lady Smith-Dorrien's Hospital Bag Fund and letter from Lady Smith-Dorrien'.
19. Winter, *Socialism and the Challenge of War*, 193.
20. IWM, WWC, ED 4/5, 'Girls' Patriotic Union of Secondary Schools, First Report, November 1914'.
21. 'Girls' Patriotic Union, First Report'.
22. Fowler, 'War Charity', 22.
23. Diary or Log Book, Stanbury Board School, Haworth, Yorkshire; see Haworth village website, http://www.haworth-village.org.uk/history/school/stanbury_school.asp, accessed 20/9/06.
24. IWM, MISC 68, Item 1056, extracts from the Log Books of East Anglian Schools, compiled by Mrs S.M. Hardy.
25. W.A. Armstrong, 'Kentish Rural Society during the First World War', in *Land, Labour and Agriculture, 1700–1920: Essays for Gordon Mingay*, eds. B.A. Holderness and M.E. Turner (London: Hambledon, 1990), 122.
26. IWM, extracts from the Log Books of East Anglian Schools.
27. 'How Did Horse Chestnuts Help the War Effort during the First World War?', IWM online collection, http://collections.iwm.org.uk/server/show/ConWebDoc.1267, accessed 20/9/06.
28. TNA, ED 10/74.
29. TNA, ED 10/74, letter from Miss Agnes Fry to Board of Education, 29 September 1917.
30. Croydon War Supplies Clearing House, Minute Book, Croydon Local Studies Library.
31. TNA, ED 10/75.
32. TNA, ED 10/74.
33. It was however revived during the Second World War; see Berry Mayall and Virginia Morrow, *You Can Help Your Country: English Children's Work during the Second World War* (London: Institute of Education, 2011), 126 and 128.
34. TNA, ED 10/73.
35. Extracts from the Log Books of East Anglian Schools.
36. Bavin, *Swindon*, 183.

37. Paul Wilkinson, 'English Youth Movements 1908–30', *Journal of Contemporary History*, Vol. 4, No. 2 (April 1969): 15; entry for 30 January 1918 in Michael MacDonagh, *In London during the Great War: The Diary of a Journalist* (London: Eyre and Spottiswode, 1935), 260.
38. J. Lewis Paton, 'War Work by Secondary Schoolboys', in Kelynack, *Pro Patria*, 11–13.
39. Wilkinson, 'English Youth Movements', 23.
40. Gill Johnson, 'Burnley: Fame of Little Girl "Soldiers"', *This is Lancashire*, 20 July 2006, www.thisislancashire.co.uk/archive/2006/07/20/Looking+Back, accessed 5/11/10.
41. '"Young Kitchener" Jennie Dies at 89', *This is Lancashire*, 4 November 1997, www.thisislancashire.co.uk/archive/1997/11/04/Lancashire+Archive/6167359, accessed 5/11/10.
42. *War Charities Act 1916: Index of Charities Registered under the Act to 31 December 1919* (London: HMSO, 1920).
43. Alderman W.H. Bowater, Lord Mayor of Birmingham, 'Busy Birmingham: Equipping the Allied Armies', *TP's Journal*, Vol. 3, No. 28 (24 April 1915): 31.
44. Alderman Daniel McCabe, Lord Mayor of Manchester, 'Manchester's Motto', *TP's Journal*, Vol. 2, No. 21 (6 March 1915): 203.
45. 'Our Day' was held in the third week of October each year on the anniversary of the Red Cross and Order of St John joining forces in 1914.
46. Mitchinson, *Saddleworth*, 56.
47. W.E. Dowding, 'The Romance of Voluntary Effort – Part IV: Salving the Stricken', *TP's Journal*, Vol. 3, No. 3 (29 May 1915): 173.
48. Bavin, *Swindon*, 183.
49. D.M. Mackie, *Forfar and District in the War* (Forfar: Forfar War Memorial Committee, 1921), 198.

NOTES TO CASE STUDY 3

1. Marwick, *Deluge*, 87.
2. Julia Bush, *Behind the Lines: East London Labour 1914–1919* (London: Merlin Press, 1984), 41 and 47.
3. Though there was a later split in the NUWSS too, specifically over attendance at the April 1915 peace conference at the Hague. See Jo Vellacott, 'Feminist Consciousness and the First World War', *History Workshop Journal*, No. 23 (1987): 81–101.
4. Millicent Garrett Fawcett, *The Women's Victory – and After: Personal Reminiscences 1911–1918* (London: Sidgwick and Jackson, 1920), 87.
5. Fraser, *Women and War Work*, 18.
6. Frances Balfour, *Dr Elsie Inglis* (London: Hodder and Stoughton, 1918), 144.
7. Fraser, *Women and War Work*, 17–18.
8. The Fund was especially focussed on the 'cheehas', men either too old or disabled to serve in the front line. Storr, *Excluded from the Record*, 216.
9. 'Women's Organisations', http://www.1914–1918.net/women.htm, accessed 20/9/06.
10. 'Women's Service under Fire', *Common Cause* (24 December 1914): 618 and (19 February 1915): 719.
11. Nicoletta Gullace, *'The Blood of Our Sons': Men, Women, and the Renegotiation of British Citizenship during the Great War* (Basingstoke: Palgrave Macmillan, 2002), 148.

12. IWM, WWC, SER 11/20, 'Account of the Life of Hon Evelina Haverfield', written by Flora Sandes.
13. Marwick, *Deluge*, 98.
14. *Daily News*, 10 January 1918.
15. Angela K. Smith, *The Second Battlefield: Women, Modernism and the First World War* (Manchester: Manchester University Press, 2000), 52.
16. Louise Miller, *A Fine Brother: The Life of Captain Flora Sandes* (London: Alma, 2012), 204 and 207.
17. Gullace, *Blood of Our Sons*, 149. Sandes's military role was not, however, approved of by the officials of the Serbian Relief Fund. See Storr, *Excluded from the Record*, 198.
18. Elsie Cameron Corbett, *Red Cross in Serbia, 1915–1919: A Personal Diary of Experiences* (Banbury: Cheney and Sons, 1964), 87.
19. Gullace, *Blood of Our Sons*, 150.
20. Janet Lee, 'A Nurse and a Soldier: Gender, Class and National Identity in the First World War Adventures of Grace McDougall and Flora Sandes', *Women's History Review*, Vol. 15, No. 1 (2006): 84.

NOTES TO CHAPTER 5

1. They raised a total of £178,950; *Central British Committee of the Red Cross, Report on Voluntary Organisations in Aid of the Sick and Wounded during the South African War* (London, HMSO, 1902), 4.
2. TNA, WO 107/21, QMG Directors Meeting minutes, 16 August 1914.
3. Sir Wodehouse Richardson, *With the Army Service Corps in South Africa* (London: Richardson and Co, 1903), 125.
4. Richardson, *With the Army Service Corps*, 126.
5. *Report on Voluntary Organisations during the South African War*, 5.
6. Captain J.C. Dunn, *The War the Infantry Knew* (London: Abacus reprint, 1994), 100.
7. Fowler, 'War Charity', 19.
8. Quoted in Ian F.W. Beckett, *Home Front 1914–1918: How Britain Survived the Great War* (Kew: National Archives, 2006), 66.
9. TNA, WO 95/71, War Diary, Director of Transport, 28 November 1914.
10. Sarah Pedersen, 'A Surfeit of Socks? The Impact of the First World War on Women Correspondents to Daily Newspapers', *Scottish Economic and Social History*, Vol. 22, No. 1 (2002): 60.
11. TNA, WO 107/21, QMG Directors Meeting minutes, 8 November 1914.
12. W.E. Dowding, 'A Study of the War-Giving', *The Contemporary Review*, Vol. CVIII, (November 1915): 634. Dowding later welcomed the formation of the DGVO's office; letter to the *Daily Telegraph*, 21 September 1915.
13. *Report of the National Scheme of Voluntary Effort Resulting from the Formation of Departments of Director General of Voluntary Organisations*, PP 1919, Cmd. 173, x (London: HMSO, 1919), 185. Hereafter *Report on the Director General of Voluntary Organisations*.
14. Debate on the Address, House of Commons, *Proceedings HoC*, 5th Series, Vol. 68, 12 November 1914, Col. 143.
15. *Proceedings HoC*, Vol. 68, 12 November 1914, Col. 144.
16. *Proceedings HoC*, Vol. 68, 12 November 1914, Col. 146.
17. *Daily Chronicle*, 2 February 1915.
18. TNA, WO 107/14.
19. TNA, WO 107/14.

20. TNA, WO 107/14, Cowans to Maxwell, 7 February 1915.
21. TNA, WO 107/14, Maxwell letter of 13 February 1915.
22. Debate on the Army Estimates, House of Commons, *Proceedings HoC*, 5th Series, Vol. 69, 10 February 1915, Col. 629. Hogge became the first President of the National Federation of Discharged and Demobilized Sailors and Soldiers in 1919.
23. *Proceedings HoC*, Vol. 69, 10 February 1915, Col. 657–58.
24. *Proceedings HoC*, Vol. 69, 10 February 1915, Col. 630.
25. TNA, WO 107/14, Maxwell to Cowans, 24 February 1915.
26. Messenger, *Call to Arms*, 470.
27. TNA, WO 107/15, letter on file.
28. TNA, WO 107/15, Cowans to Maxwell, 19 November 1915.
29. TNA, WO 107/15, Cowans to Maxwell, 30 November 1915.
30. TNA, WO 107/15, Maxwell to Cowans, 21 December 1915.
31. TNA, WO 107/15.
32. TNA, WO 107/15, letter from Lt V.E. Reynolds, 4 December 1915.
33. Corporal B.H. Jeffrey, Divisional Telegraphs, 3rd Signal Company RE, 3rd Division, letter of 31 January 1915. Centre for Kentish Studies, Acquisition 6632, Vol. 1 (henceforth Great Chart Letters).
34. *The Times*, 21 September 1915, 9.
35. *Proceedings HoC*, 5th Series, Vol. 69, 18 November 1915, Col. 2070–71.
36. *The Times*, 21 September 1915, 8.
37. *The Times*, 11 October 1915, 11.
38. G.R. Searle, *A New England? Peace and War 1886–1918* (The New Oxford History of England) (Oxford: Clarendon Press, 2004), 33.
39. Sir Francis Scott, Farewell Order, issued 4 February 1896, quoted in Lt-Col E.W.D. Ward, 'To Kumasi and Back with the Ashanti Expeditionary Force 1895–96', *Journal of the Royal United Service Institution*, Vol. XL, No. 222 (August 1896): 1030.
40. Major R.S.S. Baden-Powell, *The Downfall of Prempeh: A Diary of Life with the Native Levy in Ashanti 1895–96*, Chapter 6, http://pinetreeweb.com/bp-prempeh-01.htm, accessed 22/10/06.
41. E.W.D. Ward, *Supply and Transport on Active Service* (Dublin: Sibley and Co., 1893), 10.
42. *Army Service Corps Journal* (March 1896): 255.
43. Ward, 'To Kumasi', 1029.
44. 'Colonel Sir Edward Ward', obituary by 'An Old Brother Officer', *Journal of the Royal Army Service Corps* (1928): 682.
45. Lt-Col P.L. Binns, *The Story of the Royal Tournament* (Aldershot: Gale and Polden, 1952), 149.
46. *Dictionary of National Biography*, 1922–30, 883–84. The entry was compiled by Sir Charles Harris who became Permanent Under Secretary at the War Office in succession to Ward.
47. H.W. Nevinson, *The Diary of a Siege* (London: Methuen, 1900), entry for 19 October 1899. Nevinson was correspondent for the *Daily Chronicle*.
48. Ruari Chisholm, *Ladysmith* (London: Osprey, 1979), 193.
49. H. Babington Smith, 'Ladysmith after the Siege', *National Review*, Vol. 35 (1900): 538.
50. Field-Marshal Lord Birdwood, *Khaki and Gown* (London: Ward Lock and Co, 1941), 107.
51. Memoirs of Katherine Louisa (Oswell) Nealon, Nursing Sister at Ladysmith, 1900. Published on the website of the South African Military History Society at http://samilitaryhistory.org/dianurse.html, accessed 21/9/06. Ward named it 'Chevril' as the equine version of Bovril.

52. Speech to the Authors' Club reported in *The Times*, 23 May 1905. Ward clearly had a good sense of humour as demonstrated both in the punning title of the 'Lyre' and when a formal complaint was lodged with him by the ladies of the town who were indignant about the soldiers who bathed naked in the river on Sundays. Ward sensibly suggested that the ladies not look. Byron Farwell, *The Great Anglo-Boer War* (New York and London: W.W. Norton, 1976), 221.
53. Excerpt taken from British Battles.com, http://www.britishbattles.com/great-boer-war/ladysmith.htm, accessed 21/9/06.
54. Sir George White despatches of 2 December 1899 and 23 March 1900, quoted in the *Army Service Corps Journal* (May 1901): 45 and 47.
55. Entry dated 17 July 1900; Richardson, *With the Army Service Corps*, 136.
56. *The Times*, 12 September 1928, 7; 'Colonel Sir Edward Ward', obituary by 'An Old Brother Officer', 682.
57. Despatch from Earl Roberts to the Secretary of State for War, 2 April 1901, quoted in the *Army Service Corps Journal* (May 1901): 56.
58. *The Times*, 26 August 1903, 4. Even the official German account of the war, which was highly critical of the British in every other respect, concurred in praising the ASC. *The Official German Account of the War in South Africa Prepared by the Historical Section of the Great General Staff, Berlin*, authorised translation by Colonel W.H.H. Waters (London: John Murray, 1904), especially 7–8.
59. Captain Owen Wheeler, *The War Office Past and Present* (London: Methuen, 1914), 60.
60. 'Colonel Sir Edward Ward', obituary by 'An Old Brother Officer', 682.
61. A.H. Page, 'Supply Services in the British Army in the South African War 1899–1902' (PhD diss., Oxford, 1977), 359.
62. The War Office Reconstruction Committee comprised Esher, Admiral Sir John (Jackie) Fisher and Sir George Clarke, the former Governor of Victoria.
63. Peter Fraser, *Lord Esher: A Political Biography* (London: Hart-Davis, MacGibbon, 1973), 21.
64. Edward M. Spiers, *The Army and Society, 1815–1914* (London: Longman, 1980), 124.
65. TNA, WO 32/9224, letter from Ward to Arnold-Forster, 21 November 1904.
66. TNA, WO 32/9224, memo attached to Ward letter.
67. TNA, WO 32/8782, memo of 28 February 1905.
68. TNA, WO 32/8782, memo of 1 March 1905.
69. Simon Giles Higgens, 'How Was Richard Haldane Able to Reform the British Army? An Historical Assessment Using a Contemporary Change Management Model' (MPhil diss., University of Birmingham, 2010), 68; K.W. Mitchinson, *Defending Albion: Britain's Home Army 1908–1919* (Basingstoke: Palgrave Macmillan, 2005), 3; see also R. Blake, 'Great Britain: The Crimean War to the First World War', in *Soldiers and Governments*, ed. Michael Howard (London: Eyre and Spottiswode, 1957), 34
70. Colonel G. Williams, *Citizen Soldiers of the Royal Engineers Transportation and Movements and the Army Service Corps 1859–1965* (Ashford, Kent: Royal Corps of Transport, 1965), 26 and 33.
71. *Committee on the Employment of Ex-Soldiers and Sailors*, 1906, PP, Cd. 2991 (London: HMSO, 1906), and information from British Official Publications Collaborative Reader Information Service at bopcris.ac.uk, http://www.bopcris.ac.uk/cgi-bin/displayrec.pl?searchtext=ex+soldiers&record=/bopall/ref7397.html, accessed 21/9/06.

72. TNA, WO 32/6384, Establishment (Code 1(C)), *Report of Ward Committee on Organisation and Establishment of Civil Departments 1903.*
73. Simkins, *Kitchener's Army*, 12; Ian Worthington, 'Socialization, Militarization and Officer Recruiting: The Development of the Officers Training Corps', *Military Affairs*, Vol. 43, No. 2 (April 1979): 90–96.
74. *Interim Report of the War Office Committee on the Provision of Officers for Service with the Regular Army in War and for the Auxiliary Forces*, 1907, PP, Cd. 3294 (London: HMSO, 1907).
75. Captain Alan R. Haig-Brown, *The O.T.C. and the Great War* (London: Country Life, 1915), x (Ward wrote the Introduction); Worthington, 'Socialization, Mobilization'. It is also notable that Ward's report comments that candidates for the Army Service Corps 'would be selected from men possessing a business training'; *Interim Report of the War Office Committee on the Provision of Officers*, 17.
76. Williams, *Citizen Soldiers*, 33.
77. Michael Tadman, 'The War Office: A Study of Its Development as an Organisational System 1870–1904' (PhD diss., London, King's, 1992), 240–56.
78. Tadman, 'The War Office', 261.
79. Higgens 'How Was Richard Haldane Able to Reform the British Army?', Abstract.
80. Edward M. Spiers, *Haldane: An Army Reformer* (Edinburgh: Edinburgh University Press, 1980), 151.
81. Spiers, *Haldane*, 151; Geoff Sloan, 'Haldane's Mackindergarten: A Radical Experiment in British Military Education?', *War in History*, Vol. 19, No. 3 (2012), 322–52.
82. Ward, *Supply and Transport on Active Service*, 18, 25–26. Haldane proposed something very similar when he said, 'I have noticed in our new Universities with delight degrees established in special sciences. Why should there not be a B.Sc. degree in the science of war?' Haldane, 'On the Reform of the Army', *Army Reform and Other Addresses* (London: T. Fisher and Unwin, 1907), 36. This was in a speech given in Parliament on 8 March 1906, a few days after receiving Ward's memo.
83. Donald Cameron Watt, 'The London University Class for Military Administrators 1906–31: A Study of the British Approach to Civil-Military Relations', *LSE Quarterly*, Vol. 2, No. 2 (Summer 1988): 157–58.
84. Warwick Funnell, 'National Efficiency, Military Accounting and the Business of War', *Critical Perspectives on Accounting*, Vol. 17, No. 6 (September 2006): 732–33.
85. B.W. Blouet, *Halford Mackinder: A Biography* (College Station: Texas A&M University Press, 1987), 131; Watt, 'The London University Class', 158.
86. *Papers of Percy Noble*, Bodleian Library, MSS Autogr c 17, No. 495, letter from Webb to Ward, 23 December 1910.
87. Watt, 'The London University Class', 162–63.
88. Funnell, 'National Efficiency, Military Accounting and the Business of War', 736.
89. The nickname came from the student magazine *The Clare Market Review*. Blouet, *Halford Mackinder*, 132.
90. Lawrence R. Dicksee, *Business Methods and the War* (London: Cambridge University Press, 1915), 2. Dicksee was the first Professor of Accounting at any British University, holding the post at Birmingham.
91. Of these 42 percent achieved at least the rank of Brigadier General and they included, for example, the Director of Supplies at GHQ in France, Evan Carter, future Colonel Commandants of both the ASC and the Royal Army Ordnance Corps and Felix Ready, the future QMG to the Forces.

92. Funnell, 'National Efficiency, Military Accounting and the Business of War', 719–20 and 736.
93. D.R. Stoddart, 'Geography and War: The "New Geography" and the "New Army" in England, 1899–1914', *Political Geography*, Vol. 11, No. 1 (January 1992): 95–97; Funnell, 'National Efficiency, Military Accounting and the Business of War', 736.
94. Correlli Barnett, *Britain and Her Army 1509–1970* (London: Allen Lane, 1970), 367.
95. 'A.C.P.', *The Times*, 14 September 1928, 15. For the complimentary remarks of Sir John French on Ward's work for the War Office Sports Club see 'General French on Harmony at the War Office – The Bonds of Sport and War', *The Times*, 9 April 1913, 10.
96. W.S. Hamer, *The British Army: Civil-Military Relations 1885–1905* (Oxford: Clarendon Press, 1970), 190.
97. Arthur William Moss, *Valiant Crusade: The History of the R.S.P.C.A.* (London: Cassell, 1961), 122. Ward was also instrumental in Britain adopting humane methods of animal slaughter; see *The Times*, 10 October 1912, 3. For the role of the Special Constabulary see Clare Leon, 'Special Constables in the First and Second World Wars', *Police History Society Journal*, Vol 7 (1992): 1–41.
98. See Case Study 5.
99. *Report on the Director General of Voluntary Organisations*, 2.
100. *The Times*, 12 October 1915, 11.
101. *Scheme for Co-ordinating and Regulating Voluntary Work Organizations throughout the United Kingdom*, 2nd ed. (London: HMSO, 1 December 1915).
102. *Report on the Director General of Voluntary Organisations*, 4.
103. *Memorandum from the Office of Director-General of Voluntary Organizations* (London: HMSO, June 1917).
104. *The Times*, 11 October 1915, 11 and minutes of the Croydon War Supplies Clearing House, 12 November and 3 December 1915, Croydon Local Studies Library.
105. Councillor J.E. Rayner, Lord Mayor of Liverpool, 'Live Liverpool: The Great Maritime Metropolis', *TP's Journal*, Vol. 3, No. 35 (12 June 1915): 238.
106. William Crawford Anderson was MP for Attercliffe, Sheffield. A member of the anti-war ILP he was its Chairman between 1911 and 1913 and Chairman of the national Labour Party in 1914 and '15. As such he was a significant figure in calls for peace following the 1917 Russian Revolution, advocating the immediate formation of workers' and soldiers' councils based on the soviet model.
107. *The Times*, 11 October 1915, 11.
108. Williams, *Citizen Soldiers*, 33.
109. *Memorandum from the Office of Director-General of Voluntary Organizations*.
110. *Memorandum from the Office of Director-General of Voluntary Organizations*.
111. *British Journal of Nursing*, Vol. LIX, No. 1530 (28 July 1917).
112. *Report on the Director General of Voluntary Organisations*, 5.
113. Letter to Sir Arthur Stanley, 29 November 1915, quoted in *Report on the Director General of Voluntary Organisations*, 5.
114. *Report on the Director General of Voluntary Organisations*, 5.
115. *Report on the Director General of Voluntary Organisations*, 7.
116. Diary or Log Book, Stanbury Board School Haworth, 17 November 1916; see also Van Emden and Humphries, *All Quiet on the Home Front*, 273–74.
117. *Report on the Director General of Voluntary Organisations*, 23.
118. Alex Ogston, 'Our Wounded: Sphagnum Moss as a Dressing', *The National Review*, Vol. 67 (1916): 872.

119. Minutes of the Croydon War Supplies Clearing House, 29 September 1916, Croydon Local Studies Library.
120. *Report on the Director General of Voluntary Organisations*, 31.
121. *Report on the Director General of Voluntary Organisations*, 36.
122. *Report on the Director General of Voluntary Organisations*, 9.
123. *Report on the Director General of Voluntary Organisations*, 9.
124. Letter to Sir Edward Ward, 26 March 1919, quoted in *Report on the Director General of Voluntary Organisations*, 10.
125. David Bilton, *The Home Front in the Great War: Aspects of the Conflict 1914–1918* (Barnsley: Leo Cooper, 2004), 216.
126. TNA, HO 45/1084/308566, letter to War Charities Committee, 9 June 1916.
127. *Croydon Guild of Help Magazine*, No. 53 (September 1916): 366.
128. *The Times*, 12 October 1915, 11.
129. *Truth*, Vol. LXXIX, No. 2046 (1 March 1916).
130. IWM, WWC, BO1 2/26, DGVO Memorandum 45A.
131. IWM, MISC 88/57/1.
132. 'Prisoners' Parcels: Official Statement to the Editor of the Times', *The Times*, 31 August 1917, 9.
133. *Report on the Joint Committee to Enquire into the Organisation and Methods of the Central Prisoners of War Committee*, 1917, PP, Cd. 8615 (London: HMSO, 1917), 3.
134. *Report on the Central Prisoners of War Committee*, 4 and 8.
135. Ernest Scott, *Official Histories – First World War, Vol. XI: Australia during the War*, 7th ed. (Canberra: 1941), 704 and 719.
136. Sarah Pedersen, 'A Surfeit of Socks?', 51.

NOTES TO CASE STUDY 4

1. Grieves, *Sussex in the First World War*, ix.
2. This and subsequent extracts are taken from 'Croydon War Supplies Clearing House: Summary Report 1914–19' (probably written by Mr H. Terrell Peard, the Chairman and Joint Secretary), Croydon Local Studies Library.

NOTES TO CHAPTER 6

1. This definition has only recently been amended through the 2006 Charities Act to include a test of public benefit.
2. James J. Fishman, 'Charitable Accountability and Reform in Nineteenth-Century England: The Case of the Charity Commission', 80 *Chicago-Kent Law Review*, 724.
3. There had been non-permanent Charity Commissioners since 1818.
4. Cy près means 'as close as possible'. When a gift is made by will or trust and the named recipient of the gift does not exist, has dissolved or no longer conducts the activity for which the gift was made, then the estate or trustee must make the gift to an organisation that comes closest to fulfilling its original purpose.
5. Fishman, 'Charitable Accountability', 749.
6. Michael Chesterman, *Charities, Trusts and Social Welfare* (London: Weidenfeld and Nicolson, 1979), 70.
7. Fishman, 'Charitable Accountability', 770.
8. The actual total was nearer £9 million.

9. TNA, CHAR 3/83.
10. *Charities Emergency Bill*, 1914, Bill 399.
11. TNA, CHAR 3/83. There is a pencilled note on his speech at this point with '?60,000'. The latter would have been a more accurate figure and probably indicates the haste with which this legislation was being drafted.
12. *Proceedings HoC*, Vol. 66, 10 September 1914, Col. 691.
13. TNA, CHAR 3/83.
14. TNA, CHAR 3/83, Soames to Sir Charles Cook, 25 November 1915.
15. TNA, CHAR 3/83, Cook to Soames, 25 November 1915.
16. DeGroot, *Blighty*, 142–43, quoting *The Times* of 11 January and 13 February 1915.
17. Street collections in London were regulated by the Metropolitan Streets Act of 1903.
18. *Truth*, Vol. LXXVI, No. 1978 (18 November 1914): 924.
19. See Chapter 7.
20. *Truth*, 18 November 1914, 925.
21. See 'Beyond the range of ordinary business'.
22. *Charity Organisation Review*, No. 37 (June 1915): 284.
23. Cahalan, *Belgian Refugee Relief*, 465.
24. *Proceedings HoC*, Vol. 72, 16 June 1915, Col. 65.
25. *Proceedings HoC*, Vol. 72, 16 June 1915, Col. 65.
26. *Proceedings HoC*, Vol. 72, 22 June 1915, Col. 1046.
27. *Proceedings HoC*, Vol. 73, 23 July 1915, Col. 1817.
28. *The Times*, 28 July 1915, 9.
29. This was Herbert Cole and suggests the figure may have been quoted in connection with this case. Cole was sentenced to three months imprisonment under the Vagrancy Act in December 1915. Described as an 'author and publisher', Cole ran the bogus Patriots' League, which claimed a connection with the League of Mercy. See *The Times*, 6 December 1915, 3; *Hampshire Telegraph and Post*, 3 December 1915, 4; and 10 December 1915, 4.
30. *Proceedings HoC*, Vol. 80, 17 February 1916, Col. 227–28.
31. Scrutator, 'Wanted Charity Control', *Truth*, Vol. LXXIX, No. 2046 (1 March 1916): 351–52.
32. Though the subsequent committee took evidence from Scotland there appears to have been no intention of including Scotland in the legislation until after the passing of the War Charities Act. This would seem to be for a combination of technical and practical reasons. Scotland has different charity law and therefore would have required separate legislation and, with the possible exception of Dr Sarolea's fund mentioned later, there was far less evidence of potential misuse in Scotland.
33. TNA, HO 45/1084/308566.
34. TNA, HO 45/1084/308566.
35. TNA, HO 45/1084/308566, transcribed from F. Primrose Stevenson's shorthand notes of the meeting.
36. TNA, HO 45/1084/308566, Stevenson's notes.
37. TNA, HO 45/1084/308566, Stevenson's notes.
38. TNA, HO 45/1084/308566, Stevenson's notes.
39. TNA, HO 45/1084/308566, Stevenson's notes.
40. TNA, HO 45/1084/308566, Stevenson's notes.
41. TNA, HO 45/1084/308566, Stevenson's notes.
42. TNA, HO 45/1084/308566.
43. TNA, HO 45/1084/308566.
44. TNA, HO 45/1084/308566, note dated 15 March 1916.
45. *Report of the Committee on War Charities*, 1916, PP, Cd. 8287, vi (London: HMSO, 1916).

46. TNA, HO 45/1084/308566/32, minutes of and memoranda submitted by witnesses to the Committee on War Charities.
47. TNA, HO 45/1084/308566/32.
48. *The Times*, 21 December 1915, 17; 20 January 1916, 5; and 21 January, 1916, 28.
49. TNA, HO 45/1084/308566/32, Robert Donald typescript submission.
50. The Home Office were relatively unimpressed with her ideas, which were written 'entirely from the London point of view' and were impracticable. TNA, HO 45/1084/308566/32, 'AJE' handwritten note.
51. M.H. Mason, 'War Charities Scandals', *English Review*, Vol. 22 (April 1916): 360–72. The article contains a thinly disguised fictional account based on the French Relief Fund case.
52. TNA, HO 45/1084/308566/32.
53. TNA, HO 45/1084/308566/32, minutes of and memoranda submitted by witnesses to the Committee on War Charities, 25 May 1916.
54. TNA, HO 45/1084/308566/32, Samuel typescript submission.
55. The passage in his typescript advocating local control is marked up in the file by Home Office officials.
56. Her father was Denis Carey, Rector of Toynton All Saints, Spilsbury, Lincs. She was born on 28 July 1874 and died in 1953. *The History of the Carey Family of Guernsey*, http://www.careyroots.com, accessed 2/11/06.
57. Cahalan, *Belgian Refugee Relief*, 457.
58. *Truth*, Vol. LXXV, No. 1950 (6 May 1914): 1115.
59. *Truth*, Vol. LXXV, No. 1951 (13 May 1914): 1182.
60. *Truth*, Vol. LXXV, No. 1952 (20 May 1914): 1249.
61. Miss Mason had not long retired from her post as the second woman inspector and first senior women inspector ever appointed by the Local Government Board. Cahalan, *Belgian Refugee Relief*, 458.
62. TNA, HO 45/1084/308566/32, evidence presented to the Committee on War Charities by Robert Donald.
63. TNA, MEPO 2/1675.
64. TNA, MEPO 2/1675.
65. TNA, MEPO 2/1675, report dated 8 January 1915.
66. TNA, MEPO 2/1675, dated 2 October 1915.
67. TNA, MEPO 2/1675, telegram from Chief Inspector Blackwell, Birmingham Police, to Scotland Yard, 12 October 1916.
68. TNA, MEPO 2/1675.
69. TNA, MEPO 2/1675, letter to the Secretary of the London Chamber of Commerce, 15 November 1915.
70. *Truth*, Vol. LXXVIII, No. 2032 (1 December 1915): 877.
71. *Truth*, Vol. LXXVIII, No. 2032 (1 December 1915): 877.
72. The son of a jeweller from Gosport, John Thomas Curry was born on 10 November 1871. He had joined the Metropolitan Police in February 1893, became a Detective in 1898 and was promoted to Detective Sergeant in 1902 and DI in 1911. He left the force in November 1919 on a pension of £300 a year, his record marked as 'exemplary'. Metropolitan Police Collection, information by e-mail, 30/4/10. TNA MEPO 4/346 and 4/381.
73. TNA, MEPO 2/1675, report dated 18 November 1915.
74. TNA, MEPO 2/1675.
75. *The Times*, 26 August 1916, 3.
76. TNA, HO 45/1084/308566/32, minutes of and memoranda submitted by witnesses to the Committee on War Charities, evidence submitted by DI Curry.
77. *Report of the Committee on War Charities*, PP, 1916, Cmd. 8287, vi, 425.
78. *The Times*, 30 December 1915, 5; and 5 January 1916, 5.

79. TNA, BT 31/22964/141418.
80. TNA, MEPO 3/249.
81. The Met did not employ its first official female detective until the appointment of Inspector Lillian Wyles to the CID in 1922/23. However women detectives were 'often temporarily employed for special work' at this date; *The Times*, 30 December 1915, 5.
82. DeGroot says that the Anti-German League later changed its name to the British Empire Union but he is confused because there were *two* Anti-German Leagues. In addition to Chatterton's enterprise there was the British Anti-German League based in Birmingham. In many ways it looked nearly as bogus and also used the 'shilling' tactic. *Truth* suggested it was a 'silly game' and 'the latest device for extracting money from the pockets of patriotic simpletons' (3 February 1915). A group of its supporters later began the British Empire Union. The BEU was one of the bodies that later metamorphosed into the British Union of Fascists.
83. *Report of the Committee on War Charities*, PP, 1916, Cmd. 8287, vi, 425.
84. Originally, seven million flags were ordered but this was later increased to fourteen million.
85. *Daily Graphic*, 11 November 1915.
86. TNA, TS 18/262, report dated 9 December 1915.
87. 'An Anonymous War Fund', *Truth*, Vol. LXXVII, No. 1989 (27 January): 167; and 10 February 1915.
88. 'Entre Nous', *Truth*, Vol. LXXVII, No. 1995 (17 March 1915): 408.
89. Scrutator, 'F.R.F. Resignations', *Truth*, Vol. LXXVIII, No. 2019 (1 September 1915).
90. 'F.R.F. Resignations', 342.
91. *The Times*, 1 December 1915, 6.
92. *The Times*, 1 December 1915, 6.
93. *Truth*, Vol. LXXVIII, No. 2033 (8 December 1915): 919–20.
94. TNA, TS 18/262, report to Chief Constable of Lancashire, dated 12 January 1916.
95. TNA, TS 18/262, report to Chief Constable of Lancashire.
96. TNA, TS 18/262, report to Chief Constable of Lancashire.
97. TNA, TS 18/262, letter from Herbert Morris, Secretary of the Charity Commission to Treasury Solicitor, 24 October 1916.
98. *The Times*, 1912 *passim*.
99. There is an excellent description of the day in MacDonagh's *In London during the Great War*, 114.
100. TNA, TS 18/262, letter of 16 September 1916.
101. At the commencement of the Second World War Dickinson attempted to promote a very similar venture, the Anglo-French Ambulance Corps. See *Proceedings HoC*, 5th Series, Vol. 355, 7 December 1939, Col. 831. The Corps operated but under different management with Colonel J. Baldwin-Webb MP as Honorary Secretary; *Flight* (30 May 1940): 495.
102. TNA, MEPO 3/252.
103. *Report of Queen Alexandra's Field Force Fund 1918* (London: William Brown and Co, 1919).
104. TNA, MEPO 3/252.
105. TNA, MEPO 3/252.
106. TNA, MEPO 3/252.
107. TNA, MEPO 3/252.
108. TNA, MEPO 3/252.
109. TNA, MEPO 3/252.

110. TNA, MEPO 3/252.
111. The papers on this case were closed until 1993, those on the French Relief Fund until the following year.
112. ICAEW Fraud Advisory Panel, *Charity Fraud: Occasional Paper* (London: ICAEW, 2008), 2.
113. Jeffrey Reznick, *Healing the Nation: Soldiers and the Culture of Caregiving in Britain during the Great War* (Manchester: Manchester University Press, 2004), 34.
114. *Report of the Committee on War Charities*, PP 1916, Cmd. 8287, 425.
115. *Report of the Committee on War Charities*, PP 1916, Cmd. 8287, 425.
116. Regarding audited accounts, this regulation is actually tougher than today's law on charities where they are only required to submit accounts for external scrutiny if their income is above £25,000, the equivalent of about £500 in 1916.
117. *War Charities Act*, 1916
118. TNA HO 45/1084/308566, letter of 13 June 1916.
119. TNA, HO 45/1084/308566, minute of 26 June 1916.
120. TNA, HO 45/1084/308566/32, letter of 2 August 1916.
121. TNA, HO 45/1084/308566/32, letter of 9 August 1916.
122. For example the minutes of CWSCH.
123. Voluntary Action History Society, *The Origins of Flag Days*, http://www.vahs.org.uk/vahs/papers/vahs3.pdf , accessed 4/1/07, 10; TNA, HO 45/104546/160443.
124. *Proceedings HoC*, Vol. 85, 2 August 1916, Col. 454.
125. *Proceedings HoC*, Vol. 85, 2 August 1916, Col. 457.
126. *Proceedings HoC*, Vol. 85, 2 August 1916, Col. 459.
127. *Proceedings HoC*, Vol. 85, 2 August 1916, Cols. 462–63.
128. *Proceedings HoC*, Vol. 85, 14 August 1916, Col. 1603.
129. It was also not extended to Scotland until March 1919.
130. *Proceedings House of Lords*, 5th Series, Vol. 23, 16 August 1916, Col. 72.
131. *Proceedings HoL*, Vol. 23, 16 August 1916, Col. 75.
132. See *Sixty-Seventh Report of the Charity Commissioners*, PP, Cmd. 621.
133. LMA, LCC/PC/CHA/1/4, decision of 11 July 1917.
134. The LCC were quite pedantic on this point. The Waldensian Church Missions were told they would have to register as they stated that their appeal was for an orphanage in Italy that would be a war memorial. If they simply said it was an orphanage then they would not have been required to register. LMA, LCC/MIN 8349 (Vol. 15), Case No. 916.
135. LMA, LCC/PC/CHA/1/2, War Charities Act, 1916 – Particulars of the work done, decisions of 10, 24 and 26 October 1916 and 11 September 1917.
136. TNA, HO 45/18406/309078/49.
137. LMA, LCC/PC/CHA/1/3, letter of 21 August 1916.
138. *66th Report of the Charity Commissioners for England and Wales* (London: HMSO, 1919), 9–10.
139. LMA, LCC/PC/CHA/1/3, note to LCC by Suffield Mylius, Metropolitan Police, 21 August 1916.
140. LMA, LCC/PC/CHA/1/3, note to LCC by Suffield Mylius.
141. LMA, LCC/MIN 8337 (Vol. 3).
142. Somewhat surprisingly this same issue has been raised with regard to modern service charities with trustees on active service; see Kaye Wiggins, '"Governance Risk" for Military Charities—Organisations Served Mainly by Trustees on Front-line Service Might Not Be Being Properly Scrutinised, Experts Warn', *Third Sector* (17 August 2010).

143. LMA, LCC/MIN 8338 (Vol. 4), Case No. 638 – Koval, Ludmar, Lutsk and District Benevolent Society, report by H. Alker Tripp, 5 May 1917.
144. Report by H. Alker Tripp, 5 July 1917.
145. LMA, LCC/MIN 8347 (Vol. 13), Case No. 663; and LMA, LCC/MIN 8350 (Vol. 16), Case No. 7.
146. LMA, LCC/MIN 8338 (Vol. 4), Case No. 675 – British-American (Overseas) Field Hospital.
147. There appears to have been a genuine Petronite Syndicate in existence in Hull in 1892. Based at 9 Marmaduke Street their manager was a Mr M. Mackay; see http://www.genuki.org.uk/big/eng/YKS/Misc/Transcriptions/ERY/Hull1892StreetsM.html, accessed 9/1/2011.
148. *Proceedings HoC*, Vol. 234, 28 January 1930, Cols. 934–36, quoted in Elizabeth Macadam, *The New Philanthropy: A Study of the Relations between the Statutory and Voluntary Social Services* (London: George Allen and Unwin, 1934), 37. It was none other than Herbert Samuel who 'talked up' the effects of the Act and it is possible that he might have been including those who were uncertain whether they required registration or not (for example whether their appeal was public) which could have pushed the total up to this kind of figure.
149. *66th Report of the Charity Commissioners for England and Wales* (London: HMSO, 1919), 9.
150. The five were: the Khaki Prisoners of War Fund; the Stick Crutch Fund; the International Bible Institute War Relief Fund; the British American (Overseas) Field Hospital (LMA, LCC/PC/CHA/1/2) and the Bob Sievier Charity Fund (TNA, HO 45/18406/319028/17).
151. TNA, HO 45/18406/319028/19; LMA, LCC/MIN 8338 (Vol. 4), Case No. 591, War Lectures Committee.
152. Lady Randolph Churchill, *Women's War Work* (London: Arthur Pearson, 1916), Chapter 6.
153. TNA, HO 45/18406/319028/42, letter from Sir Edward Troup to Sir Edward Henry.
154. TNA, MEPO 2/1732, report of 6 November 1917.
155. Joe Saxton, Gimme, *Gimme, Gimme! A guide for organisations new to fundraising or just starting out raising money* (London, nfp Synergy, 2011), 12.
156. TNA, MEPO 2/1729, Inspector Curry's report of 25 September 1917; LMA, LCC/MIN 8347 (Vol. 13), Case No. 643 – Westminster Entertainments for Wounded Soldiers and Case No. 691 – Red Star Society.
157. *The Times*, 19 October 1917, 3.
158. TNA, MEPO 2/1729, signed statement by Mrs Hodge.
159. TNA, MEPO 2/1729, letter of 31 August 1917.
160. TNA, MEPO 2/1729, report of 25 September 1917.
161. *The Times*, 19 October 1917, 3.
162. TNA, MEPO 2/1729, report of 31 October 1917.
163. TNA, MEPO 2/1729, letter of 9 March 1918.
164. *The Times*, 1 November 1919, 4. 1919 was the year of one of Marshall Hall's greatest triumphs when 'the great defender' obtained an acquittal in the case of *Rex v Ronald Light*, known as the Green Bicycle Murder.
165. TNA, MEPO 2/1729, letter to Reginald Poole.
166. *64th Report of the Charity Commissioners for England and Wales* (London: HMSO, 1917), 8.
167. TNA, HO 45/319028/54, memorandum dated 31 August 1925.
168. PP *Report of the Home Office Departmental Committee on the Supervision of Charities* (Cunliffe Committee), 1927, vii, Cmd. 2823, 14.

169. TNA, HO 45/309028/49.
170. LMA, LCC/MIN 8350 (Vol. 16), Case No. 21a.
171. Helen McCartney, *Citizen Soldiers: The Liverpool Territorials in the First World War* (Studies in the Social and Cultural History of Modern Warfare 22) (Cambridge: Cambridge University Press, 2005), 249–50; see also William Philpott, *Bloody Victory: The Sacrifice on the Somme* (London: Abacus, 2009), 551.
172. See Storr, *Excluded from the Record*, 216–20.
173. PP *64th Annual Report of the Charity Commission*, 1917–18, viii, Cd. 8521, 8.
174. Cunliffe Committee, 5.
175. Cunliffe Committee, 24 and 27.
176. Cunliffe Committee, 31.
177. Cunliffe Committee, 43.
178. TNA, HO 45/16220.
179. See *The Times*, 30 November, 1939, 4; 12 January, 1940, 4; 13 January, 1940, 3. Hutchings organised the DGVO in exactly the same way as Ward.
180. Geoffrey Finlayson, 'A Moving Frontier: Voluntarism and the State in British Social Welfare 1911–1949', *Twentieth Century British History*, Vol. 1, No. 2 (1990): 195.
181. Finlayson, 'Moving Frontier', 196.
182. Andrew Latcham, 'Journeys End: Ex Servicemen and the State during and after the Great War' (PhD diss., Oxford, 1997), 16.
183. See Matthew Hilton and James McKay (eds.), *The Ages of Voluntarism, How We Got to the Big Society* (Oxford: Oxford University Press, 2011), notably the chapters by Nicholas Deakin and Justin Davis Smith, 'Labour, Charity and Voluntary Action: The Myth of Hostility' and Virginia Berridge and Alex Mold, 'Professionalisation, New Social Movements and Voluntary Action in the 1960s and 1970s'.
184. TNA, HO 279/73, War Charities Act 1940, Home Office Comments on Goodman Committee Recommendations, memorandum dated 24 October 1977.
185. TNA, HO 45/319028/54, memorandum dated 31 August 1925.
186. ICAEW, *Charity Fraud*, 2.
187. 'Watchdog Failing to Halt Charity Fraud Say MPs', *Independent*, 7 August 2000; Sophie Hudson, 'Parliamentary Motion Calls on Police to Tackle Bogus Charity Collectors', *Third Sector*, 9 September 2010.
188. 'Five Charged in Charity Fraud Case', *Independent*, 28 August 2002; *Newcastle Chronicle*, 2002, *passim*.
189. 'E-Mail Scams Exploit Haiti Quake', BBC News, 16 February 2010.
190. 'E-Mail Scams Exploit Haiti Quake'.
191. Cahalan, *Belgian Refugee Relief*, 496.

NOTES TO CASE STUDY 5

1. *Percy Noble Papers*, Nos. 451–464, 481 and 1514.
2. TNA, WO 95/28, QMG War Diary, 12 November 1915.
3. Haig to Ward, 18 November 1915, *Report of the Work of the Camps Library*, PP 1919, Cmd. 174 (London: HMSO, 1919), 3.
4. *Report of the Work of the Camps Library*, 9.
5. *Report of the Work of the Camps Library*, 9. The existence of the *Guide to Germany* was first mentioned in 1915 by W.E. Dowding in his report 'The

Romance of Voluntary Effort: Part III – For Our Soldiers and Sailors', *TP's Journal* (15 May 1915).
6. *Daily Telegraph*, 28 January 1915. Quoted in Theodore Wesley Koch, *Books in Camp, Trench and Hospital* (London: Dent, 1917), reprinted from the *Library Journal* (July–August 1917): 7.
7. Koch, *Books in Camp*, 7.
8. *Report of the Work of the Camps Library*, 12.
9. Ysenda Maxtone Graham, *The Real Mrs Miniver: Jan Struther's Story* (London: John Murray, 2001), 20. Struther was Eva Ansthruther's daughter and Maxtone Graham is her great-granddaughter. I am also grateful to Robert Maxtone-Graham, Dame Eva's grandson, for further information.

NOTES TO CHAPTER 7

1. It is worthwhile first to give a comparison between the value of money from the First World War period and today to give some idea of the scale of voluntary effort. In 2013 £1 from 1914 would be worth about £72 but because of wartime inflation, £1 from 1916 would equal around £50 today and by 1918 would only be worth £38. To put it another way the Disasters Emergency Committee Tsunami Earthquake Appeal (following the Asian tsunami of Christmas 2004) raised £372 million. A similar effort in 1914 would have raised £5.2 million, almost what was raised for the National Relief Fund alone. In most cases hereafter I use the 'median' comparison from 1916 of £1 equals £50. These figures are calculated against the retail price index. If one used average earnings instead the comparisons would be around £1 = £300 and so the comparative amounts quoted hereafter would need to be multiplied approximately sixfold. The latter would be more accurate for the *value* of giving (or the cost to the individual giver), the former for its *purchasing power*. Measuring Worth, http://www.measuringworth.com, accessed 10/4/13.
2. Of this, actual donations were £16,510,023; *Red Cross Reports*, Nos. 58 and 70. At the commencement of the war the British Red Cross Society and the Order of St John established a joint committee to administer the *Times* Fund and coordinate their activities.
3. Messenger, *Call to Arms*, 469. His source is the 12th edition of the *Encyclopaedia Britannica*, Vol. XXXII (London and New York: 1922), 1062. This entry was written by Agnes Conway, Hon Curator of the Women's Work section of the Imperial War Museum whose research was both extensive and intensive and so this estimate can be viewed with some confidence.
4. J.G. Fuller, *Troop Morale and Popular Culture in the British and Dominion Armies 1914–18* (Oxford: Clarendon Press, 1990), 83.
5. Snape, *God and the British Soldier*, 208–9.
6. Deborah Cohen, *The War Come Home: Disabled Veterans in Britain and Germany, 1914–1939* (Berkeley: University of California Press, 2001), 135–36.
7. Cohen, *War Come Home*, 119.
8. A rough and ready calculation of the number of charities that were newly created compared to ones that already existed and turned their activities to war-related work is provided in Kelynack's *Pro Patria*. Probably the most comprehensive contemporary reference to wartime charities, Kelynack includes 132 organisations in his survey of which forty (30 percent) were pre-existing. If this were an accurate reflection then there would have been just over 23,000 war-related charities (it almost certainly was not, as Kelynack only includes organisations with national coverage).

9. This is a sensible date as the figures include Scotland which did not come under the auspices of the Act until March 1919.
10. PP *61st Report of the Charity Commissioners of England and Wales*, 1914, xv, Cd. 7310, 785.
11. In contrast, Australia produced an excellent official history of wartime charitable effort: Ernest Scott, *Official Histories – First World War, Vol: XI: Australia during the War*, 7th ed. (Sydney: Angus and Robertson, 1941). This demonstrates that the total raised in Australia by those organisations officially recorded was £13,802,301 or £2.80 per head of population. These figures are useful to compare with my estimates for the UK.
12. Dowding, 'Study of the War-Giving', 630.
13. C.F.G. Masterman, 'The Temper of the People', *Contemporary Review*, Vol. 108 (July 1915): 7.
14. Masterman, 'Temper', 7.
15. The book was probably abandoned due to his ill health as Dowding died in October 1917.
16. Dowding, 'Study of the War-Giving', 628–30.
17. *Proceedings of the House of Commons* (Hansard), 5th Series, Vol. 76, 8 December 1915, Col. 1391.
18. *Truth*, Vol. LXXVIII, No. 2032 (1 December 1915): 873.
19. TNA, MEPO 2/1675, report by Detective Inspector Curry, 18 November 1915. It is unclear whether this is the police source used by Anderson and *Truth*. The statement was made by Treasury Counsel Herbert Muskett in the case of Millie Back (see Chapter 6, 'Beyond the range of ordinary business') quoted in *The Times* report 'Twenty Millions for War Funds', 23 November 1915, 5. Another estimate was one of 'over £30 million' raised by early summer 1916, quoted by E.C. Price in the *Charity Organisation Review* (August 1916): 47. It is possible, though perhaps unlikely, that the source of all of these estimates was Dowding's calculation.
20. *Daily Chronicle*, 15 February 1916.
21. Another example is Huddersfield. There were twenty-five war-related charities in Huddersfield in November 1915 when the local newspaper contended 'that Huddersfield stands at the head of all the municipalities in the country in the amount of money raised on behalf of war funds.' *Huddersfield Chronicle*, 13 November 1915, quoted in Pearce, *Comrades of Conscience*, 89.
22. Wilson, *Myriad Faces of War*, 775.
23. Jay Winter, 'Army and Society: The Demographic Context', in Beckett and Simpson, *A Nation in Arms*, 208. Winter is supported by other authorities including Bernard Waites, *A Class Society at War: England 1914–18* (Berg: Leamington Spa, 1987) and Alastair Reid, 'World War 1 and the Working Class in Britain', in *Total War and Social Change*, ed. Arthur Marwick (London and Basingstoke: Macmillan, 1988).
24. Beth Egan, *The Widow's Might: How Charities Depend on the Poor* (London: Social Market Foundation, 2001), 14; University of Manchester study, http://www.manchester.ac.uk/aboutus/news/display/?id=9782, accessed 25/5/13.
25. John Morgan, 'Financing Public Goods by Means of Lotteries', *The Review of Economic Studies*, Vol. 67, No. 4 (October 2000): 777–78.
26. Quoted in Frank Prochaska, *Christianity and Social Service in Modern Britain: The Disinherited Spirit* (Oxford: Oxford University Press, 2006), 20.
27. Prochaska, *Christianity and Social Service*, 20–21.
28. Tony Allen, in his pamphlet *Charity Flags and Flag Days 1914–1918* (York: Holgate Publications, 1999), 2, says £25 million was raised through this means during the war though he does not say from where this figure comes.

If true, it would again suggest that my final minimum total could be a significant underestimate.

29. Armstrong, 'Kentish Rural Society during the First World War', 123.
30. The figure for Glasgow is estimated as follows: Figures given in the *Glasgow Herald* are that the city had raised £4,000,000 by the end of the war. However, this included the monetary value of 'clothing, food, and comforts despatched to the troops' which was £240,275 after two years (9 percent). They also included some, though relatively few, funds raised nationally across the whole of Scotland (like those for Belgian refugees). I have reduced the overall figure by £500,000 (12.5 percent) to compensate. 'War Philanthropy: Glasgow Raises £4,000,000', *Glasgow Herald*, 26 December 1919, 3. The article concludes that they consider the overall figures to be an underestimate as the figure to the end of 1915 excluded 'private committees ... connected with Churches and individual regiments' and 'in kind' contributions. The former could be quite considerable as, in some areas, they accounted for up to 20 percent of charities.
31. W.E. Dowding discussed this issue in an unpublished article draft ('Town or Country: Which Is the More Generous?', IWM, WWC BO2 49/4) concluding that the closer personal relationships existing in rural areas might be more effective.
32. 'War Philanthropy', *Glasgow Herald*; and John S. Samuel, *European War: Statement of the Funds Raised in Glasgow for War Relief Purposes from August 1914 to December 1915 Prepared for the Lord Provost* (Glasgow: City Chambers, 1916).
33. IWM WWC, BO2 52/17, W.E. Dowding draft of unpublished book on flag days; Thomas Dunlop, 'Go-Ahead Glasgow: The generosity of a great city', *TP's Journal*, Vol. 2, No. 25, 3 April 1915, 323. Dowding also indicated that Glasgow newspaper funds were especially effective. W.E. Dowding, 'The Romance of Voluntary Effort – Part VI: How the Press Has Helped', 260.
34. Gregory, *The Last Great War*, 228.
35. Glasgow was also one of the main centres of anti-war opposition and of the shop stewards movement.
36. The British population was around forty-six million, including Ireland (4.3 million) which, admittedly, is something of a 'special case'.
37. It is also noticeable how close this amount comes to the Australian figure of £2.80 per head that we noted earlier.
38. Sheffield, *Leadership in the Trenches*, 82.
39. Sheffield, *Leadership in the Trenches*, 83.
40. The 'Glasgow calculation' is £240,000 ÷ 24 (months) × 52 (months, the duration of war) ÷ 784,000 (population of Glasgow) × 46,000,000 (total population of GB) = £30,510,204.
41. Turner, *Dear Old Blighty*, 134.
42. *63rd Report of the Charity Commission for England and Wales*, 1916 (London: HMSO, 1916).
43. Searle, *A New England?*, 300.
44. Robert H. Bremner, *American Philanthropy* (Chicago: University of Chicago Press, 1960), 169–70.
45. Dowding, 'Study of the War-Giving', 628.
46. Geoffrey Finlayson, *Citizen, State and Social Welfare in Britain 1830–1990* (Oxford: Clarendon Press, 1994), 209.
47. Keith Laybourn, *The Guild of Help and the Changing Face of Edwardian Philanthropy* (Lewiston/Queenstown/Lampeter: Edwin Mellen Press, 1994), 130; W.E. Dowding, 'The Romance of Voluntary Effort – Part 3: For Our Soldiers and Sailors', *TP's Journal*, Vol. 3, No. 31 (15 May 1915): 119; and Bowater, 'Busy Birmingham', 34.

48. Gregory, *The Last Great War*, 98.
49. Cohen, *War Come Home*, 30.
50. For example, DeGroot, *Blighty*, 64.
51. W.F. Markwick, *Stamford and the Great War* (Stamford: Dolby Brothers, 1919), 23.
52. William Herbert Scott, *Leeds in the Great War 1914–1918: A Book of Remembrance* (Leeds: Leeds Libraries and Arts Committee, 1923), 35.
53. Michael J. Moore, 'Social Work and Social Welfare: The Organization of Philanthropic Resources in Britain, 1900–1914', *Journal of British Studies*, Vol. 16, No. 2 (Spring 1977): 93.
54. TNA, CHAR 4/1 to 4/21, *Registers of Individual Charities*.
55. Charity Commission Register, http://www.charitycommission.gov.uk/find-charities, accessed 14/6/10.
56. Martin Stephen, *The Price of Pity: Poetry, History and Myth in the Great War* (London: Leo Cooper, 1996), 99.
57. G.D.H. Cole, *Labour in War Time* (London: G. Bell and Sons, 1915), 95, quoted in Graham Wootton, *The Politics of Influence: British Ex-Service-men, Cabinet Decisions and Cultural Change* (London: Routledge and Kegan Paul, 1963), 33.
58. Richard Holmes emphasises this point in several of his books, notably *Acts of War: The Behaviour of Men in Battle* (London: Cassell, 2003), first published as *Firing Line* (1985).
59. Janet S.K. Watson, *Fighting Different Wars: Experience, Memory, and the First World War in Britain* (Cambridge: Cambridge University Press, 2004), 300; and *The Wipers Times* (London: Little Books, 2006), 105, 119 and 133.
60. Nicholas Hiley, '"You Can't Believe a Word You Read": Newspaper Reading in the British Expeditionary Force, 1914–18', in *Studies in Newspaper and Periodical History, 1994 Annual,* eds. Michael Harris and Tom O'Malley (Westport, CT: Greenwood Press, 1996), 99–100.
61. Notably expressed in 'War Relief and War Service'.
62. Masterman, 'Temper', 10–11.
63. Letter to the *Daily Telegraph*, 21 September 1915. This view is supported by Bruce Scates, 'The Unknown Sock Knitter: Voluntary Work, Emotional Labour, Bereavement and the Great War', *Labour History* (Australia), Vol. 81 (2001): 29–50.
64. Dowding, 'Study of the War-Giving', 632–33.
65. Cohen, *War Come Home*, 17.
66. Cohen, *War Come Home*, 8 and 214.
67. Gregory, *The Last Great War*, 135.
68. Quoted in Max Arthur, *Forgotten Voices of the Great War* (London: Ebury Press, 2002), 172.
69. Snape, *God and the British Soldier*, 209.
70. Snape, *God and the British Soldier*, 219; and T. Lever, *Clayton of Toc H* (London: John Murray, 1971), 70.
71. Snape, *God and the British Soldier*, 213.
72. Snape, *God and the British Soldier*, 216. Snape also quotes examples from D.H. Barber, *The Church Army in World War Two* (London: SPCK, 1946), 8, and from Mass Observation, *Report on Feelings about the Salvation Army*, Mass Observation Archives, University of Sussex, FR 1421.
73. H.M. Walbrook, *Hove and the Great War: A Record and a Review Together with the Roll of Honour and List of Distinctions* (Hove: Cliftonville Press, 1920).
74. IWM, MISC 16, Item 351, letters from soldiers to a small girl who had sent them knitted comforts.

75. Frederick William Harvey, *Comrades in Captivity: A Record of Life in Seven German Prison Camps* (London: Sidgwick and Jackson, 1920), 65.
76. Great Chart Letters, Vol. 2.
77. Great Chart Letters, Vol. 5.
78. Great Chart Letters, Vol. 5.
79. Grieves, *Sussex in the First World War*, 76–84.
80. Jessica Meyer (ed.), *British Popular Culture and the First World War* (History of Warfare Vol. 48) (Leiden and Boston: Brill, 2008), 8.
81. Peter Simkins, 'Everyman at War: Recent Interpretations of the Front Line Experience', in *The First World War and British Military History*, ed. Brian Bond (Oxford: Clarendon, 1991), 302.
82. Jay Winter, 'Popular Culture in Wartime Britain', in *The Arts, Entertainment and Propaganda 1914–1918*, eds. Aviel Roshwald and Richard Sites (Cambridge: Cambridge University Press, 1999), 347–48.

NOTES TO CASE STUDY 6

1. Alan Borg, *War Memorials from Antiquity to the Present* (London: Leo Cooper, 1991), ix.
2. Gregory, *The Last Great War*, 257.
3. Significant contributions include Jay Winter, *Sites of Memory, Sites of Mourning: The Great War in European Cultural History* (Cambridge: Cambridge University Press, 1995); Catherine Moriarty, 'Private Grief and Public Remembrance: British First World War Memorials', in *War and Memory in the Twentieth Century*, eds. Martin Evans and Ken Lunn (Oxford: Berg, 1997), 125–42; Mark Connelly, *The Great War Memory and Ritual: Commemoration in the City and East London 1916–1939* (Woodbridge: Royal Historical Society and Rochester: Boydell Press, 2002); and Dan Todman, *The Great War: Myth and Memory* (London and New York: Hambledon and London, 2005).
4. Moriarty, 'Private Grief and Public Remembrance', 127–28.
5. MacDonagh, *In London during the Great War*, 146; and Martin Pugh, *We Danced All Night: A Social History of Britain between the Wars* (London: Bodley Head, 2008), 6–7.
6. Allyson Booth, *Postcards from the Trenches: Negotiating the Space between Modernism and the First World War* (Oxford: Oxford University Press, 1997), 22.
7. Gregory, *The Last Great War*, 255.
8. Mark Connelly, 'The Biggest Single Piece of Work since the Pharaohs: The Work of the Imperial War Graves Commission 1917–39', paper given at the National Army Museum, 1 November 2008.
9. Gregory, *The Last Great War*, 261.
10. Moriarty, 'Private Grief and Public Remembrance', 127.
11. Mitchinson, *Saddleworth*, 57. They got the cenotaph, an impressive sandstone needle erected on the moors above the town.
12. This was certainly true in Todmorden; see Lee, *Todmorden and the Great War*, 201–16.
13. Moriarty, 'Private Grief and Public Remembrance', 127.
14. See for example the Dover War Memorial Project, http://www.doverwarmemorialproject.org.uk/Casualties/MissingNames/CasualtiesMissing.htm, or those in Craven or Abergele, http://www.allbusiness.com/government/government-bodies-offices-regional/14049692-1.html and http://www.rhyljournal.co.uk/news/87305/abergele-considers-new-war-memorial-names.aspx. All accessed 21/4/10.

15. *The Hall in the Garden: Freemasons' Hall and Its Place in London* (Hersham: Ian Allen, 2006), 59–62. Fund-raising events included the largest sit-down meal ever served, to 7,000 people at Olympia in August 1925.

NOTES TO CHAPTER 8

1. Stevenson, *British Society 1914–1945*, 58.
2. John A. Fairlie, *British War Administration* (Carnegie Endowment for International Peace, Division of Economics and History, Preliminary Economic Studies of the War No. 8) (New York: Oxford University Press, 1919), 271–95.
3. Jose Harris, *Private Lives, Public Spirit: Britain 1870–1914* (Oxford: Oxford University Press, 1993), 11–12.
4. Rodney Lowe, 'Government', in *The First World War in British History*, eds. Stephen Constantine, Maurice W. Kirby and Mary B. Rose (London, New York, Sydney and Auckland: Edward Arnold, 1995), 29.
5. Rex Pope, *War and Society in Britain 1899–1948* (London and New York: Longman, 1991), 31.
6. *History of the Ministry of Munitions*, Vol. VII, Pt. 1, quoted in Marwick, *Deluge*, 166.
7. DeGroot, *Blighty*, 79. Thane agrees that intervention was 'haphazard rather than planned'; *The Foundation of the Welfare State* (London: Longman, 1982), 136, as does Stevenson who characterises intervention as ad hoc and 'dictated largely by expediency, with little thought for long-term consequences or social implications'; *British Society 1914–1945*, 67.
8. Marwick, *Deluge*, 156.
9. John M. Bourne, *Britain and the Great War 1914–1918* (London: Edward Arnold, 1989), 192–93.
10. Gregory, *The Last Great War*, 110.
11. Gregory, *The Last Great War*, 110–11.
12. Robb, *British Culture and the First World War*, 77.
13. Marwick, *Deluge*, 174.
14. John Holford, *Reshaping Labour: Organisation, Work and Politics: Edinburgh in the Great War and After* (London: Croom Helm, 1988), 152.
15. Holford, *Reshaping Labour*, 105.
16. Noel Whiteside, 'Concession, Coercion or Cooperation? State Policy and Industrial Unrest in Britain, 1916–1920', in *Strikes, Social Conflict and the First World War, an International Perspective*, eds. Leopold Haimson and Giulio Sapelli (Milan: Feltrinelli, 1992), 110.
17. Bourne, *Britain and the Great War*, 195.
18. See Harris, *Private Lives, Public Spirit*, especially Chapter 7, 'Society and the State', for the national picture. For a local example of this relationship, see Helen Elizabeth Meller's study of Bristol, *Leisure and the Changing City, 1870–1914* (London: Routledge and Kegan Paul, 1976), 74–77. Bernard Harris considers the development of state intervention in social welfare in *Origins of the British Welfare State*, Chapter 2. He also discusses the historical relationship between state provision and voluntary action in 'Voluntary Action and the State in Historical Perspective', *Voluntary Sector Review*, Vol. 1, No. 1, 25–40. I would agree with his view that there has been a 'partnership' between the state and voluntary action for at least 200 years, though the nature and degree of that partnership has changed.
19. Kidd, *State, Society and the Poor*, 108.
20. Gordon Phillips, 'The Social Impact', in *The First World War in British History*, eds. Constantine et al., 140.

21. John Turner, 'Change and Inertia in Politics', in *Change and Inertia: Britain under the Impact of the First World War*, eds. Hartmut Berghoff and Robert von Friedeburg (Bodenheim: Philo Cop, 1998), 159.
22. Turner, 'Change and Inertia', 158.
23. Turner, 'Change and Inertia', 158–59.
24. Keith Laybourn, 'Social Welfare: Public and Private, 1900–1939', in *A Companion to Early Twentieth-Century Britain* (Blackwell Companions to British History), ed. Christopher John Wrigley (Oxford: Blackwell Publishers, 2003), 373–87.
25. Laybourn, 'Social Welfare: Public and Private', 374.
26. Robert Humphreys, *Poor Relief and Charity 1869–1945: The London Charity Organisation Society* (London and Basingstoke: Macmillan, 2001), 143. The COS eventually became the Family Welfare Association in 1946. For a more nuanced view of the changes in the COS see Philips, 'The Social Impact', 133–38.
27. Laybourn, 'Social Welfare: Public and Private', 379. He also makes some errors of fact such as asserting that the Soldiers' and Sailors' Family Association was a new body formed during the war when it had been in existence since 1885.
28. Laybourn, *The Guild of Help*, 150–51.
29. Lowe, 'Government', 42.
30. Finlayson, 'A Moving Frontier', 184.
31. See Jose Harris, 'Political Thought and the Welfare State 1870–1940: An Intellectual Framework for British Social Policy', *Past and Present*, No. 135 (May 1992): 134–35. Harris sees the 1920s as being one of 'great vitality and innovation in the sphere of voluntary service and in co-operation between public and voluntary sectors.'
32. Prochaska, *The Voluntary Impulse*, 76.
33. Jay Winter, *The Great War and the British People* (Basingstoke: Palgrave Macmillan, 2003), 21.
34. Finlayson, *Citizen, State and Social Welfare*, 221.
35. Finlayson, 'Moving Frontier', 202.
36. Quoted in Elizabeth Macadam, *The New Philanthropy: A Study of the Relations between the Statutory and Voluntary Social Services* (London: Allen and Unwin, 1934), 67–68.
37. There is, for example, no reference to the DGVO in the standard history of the NCSS; Margaret Brasnett, *Voluntary Social Action: A History of the National Council of Social Service 1919–1969* (London: NCSS, 1969). Some evidence of links is provided by the fact that Sir Edward Ward had worked closely with the Social Welfare Association for London before the war on the employment of ex-soldiers; see *The Times*, 6 December 1913, 4.
38. See Moore, 'Social Work and Social Welfare', 85–104.
39. Liam Delaney and Emily Keaney, 'Sport and Social Capital in the United Kingdom: Statistical Evidence from National and International Survey Data', Department for Culture, Media and Sport (December 2005): 3. Pierre Bourdieu is more explicit on this issue and his ideas here form an important adjunct to Putnam's (who somewhat neglects this point). Bourdieu, *Distinction: A Social Critique of the Judgement of Taste* (London: Routledge and Kegan Paul, 1984).
40. Eric J. Leed, 'Class and Disillusionment in World War I', *Journal of Modern History*, Vol. 50 (1978): 695–96.
41. Sheffield, *Leadership in the Trenches*, 125; and Wilfred Trotter, *Instincts of the Herd in War and Peace*, 1919, available at http://www.onread.com/book/Instincts-of-the-Herd-in-Peace-And-War-179334, accessed 23/5/10, especially 201–11. Trotter contrasts England with Germany in this respect.

42. TNA, NSC 7/38.
43. TNA, NSC 7/38.
44. MacDonagh provides a vivid description; *In London during the Great War*, 320–21. The idea was revived to help raise funds for World Refugee Day in 2008 when the square was turned into a refugee camp. Seehttp://www. theroadtothehorizon.org/2008/06/news-june-20-world-refugee-day.html, accessed 25/10/13.
45. *The Times*, 18 April 1918, 3.
46. Ian Beckett, *The Great War 1914–1918* (Harlow: Pearson, 2001), 254.
47. TNA, NSC 7/36.
48. Beckett, *The Great War*, 254.
49. David Englander, 'Soldiering and Identity: Reflections on the Great War', *War in History*, Vol. 1, No. 3 (1994): 312.
50. McCartney, *Citizen Soldiers*, 17.
51. McCartney, *Citizen Soldiers*, 8.
52. Bourne, 'The British Working Man in Arms', 340.
53. Bourne, 'The British Working Man in Arms', 341. See also from the period of the Second World War, Frank P. Chambers, *The War behind the War 1914–1918: A History of the Political and Civilian Front* (New York: Harcourt Brace, 1939), 256; Stevenson, *British Society 1914–1945*, 453; and, in a rather different context, Geoffrey Best, 'The Militarization of European Society 1870–1914', in *The Militarization of the Western World,* ed. John R. Gillis (New Brunswick, NJ: Rutgers University Press, 1989), 29.
54. Bourne, 'The British Working Man in Arms', 349.
55. Peter Liddle, 'British Loyalties: The Evidence of an Archive', in *Facing Armageddon*, 534–36.
56. Adam R. Seipp, *The Ordeal of Peace: Demobilization and the Urban Experience in Britain and Germany 1917–1921* (Farnham: Ashgate, 2009), 66.
57. Dowding, 'A Study of the War-Giving', 632–33.
58. Harrison, *Peaceable Kingdom*; and Prochaska, *The Voluntary Impulse*.
59. See Chapter 2.
60. Alan J. Kidd, 'Philanthropy and the "Social History Paradigm"', *Social History* (London), No. 21 (1996): 180–192.
61. Anthony Mor-O'Brien, 'A Community in Wartime: Aberdare and the First World War' (PhD diss., University of Wales, 1986), Summary.
62. Mor-O'Brien, 'A Community in Wartime', 174–75.
63. Brett Fairbairn, 'Economic and Social Developments', and Edward Ross Dickinson, 'The Bourgeoisie and Reform', both in *Imperial Germany 1871–1918,* ed. James Retallack (Oxford: Oxford University Press, 2008), 68 and 153.
64. Jeffrey Verhey, 'War and Revolution', in Retallack, *Imperial Germany*, 250; and Roger Chickering, *Imperial Germany and the Great War* (Cambridge: Cambridge University Press, 1998), 116. Chickering notes that close to thirty billion Libesgaben or 'care packages' were exchanged between soldiers and home during the war.
65. Thane, *The Foundation of the Welfare State*, 107.
66. Michael Howard considers the Ludendorff-led regime as 'intrinsically racist and explicitly anti-democratic'; 'The First World War Reconsidered', in *The Great War and the Twentieth Century*, eds. Jay Winter, Geoffrey Parker and Mary Habeck (New Haven, CT: Yale University Press, 2000), 28. Brian Bond goes further by saying that 'the generals anticipated the Nazis in pressing for the complete militarization of German society'; *War and Society in Europe 1870–1970* (Bungay, Suffolk: Fontana, 1984), 118. Martin Kitchen emphasises the similarity between the civilian politicians and the generals with both aiming to become 'a world power with significant territorial additions';

'Hindenburg, Ludendorff and the Crisis of German Society 1916–1918', in *Men at War: Politics, Technology and Innovation in the Twentieth Century*, eds. Timothy Travers and Christon Archer (Chicago: Precedent, 1982), 37.

67. Roger Chickering, 'Militarism and Radical Nationalism', in Retallack, *Imperial Germany*, 204. For the counter-argument see Albrecht Ritschl, 'Germany's Economy at War, 1914–1918 and Beyond', in *The Economics of World War I*, eds. S.N. Broadberry and Mark Harrison (Cambridge: Cambridge University Press, 2005), 45–73; and Keith Allen, 'Food and the German Home Front: Evidence from Berlin', in *Evidence, History and the Great War: Historians and the Impact of 1914–18*, ed. Gail Braybon (Oxford: Bergmann, 2003), 172–97.

68. Kitchen, 'Hindenburg, Ludendorff and the Crisis of German Society', 38.

69. Beckett, *The Great War*, 264.

70. Beckett, *The Great War*, 276.

71. Winter and Robert, *Capital Cities at War*, 16.

72. Philpott, *Bloody Victory*, 91.

73. Verhey, 'War and Revolution', 251–52; and Wilhelm Deist, 'The Military Collapse of the German Empire: The Reality behind the Stab-in-the-Back Myth', *War in History*, Vol. 3, No. 2 (April 1996): 186–207.

74. 'Looking Forward', in Retallack, *Imperial Germany*, 269.

75. Philpott, *Bloody Victory*, 452.

76. For further support for the thesis that social capital in Germany was eroded during the war and the mechanisms at work, see Richard M. Wall and Jay M. Winter (eds.), *The Upheaval of War: Family, Work and Welfare in Europe 1914–18* (Cambridge: Cambridge University Press, 1987), 11–12, 38, 40–41, 53, 141 and 216; Helmut Anheier and Jeremy Kendall, 'Interpersonal Trust and Voluntary Associations: Examining Three Approaches', *British Journal of Sociology*, Vol. 53, No. 3 (September 2002): 355; Robert E. Hall and Charles I. Jones, 'Why Do Some Countries Produce So Much More Output per Worker than Others?', *Quarterly Journal of Economics*, Vol. 114, No. 1 (February 1999): 83–116; and Joe Wallis, Paul Killerby and Brian Dollery, 'Social Economics and Social Capital', *International Journal of Social Economics*, Vol. 31, No. 3 (2004): 239–58.

77. Seipp, *The Ordeal of Peace*, 46.

78. Helen McCarthy, 'Associational Voluntarism in Interwar Britain', in Hilton and McKay, *The Ages of Voluntarism*, 49.

79. Bernard Harris, 'Voluntary Action and the State in Historical Perspective', 33.

80. McCarthy, 'Associational Voluntarism in Interwar Britain', 57.

81. McCarthy, 'Associational Voluntarism in Interwar Britain', 67.

82. Cohen, *War Come Home*, 5. Pensions became a statutory right in late 1919. Operation of war pensions provided yet another example of massive voluntary effort as they required 1,200 local committees involving 100,000 voluntary members. Gregory, *The Last Great War*, 264.

83. Eric J. Leed, *No Man's Land: Combat and Identity in World War I* (Cambridge: Cambridge University Press, 1979), 204–13.

84. Latcham, 'Journeys End', suggests this was indicative of a general 'pent-up violence', 116. Charles Kimball, 'The Ex-Service Movement in England and Wales 1916–1930' (PhD diss., Stanford University, 1991), 62–63, is more persuasive in his analysis and refutes this point. The latter is supported by Cohen, *The War Come Home*, 26.

85. Stephen Ward, 'The British Veterans' Ticket of 1918', *Journal of British Studies*, Vol. 8 (November 1968): 169.

86. Cohen, *War Come Home*, 7–8. Kimball strongly supports this view in 'The Ex-Service Movement in England and Wales'.
87. Cohen, *War Come Home*, 58–59.
88. Cohen, *War Come Home*, 189. Again Kimball supports this argument; 'The Ex-Service Movement in England and Wales', 270, and Stephen Ward, in his introduction to *The War Generation: Veterans of the First World War* (Port Washington, NY: Kennikat Press, 1975), is another who concludes 'that veterans reflected the social, economic, intellectual and political divisions within their individual nations' rather than their communality of experience as soldiers. Despite his criticisms of outdated philanthropy, Adrian Gregory is also in agreement; *The Last Great War*, 266.
89. McCarthy, 'Associational Voluntarism in Interwar Britain', 47–68.
90. A recent example is Juliet Nicholson, *The Great Silence 1918–1920: Living in the Shadow of the Great War* (London: John Murray, 2009), whose evidence is highly anecdotal and whose arguments begin with a flawed view of the war years.
91. Hilton and McKay, *The Ages of Voluntarism*, 21.

NOTES TO THE AFTERWORD

1. Watson, Fighting Different Wars, 2.
2. Wilson, Myriad Faces of War, 851.
3. 'Justice Is Justice, Even 80 Years Late', 17 March 1998, 20. The article was supporting the campaign to pardon those 'shot for cowardice' during the war.
4. Michael Howard, 'The Art of the Tat: Review of Modris Ekstein's Rite of Spring: The Great War and the Birth of the Modern Age', Times Literary Supplement, 9–15 February (1990): 138.
5. David Lloyd George, War Memoirs, Vol. VI (London: Ivor Nicholson and Watson, 1936), 3408.
6. Contrary to received opinion this term was used extensively during the First World War. Perhaps the term's first use was, rather inaccurately, during the Crimean War in a Times leader (5 May 1854), 8. In the First World War its first use may have been by H.G. Wells in a letter to The Times supporting the raising of a citizen's army for home defence (31 October 1914), 9.

Bibliography

IMPERIAL WAR MUSEUM

MISC 68—ITEM 1056, Extracts from the Log Books of East Anglian Schools.
MISC 351, Letters from two men on active service to schoolgirl Lucy Bateson re comforts.
MISC 930, Letters to Liverpool schoolgirl re comforts.
MISC 2785, Letter of December 1915 from Lieutenant to seven-year-old schoolgirl re comforts.
88/57/1, Britland, B, Transcripts of letters with frequent mention of comforts for PoWs.
95/38/1, Papers of Miss B. Whitby, Nottingham and Notts Comforts for Troops Fund.
WWC, BO 2 49/4, Dowding, W.E., 'Town or Country? Which is the more generous', Unpublished ms.
Women, War and Society 1914–1918 Collection, Many references.

NATIONAL ARCHIVES

BT 31/22964/141418, Heroes Poultry Farms Ltd, 1915, File of dissolved company.
CHAR 3/83, Charities Emergency Bill 1914.
CHAR 3/85, War Charities Act 1916.
CHAR 4, Charity Commission: War Charities: Binders of Basic Information.
CHAR 4/1 to 4/21, Registers of individual charities.
CHAR 4/24, Subject index of the registers.
ED 10/73, 74 and 75, Contributions of schoolchildren to the war effort: Collections of fruit (73), horse chestnuts (74) and waste paper (75).
ED 24/2032–2, Children's collections of chestnuts and acorns.
HO 45/10488/111251, Charities: Street collections generally; mainly in the Metropolitan Police District, 1903–16.
HO 45/10546/160443, Charities: Street collections—law affecting the provinces, 1907–16.
HO 45/10787/298101, Official views on the premium bond scheme advocated by Horatio Bottomley.
HO 45/10804/308566, Commissions and Committees: War Charities Committee, 1916–19.
HO 45/10885/346885, Criminal: Street Musicians, etc, falsely representing themselves as ex-servicemen, 1917.

HO 45/11217, Charities: Advisory Committee on Street Collections and Regulations for Metropolitan Police District, 1920–23.

HO 45/13806, Baronets: Ward of Wilbraham Place, 1928–30.

HO 45/16220, Charities: Collecting Charities (Regulation) Bill, 1929.

HO 45/18406, Charities: War Charities Act 1916 and Bill of 1940.

HO 45/18971, Betting and Gambling: 'Golden Ballot' and various other tombolas and lotteries run for war charities. Lotteries (War Charities) Bill 1918. 1915–20.

MAF 60/243, The effect of food queues at home on men at the front drawn up by Sydney Walton for Lord Rhondda.

MEPO 2/1675, Charities: Belgian Soldiers Fund, 1915–17.

MEPO 2/1704, Street collections: Permits for collections in parks and open spaces, 1916–17.

MEPO 2/1729, Investigation of charity 'scandal'—the 'Red Star Society'.

MEPO 2/1732, Investigation of charity 'scandal'—'Tubs for Tommies'.

MEPO 3/249, Thomas Alroy alias Thomas alias Johnson: Bogus charity frauds, 1915.

MEPO 3/252, Fraudulent collections by bogus 'Captain Illingworth' for Queen Alexandra's Field Force Fund.

MT 6/2468/10, Treasury concerns re free conveyance of comforts for Canadian troops.

TS 18/262, French Relief Fund.

WO 32/6384, Establishment (Code 1(C)): Report of Ward Committee on Organisation and Establishment of Civil Departments, 1903.

WO 32/9224, Army Council (Code 1(B)): Proposals concerning proceedings and procedure duties of Secretary, 1904–05.

WO 95/3963, War Diary: Headquarters Branches and Services: Inspector General, December 1915.

WO 107, Office of the Commander-in-Chief and War Office: Quartermaster General's Department: Correspondence and Papers.

WO 107/14, Stores and equipment, January–June 1915.

WO 107/15, General Correspondence, July 1915–June 1916.

WO 107/16, General Correspondence, July 1916 –March 1919.

WO 123/57, Army Orders, War Office, 1915.

WO 163/21, Army Council Minutes and Précis, August 1914–December 1916.

WO 163/46, Army Council Meetings 120–80, May 1915–January 1916.

WO 163/746, Minutes of proceedings of the Permanent Executive Committee of the War Office (5 January to 4 March 1904) and important Treasury and War Office Decisions, 1904–06.

WO 1017/21, Director of Supply and Transport: General correspondence, 1914–15.

LONDON METROPOLITAN ARCHIVES

A/FH/F15/001/001–2, Diary of Edith Marjorie Bunbury, charity worker, 1914–15.

LCC/PC/CHA/1/1, War Charities Act 1916—General Papers, 1916–39.

LCC/PC/CHA/1/2, War Charities Act 1916—Particulars of the work done.

LCC/PC/CHA/1/3, War Charities Act 1916—Correspondence re 1916 Act between L.C.C. and Charity Commissioners, 1916.

LCC/PC/CHA/1/4, War Charities Act 1916—Precedents, 1916–22.

LCC/PC/CHA/4/1–17, Charities registered with the LCC under the War Charities Act 1916.

LCC/MIN 8335 to 8424, Correspondence relating to applications for registration or exemption under the War Charities Act. .

LMA LCC/MIN 8346, Case 302, Church Army, The Church Army 'Blue Book': Annual Report of the Church Army including the special war work of the Society during the Great War, 1913–15, 1915–16, 1916–17, 1917–18, Cowley, Oxford, Church Army Press, 1915–18.

NATIONAL ARMY MUSEUM

NAM 1961–12–96, The 'Ladysmith Lyre'.

NAM 1963–09–114, Letter to his mother in the form of a Diary by Army School-master William H. Gilbert—The Siege and Relief of Ladysmith.

NAM 1969–19–19, Letter of Private Alf Down, C Company, 1st Bt King's Royal Rifles, to his mother re the Siege of Ladysmith.

NAM 1982–02–06, Despatches and Diary of Arthur Hutton, Reuters Correspondent re Siege of Ladysmith.

NAM 2005–06–737, Postcard from Lt Llewellyn W. Atcherley, ASC, Ashanti War.

OTHER ARCHIVES

Bodleian Library: Papers of Percy Noble, MSS Autogr c17 and b 11.

Bodleian Library: Letters of Henry Nevinson, MS Eng Lett c 278.

Bodleian Library: MS Eng Lett d 388.

Croydon Local Studies Library, Minutes of the Croydon War Refugee Committee (compiled by the Hon Sec Miss Muriel Scarff).

Croydon Local Studies Library, Croydon War Supplies Clearing House, Minute Book.

Croydon Local Studies Library, Croydon War Supplies Clearing House: Summary Report, 1914–19, probably written by Mr H. Terrell Peard.

Centre for Kentish Studies, Acquisition 6632, Great Chart Sailor's and Soldier's War Fund, Letters to family and friends, 1915–18.

London School of Economics, Wallas 6/12, Wallas's notes for his lectures for the Army Administration Class.

Royal Logistic Corps Museum, Archives of the Royal Army Service Corps.

PARLIAMENTARY PAPERS AND GOVERNMENT PUBLICATIONS

The Parliamentary Debates Official Report House of Commons (various years).

The Parliamentary Debates Official Report House of Lords (various years).

Bill to enable the income of certain charities to be applied temporarily to the Prince of Wales's National Relief Fund, 1914 (399).

Bill intituled an Act to legalise in certain cases Lotteries promoted by War Charities, 1918 (86) ii 243.

Bill/Act to provide for the registration of Charities for purposes connected with the present War (War Charities Bill, Lord's Amendments and Act), 1916.

War Charities Act, Index of Charities Registered Under the Act, HMSO, 1916 to 1921.

Bill/Act to provide for the registration of war charities; to amend in connection therewith the House to House Collections Act, 1939; and for purposes connected with the matters aforesaid, 1940.

Report of the Committee on War Office Organisation appointed by the Secretary of State for War, 1901, xl, Cd. 580 and 581.

Committee on the Employment of Ex-Soldiers and Sailors, 1906, Cd. 2991.

Interim Report of the War Office Committee on the Provision of Officers for Service with the Regular Army in War and for the Auxiliary Forces, 1907, Cd. 3294.

Report of the Advisory Board, London School of Economics, on the First Course at the London School of Economics, January to July 1907, for the Training of Officers for the Higher Appointments on the Administrative Staff of the Army and for the charge of Departmental Services, 1907, Cd. 3696.

Second Course, October 1907 to March 1908. 1908, Cd. 4055.

Third Course, October 1908 to March 1909. 1909, Cd. 4610.

Fourth Course, October 1909 to March 1910. 1910, Cd. 5213.

Fifth Course, October 1910 to March 1911. 1911, Cd. 5597.

Sixth Course, 5th October 1911 to 27th March 1912. 1912–13, Cd. 6285.

Seventh Course, 3rd October 1912 to 19th March 1913. 1913, Cd. 6693.

Eighth Course, 6th October 1913 to 25th March 1914. 1914, Cd. 7442.

Census Returns of England and Wales, 1911, giving details of Areas, Houses, Families or separate occupiers, and Population: General Report, with Appendices (Population: Census Returns, 1911), 1917–18, Cd. 8491.

Annual Reports of the Charity Commission   61st, 1914, xv, Cd. 7310.

62nd, 1914–16, xi, Cd. 7835.

63rd, 1916, vi, Cd. 8211.

64th, 1917–18, viii, Cd. 8521.

65th, 1918, vii, Cd. 9008.

66th, 1919, xi, Cmd. 82.

67th, 1920, xiii, Cmd. 621.

68th, 1921, ix, Cmd. 1198.

Memorandum on the steps taken for the prevention and relief of distress due to the war, 1914, lxxi, Cd. 7603.

First report of the Departmental Committee appointed by the President of the Local Government Board to consider and report on questions arising in connection with the reception and employment of the Belgian refugees in this country, 1914, vii, Cd. 7750.

Report on the special work of the Local Government Board arising out of the War, up to 31st December 1914, 1914–16, xxv, Cd. 7763.

Special War Work. Local Government Board Report, 1916, Cd. 8195.

Report of the special work of the Local Government Board arising out of the war (up to 31st December 1914), 1915, xxv, Cd. 7763.

Forty-fifth Annual Report of the Local Government Board, 1916, Cd. 8331, 8309, 8332.

Special War Work: Forty-sixth Annual Report of the Local Government Board, 1917–18, Cd. 8697.

Special War Work: Forty-seventh Annual Report of the Local Government Board, 1918, Cd. 9157.

Report on the administration of the National Relief Fund up to 31st March 1915, 1914–16, Cd. 7756.

Report by the Scottish Advisory Committee on the administration of the National Relief Fund in Scotland up to 31st March 1915, 1914–16, Cd. 8129.

Report on the administration of the [National Relief] Fund up to September 1915, 1916, Cd. 8169.

Report by the Scottish Advisory Committee on the administration of the National Relief Fund in Scotland up to September 1915, 1916, Cd. 8227.

Report on the administration of the [National Relief] Fund up to March 1916, 1916, Cd. 8286.

Report on the administration of the [National Relief] Fund up to September 1916, 1917–18, Cd. 8449.

Report on the administration of the [National Relief] Fund up to March 1917, 1917–18, Cd. 8621.

Report on the administration of the [National Relief] Fund up to September 1917, 1917–18, Cd. 8920.

Report on the administration of the [National Relief] Fund up to March 1918, 1918, Cd. 9111.

Report on the administration of the [National Relief] Fund up to September 1918, 1919, Cmd. 16.

Report on the administration of the [National Relief] Fund up to June 1919, 1919, Cmd. 356.

Final Report of the National Relief Fund, March 1921, 1921, Cmd. 1272.

Final statement of the accounts of the National Relief Fund up to 16th April 1923, 1923, Cmd. 1955.

Report of the Committee on War Charities, 1916, Cd. 8287.

Report on the Joint Committee to enquire into the organisation and methods of the Central Prisoners of War Committee, 1917, Cd. 8615.

Scheme for Co-ordinating and Regulating Voluntary Work Organizations throughout the United Kingdom, 2nd ed., HMSO, 1 December 1915.

Report on the National Scheme of Co-ordination of Voluntary Effort resulting from the formation of the Department of the Director-General of Voluntary Organisations, 1919, x, Cmd. 173.

Appendix No. 3—Detailed particulars of the work of each recognised Association.

Appendix No. 4—A summary showing the nature and quantity of each class of article provided by Associations.

Appendix No. 5—A general summary of all gifts supplied through the medium of the Director-General of Voluntary Organizations.

Report of the work of the Camps Library connected with the supply of literature to the troops during the war, 1919, x, Cmd. 174.

Report on the Service of the Metropolitan Special Constabulary, 1914, 1920, xxii, Cmd. 536.

Report of the Home Office Departmental Committee on the Supervision of Charities, 1927, vii, Cmd. 2823.

NEWSPAPERS, MAGAZINES AND PAMPHLETS

Daily Chronicle, Various dates.

Daily Mail, Various dates.

Daily Telegraph, Various dates.

The Times, Various dates.

TP's Journal of Great Deeds of the Great War, 17 October 1914 to May 1917 weekly to end 1915, monthly thereafter.

Truth, Various dates.

The American Women's War Relief Fund: Report of Work August 1914–August 1915.

The Ladysmith Bombshell, Ladysmith, Natal, South Africa, 1–8 (18 November 1899–8 January 1900).

The Wipers Times, the complete series of the famous wartime trench newspaper. London, Little Books, 2006.

BOOKS

Armitage, F.P. *Leicester 1914–1918: The wartime story of a Midlands town*, Leicester: Backus, 1933.
Armstrong, Walter Alan. 'Kentish Rural Society during the First World War', in Holderness, B.A. and Turner, M.E. (eds.), *Land, Labour and Agriculture, 1700–1920: Essays for Gordon Mingay*, London: Hambledon, 1990.
Balfour, Frances Lady. *Dr Elsie Inglis*, London: Hodder and Stoughton, 1918.
Bannister, Andrew. *One Valley's War: Voices from a Yorkshire community in the Great War and its aftermath, 1914–18*, Pudsey: Outremer Publishing, 1994.
Barnett, Margaret. *Voluntary Social Action: A history of the National Council of Social Service 1919–1969*, London: NCSS, 1969.
Bavin, W.D. *Swindon's War Record*, Swindon: Drew, 1922.
Beadon, Roger H. *The Royal Army Service Corps, Vol. 2*, London: Naval and Military Press reprint, 2004 (f.p. Cambridge University Press, 1930–31).
Beaven, Brad. *Leisure, Citizenship and Working-class Men in Britain, 1850–1945*, Manchester: Manchester University Press, 2005.
Becker, Jean-Jacques. *The Great War and the French People*, Leamington Spa: Berg, 1980.
Becker, Jean-Jacques. '"That's the Death Knell of Our Boys . . ."', in Fridenson, Patrick (ed.), *The French Home Front 1914–1918*, Providence RI: Berg, 1992.
Beckett, Ian and Simpson, Keith (eds.). *A Nation in Arms: A social study of the British Army in the First World War*, Manchester: Manchester University Press, 1985.
Beckett, Ian F.W. *The Great War 1914–1918*, Harlow: Pearson, 2001.
Beckett, Ian F.W. *Home Front 1914–1918: How Britain Survived the Great War*, Kew: National Archives, 2006.
Berghoff, Hartmut and Friedeburg, Robert von (eds.). *Change and Inertia: Britain under the impact of the First World War*, Bodenheim: Philo Cop., 1998.
Best, Geoffrey. 'The Militarization of European Society 1870–1914', in Gillis, John R. (ed.), *The Militarization of the Western World*, New Brunswick NJ: Rutgers University Press, 1989.
Bilton, David. *The Home Front in the Great War: Aspects of the conflict 1914–1918*, Barnsley: Leo Cooper, 2004.
Binns, Lt-Col P.L. *The Story of the Royal Tournament*, Aldershot: Gale and Polden, 1952.
Blouet, B.W. *Halford Mackinder: A biography*, College Station: Texas A&M University Press, 1987.
Bond, Brian. *War and Society in Europe 1870–1970*, Bungay, Suffolk: Fontana, 1984.
Bond, Brian (ed.). *The First World War and British Military History*, Oxford: Clarendon, 1991.
Bond, Brian. *The Unquiet Western Front: Britain's role in literature and history*, Cambridge: Cambridge University Press, 2002.
Booth, Allyson. *Postcards from the Trenches: Negotiating the space between modernism and the First World War*, Oxford: Oxford University Press, 1997.
Bourne, John M. *Britain and the Great War 1914–1918*, London: Edward Arnold, 1989.
Bourne, John, Liddle, Peter and Whitehead, Ian (eds.). *The Great World War 1914–45, Vol. 2: Who Won? Who Lost?*, London: HarperCollins, 2000.
Bowden, Samuel H. *The History of the Australian Comforts Fund*, Sydney: Scotow and Presswell, 1922.

Bradford Khaki Club. *Wonderful Story of Voluntary Labour during the Great War*, Bradford: Author, 1920(?).

Braybon, Gail. *Women Workers in the First World War*, London: Croom Helm, 1981.

Braybon, Gail (ed.). *Evidence, History and the Great War: Historians and the impact of 1914–18*, Oxford: Bergmann, 2003.

Brazier, R.H. and Sandford, E. *Birmingham and the Great War*, Birmingham: Cornish Brothers, 1921.

Brown, Ian Malcolm. *British Logistics on the Western Front 1914–1919*, Westport CT: Praeger, 1998.

Brownlie, Maj John. *The Great War: New Kilpatrick's response to the call of the King*, Glasgow: Samuel A.C. Todd, 1916.

Burk, Kathleen (ed.). *War and the State: The transformation of British government, 1914–1919*, London: Allen and Unwin, 1982.

Bush, Julia. *Behind the Lines: East London labour 1914–1919*, London: Merlin Press, 1984.

Cahalan, Peter. *Belgian Refugee Relief in England during the Great War*, New York and London: Garland, 1982.

Campbell, Rev Andrew. *Crieff in the Great War*, Edinburgh: Constable, 1925.

Campion, P. *The Honourable Women of the Great War and the Women's (War) Who's Who*, Bournemouth: W. Mate, 1919.

Cartmell, Harry. *For Remembrance: An account of the part played by Preston in the war*, Preston: George Toulmin and Sons, 1919.

Cecil, Hugh and Liddle, Peter H. (eds.). *Facing Armageddon: The First World War experienced*, London: Leo Cooper, 1996.

Chalfont, Lord Alan. *The Royal Tournament 1880–1980*, Westerham: Westerham Press, 1980.

Chambers, Frank P. *The War behind the War 1914–1918: A history of the political and civilian fronts*, New York: Harcourt Brace, 1939.

Charity Organisation Society. *The Annual Charities Register and Digest*, 22nd ed. 1913 to 31st ed. 1922, London: Longmans and Charity Organisation Society, 1897–1964.

Charity Organisation Society. *Archives of the Charity Organization Society 1869–1938, Part 1*, London: Harvester, 1984.

Chesterman, Michael. *Charities, Trusts and Social Welfare*, London, Weidenfeld and Nicolson, 1979.

Chickering, Roger. *Imperial Germany and the Great War*, Cambridge: Cambridge University Press, 1998.

Chisholm, Ruari. *Ladysmith*, London: Osprey, 1979.

Churchill, Lady Randolph. *Women's War Work*, London: Arthur Pearson, 1916.

Clark, Rev Andrew. *Echoes of the Great War: The diary of the Reverend Andrew Clark 1914–1919*, ed. by James Munson, Oxford: Oxford University Press, 1988.

Clayton, John T. *Craven's Part in the Great War*, J.T. Clayton, 1919.

Cobb, Paul and Tessa. *Lechlade and the Great War, 1914–18: An account of village life during the First World War and the stories behind the names on the war memorial*, Lechlade: Lechlade Historical Society, 1998.

Coetzee, Frans and Shevin-Coetzee, Marilyn (eds.). *Authority, Identity and the Social History of the Great War*, Providence RI: Berghahn Books, 1995.

Cohen, Deborah. *The War Come Home: Disabled veterans in Britain and Germany, 1914–1939*, Berkeley: University of California Press, 2001.

Colls, Robert and Dodd, Philip (eds.). *Englishness: Politics and culture 1880–1920*, London: Croom Helm, 1986.

Condell, Diana and Liddiard, Jean. *Working for Victory? Images of women in the First World War*, London: Routledge and Kegan Paul, 1987.

Conference on War Relief and Personal Service Organised by Charity Organisation Societies and Guilds of Help, Caxton Hall, Westminster, June 10–12, 1915, London: Longmans, 1915.

Connelly, Mark. *The Great War Memory and Ritual: Commemoration in the City and East London 1916–1939,* Woodbridge: Royal Historical Society and Rochester: Boydell Press, 2002.

Constantine, Stephen, Kirby, Maurice W. and Rose, Mary B. (eds.). *The First World War in British History,* London, New York, Sydney and Auckland: Edward Arnold, 1995.

Coote, William Alexander. *A Romance of Philanthropy: Being a record of some of the principal incidents connected with the exceptionally successful thirty years' work of the National Vigilance Association,* London: National Vigilance Association, 1916.

Copping, Arthur E. *Tommy's Triangle,* London: Hodder & Stoughton, 1917.

Corbett, Elsie Cameron. *Red Cross in Serbia, 1915–1919: A personal diary of experiences,* Banbury: Cheney and Sons, 1964.

Cornes, Cathryn and Hughes-Wilson, John. *Blindfold and Alone: British military executions in the Great War,* London: Cassell, 2001.

Coutts, Frederick. *The History of the Salvation Army, Vol. 6, 1914–46: The better fight,* London: Hodder and Stoughton, 1973.

Cronin, James E. 'Strikes and Power in Britain 1870–1920', in Haimson, L. and Tilly, C. (eds.), *Strikes, Wars and Revolutions in an International Perspective,* Cambridge: Cambridge University Press, 1989.

Crosby, Arthur Joseph. *Extracts from Notes Taken on the Boer Campaign 1899–1900,* Ladysmith: Ladysmith Historical Society, 1976 (rpt 1993).

Cullerton, Claire A. *Working Class Culture, Women and Britain 1914–1921,* New York: St Martin's Press, 1999.

Dakers, Caroline. *The Countryside at War 1914–1918,* London: Constable, 1987.

Davis Smith, Justin. 'The Voluntary Tradition: Philanthropy and self-help in Britain 1500–1945', in Davis Smith, J., Rochester, C. and Hedley, R. (eds.), *An Introduction to the Voluntary Sector,* London: Routledge, 1995.

DeGroot, Gerard J. *Blighty: British society in the era of the Great War,* London: Longman, 1996.

Devereux, Joseph and Sacker, Graham. *Leaving All That Was Dear: Cheltenham and the Great War 1914–1918,* Cheltenham: Promenade Publications, 1997.

de Vries, Jacqueline. 'Women's Voluntary Organizations in World War I', in Grayzel, Susan (ed.), *Introductory Essays to the Microfilm Collection 'A Change in Attitude: Women, war and society, 1914–1918',* Woodbridge CT: Thomson Gale, 2005.

Dicksee, Lawrence R. *Business Methods and the War,* London: Cambridge University Press, 1915.

Dimmock, F. Haydn. *The Scouts' Book of Heroes: A record of Scouts' work in the Great War with a foreword by Robert Baden-Powell,* London: Pearson, 1919.

Dollery, Brian E. and Wallis, Joe L. *The Political Economy of the Voluntary Sector: A reappraisal of the competitive institutional advantage of voluntary organizations,* Cheltenham and Northampton MA: Edward Elgar, 2003.

d'Ombrain, Nicholas. *War Machinery and High Policy: Defence administration in peacetime Britain 1902–1914,* Oxford: Oxford University Press, 1973.

Dony, John G. 'The 1919 Peace Riots in Luton', in *Worthington George Smith and Other Studies: Presented to Joyce Godber,* Bedford: Bedfordshire Historical Record Society, Vol. 57, 1978.

Driver, Nurse Kate. *Experience of a Siege: A Nurse looks back on Ladysmith,* rev. ed., Ladysmith: Ladysmith Historical Society, 1994.

Dunn, Capt James C. *The War the Infantry Knew: A chronicle of service in France and Belgium with the Second Battalion His Majesty's Twenty-Third Foot, the Royal Welch Fusiliers founded on personal records, recollections and reflections, assembled, edited and partly written by one of their medical officers,* London: P.S. King Ltd, 1938 (Abacus rpt, 1994).

Eades, Tom. *The War Diary and Letters of Corporal Tom Eades 1915–1917,* ed. by Frances Eades, Cambridge: Cambridge Aids to Learning, 1972.

Edgington, M.A. *Bournemouth and the First World War: The evergreen valley 1914–1919,* Bournemouth: Bournemouth Local Studies Publications, 1985.

Elbourne, Edward Tregaskiss. *Factory Administration and Cost Accounts: A reference book of the principles and practice of industrial administration and costing for present day requirements,* 3rd ed., London: Longmans Green, 1921.

Fairholme, Edward G. and Pain, Wellesley. *A Century of Work for Animals: The history of the RSPCA 1824–1924,* London: John Murray, 1924.

Fairlie, John A. *British War Administration* (Carnegie Endowment for International Peace, Division of Economics and History, Preliminary Economic Studies of the War, No. 8), New York: Oxford University Press, 1919.

Fawcett, Millicent Garrett. *The Women's Victory and After: Personal reminiscences 1911–1918,* London: Sidgwick and Jackson, 1920.

Field, Rev Lawrence P. *The Souvenir Book of Eye: Being some records of the Great War 1914–1919: From the Parish of Eye, in the Soke of Peterborough and in the county of Northampton,* Eye: Eye Patriotic Association, 1920.

Finlayson, Geoffrey. *Citizen, State and Social Welfare in Britain 1830–1990,* Oxford: Oxford University Press, 1994.

Firth, John B. *Dover and the Great War,* Dover: Alfred Leney and Co, 1920.

Fraser, Derek. *The Evolution of the British Welfare State,* London: Macmillan, 1973.

Fraser, Helen. *Women and War Work,* New York: G. Arnold Shaw, 1918.

Fuller, J.G. *Troop Morale and Popular Culture in the British and Dominion Armies 1914–18,* Oxford: Clarendon Press, 1988.

Fussell, Paul. *The Great War and Modern Memory,* Oxford: Oxford University Press, 1975.

Gallacher, William. *Revolt on the Clyde. An autobiography,* 4th ed. with an Introduction by Michael McGahey, London: Lawrence and Wishart, 1978 (f.p.1936).

Gates, William G. *Portsmouth and the Great War,* Portsmouth: Evening News and Hampshire Telegraph, 1919.

Gauld, H. Drummond. *The Truth from the Trenches,* London: Arthur H. Stockwell, 1922.

Gay, George I. *The Commission for Relief in Belgium, Statistical Review of Relief Operations: Five years November 1, 1914 to August 31, 1919,* Stanford CA: Stanford University Press, 1925.

George, Michael and Christine. *Dover and Folkestone during the Great War,* Barnsley: Pen and Sword, 2008.

Gilbert, Bentley B. *British Social Policy 1914–1939,* London: Batsford, 1970.

Gleason, Arthur. *What the Workers Want: A study of British labor,* New York and London: Garland, 1985 (f.p. New York: Harcourt, Brace and Howe, 1920).

Gooch, John. 'Britain and the Boer War', in Andreopoulos, George J. and Selesky, Harold E. (eds.), *The Aftermath of Defeat: Societies, armed forces and the challenge of recovery,* New Haven CT: Yale University Press, 1994.

Gooch, John. 'Adversarial Attitudes: Servicemen, politicians and strategic policy 1899–1914', in Smith, Paul (ed.), *Government and the Armed Forces in Britain 1856–1990,* London: Hambledon Press, 1996.

Gosden, Peter H.J.H. *Self-Help: Voluntary associations in the nineteenth-century*, London: Batsford, 1973.

Graham, P Anderson (ed.). *Iwerne Minster before, during and after the Great War*, n.p., 1923.

Grayzel, Susan (ed.). *Introductory Essays to the Microfilm Collection 'A Change in Attitude: Women, war and society, 1914–1918'*, Woodbridge CT: Thomson Gale, 2005.

Gregory, Adrian. *The Silence of Memory: Armistice Day 1919–1946*, Oxford: Berg, 1994.

Gregory, Adrian. *The Last Great War: British society and the First World War*, Cambridge: Cambridge University Press, 2008.

Grieves, Keith (ed.). *Sussex in the First World War*, Lewes: Sussex Record Society, Vol. 84, 2004.

Gullace, Nicoletta F. *The Blood of Our Sons: Men, women, and the renegotiation of British citizenship during the Great War*, New York and Basingstoke: Palgrave-Macmillan, 2002.

Haig-Brown, Capt Alan R. *The O.T.C. and the Great War*, London: Country Life, 1915.

Haimson, Leopold and Sapelli, Giulio (eds.). *Strikes, Social Conflict and the First World War: An international perspective*, Milan: Feltrinelli, 1992.

Halsey, Albert H. *Change in British Society: From 1900 to the present day*, Oxford: Oxford University Press, 1978.

Halsey, Albert H. (ed.). *British Social Trends since 1900: A guide to the changing social structure of Britain*, rev. ed., Basingstoke and London: Macmillan, 1988.

Hamer, William S. *The British Army: Civil-military relations 1885–1905*, Oxford: Clarendon Press, 1970.

Hammerton, J.A. (ed.). *Mr Punch in Wartime* (The New Punch Library, No 20), London: Educational Book Company, 1920(?).

Hammond, Matthew Brown. *British Labor Conditions and Legislation during the War* (Carnegie Endowment for International Peace, Division of Economics and History, Preliminary Economic Studies of the War, No. 14), New York: Oxford University Press, 1919.

Harris, Bernard. *The Origins of the British Welfare State: Social welfare in England and Wales 1800–1945*, Basingstoke: Palgrave Macmillan, 2004.

Harris, Sir Charles. *Viscount Haldane of Cloan: The man and his work*, Oxford: Oxford University Press, 1928.

Harris, Jose. *Private Lives, Public Spirit: Britain 1870–1914*, Oxford: Oxford University Press, 1993.

Harrison, Brian. *Peaceable Kingdom: Stability and change in modern Britain*, Oxford: Clarendon, 1982.

Harrison, Royden. 'The War Emergency Workers' National Committee, 1914–1920', in Saville, John and Briggs, Asa (eds.), *Essays in Labour History, Vol. 2*, London: Macmillan, 1971.

Harvey, Frederick William. *Comrades in Captivity: A record of life in seven German prison camps*, London, Sidgwick and Jackson, 1920.

Henniker, Col A.M. *Transportation on the Western Front 1914–1918*, rpt Nashville TN and London: Battery Press and Imperial War Museum, n.d. (f.p. London: HMSO, 1937).

Heron-Allen, Edward. *Edward Heron-Allen's Journal of the Great War: From Sussex shore to Flanders fields*, ed. by Brian W. Harvey and Carol Fitzgerald, Lewes: Sussex Record Society, Vol. 86, 2002.

Hibberd, Dominic. *Context and Commentary: The First World War*, London: Macmillan, 1990.

Higonnet, Margaret, Jenson, Jane, Michel, Sonya and Weitz, Margaret Collins (eds.). *Behind the Lines: Gender and the two world wars,* New Haven CT: Yale University Press, 1987.

Hiley, Nicholas. '"You Can't Believe a Word You Read": Newspaper reading in the British Expeditionary Force, 1914–18', in Harris, Michael and O'Malley, Tom (eds.), *Studies in Newspaper and Periodical History, 1994 Annual,* Westport, CT: Greenwood Press, 1996.

Hilton, Matthew and McKay, James (eds.). *The Ages of Voluntarism: How we got to the Big Society,* Oxford: Oxford University Press, 2011.

Holford, John. *Reshaping Labour: Organisation, work and politics: Edinburgh in the Great War and after,* London: Croom Helm, 1988.

Holmes, Richard. *Acts of War: The behaviour of men in battle,* London: Cassell, 2003 (f.p. as *Firing Line,* 1985).

Holmes, Richard. *Tommy: The British soldier on the Western Front 1914–1918,* London: HarperCollins, 2004.

Holton, Sandra Stanley. *Feminism and Democracy: Women's suffrage and reform politics in Britain, 1900–1918,* Cambridge: Cambridge University Press, 1986.

Hore, C.F. Adair. *War and Peace Charities: The mobilisation of voluntary effort,* London: P.S. King and Son, 1916.

Horn, Pamela. *Rural Life in England in the First World War,* Dublin: Gill and Macmillan, 1984.

Howard, Michael (ed.). *A Part of History: Aspects of the British experience of the First World War,* London: Continuum, 2008.

Howe, W.F. (ed.). *Howe's Classified Directory to the Metropolitan Charities,* 38th ed., 1913 to 44th ed., 1919, London, 1913–19.

Howell, Chris. *No Thankful Village: The impact of the Great War on a group of Somerset villages—a microcosm,* Chilcompton, Bath: Fickle Hill, 2002.

Humphreys, Robert. *Poor Relief and Charity 1869–1945: The London Charity Organisation Society,* London and Basingstoke: Macmillan, 2001.

Hurwitz, Samuel J. *State Intervention in Great Britain: A study of economic control and social response 1914–1919,* New York: Columbia University Press, 1949.

Jennings, Maj-Gen W.E. *War Relief Work in the Bombay Presidency,* Bombay: Times Press, 1919.

Jensen, Geoffrey and Wiest, Andrew (eds.). *War in the Age of Technology: Myriad faces of modern armed conflict,* New York and London: New York University Press, 2001.

Johnson, Paul. *Saving and Spending: The working class economy in Britain 1870–1939,* Oxford, Clarendon, 1985.

Jones, A.E. *A Small School in the Great War: The story of Sutton County School and its old boys in World War 1,* Carshalton, Surrey: Author, 1975.

Kelynack, T.N. (ed.). *Pro Patria: A guide to public and personal service in war time,* London: John Bale, 1916.

Kennedy, Maj J.H. *Attleborough in War Time: With short concurrent history of the Great War,* London and Norwich: London and Norwich Press, 1919.

Kennedy, Paul and Nicholls, Anthony (eds.). *Nationalist and Racialist Movements in Britain and Germany before 1914,* London: Macmillan in association with St Antony's College, Oxford, 1981.

Kidd, Alan. *State, Society and the Poor in Nineteenth Century England,* London and Basingstoke: Macmillan, 1999.

Kissin, S.F. *War and the Marxists: Socialist theory and practice in capitalist war, Vol. 1: 1848–1918,* London: Andre Deutsch, 1988.

Kitchen, Martin. 'Hindenburg, Ludendorff and the Crisis of German Society 1916–1918', in Travers, Timothy and Archer, Christon (eds.), *Men at War:*

Politics, technology and innovation in the twentieth century, Chicago: Precedent, 1982.

Koch, Theodore W. *Books in Camp, Trench and Hospital,* London: Dent, 1917.

Kocka, Jurgen. *Facing Total War: German society 1914–1918,* Cambridge MA: Harvard University Press, 1973.

Knubley, E.P. *The Record of the Parish of Steeple Ashton Including the Tithing of Great Hinton in the County of Wilts in Relation to the Great War, 1914–1919,* Trowbridge: Massey, 1919.

The Labour Year Book, London: Co-operative Press, 1916.

Lavalette, Michael and Mooney, Gerry (eds.). *Class Struggle and Social Welfare,* New York: Routledge, 2000.

Laybourn, Keith. *The Guild of Help and the Changing Face of Edwardian Philanthropy,* Lewiston/Queenstown/Lampeter: Edwin Mellen Press, 1994.

Laybourn, Keith and Reynolds, Jack. *Liberalism and the Rise of Labour 1890–1918,* London: Croom Helm, 1984.

Lee, John A. *Todmorden and the Great War 1914–1918: A local record,* Todmorden: Waddington and Sons, 1922.

Leed, Eric J. *No Man's Land: Combat and identity in World War I,* Cambridge: Cambridge University Press, 1979.

Leeds, Herbert (ed.). *Peace Souvenir Norwich War Record,* Norwich: Jarrold and Sons(?), 1919.

Lewis, Jane. *Women in England, 1870–1950: Sexual divisions and social change,* Brighton: Wheatsheaf, and Bloomington: Indiana University Press, 1984.

Lewis, Jane. *Women and Social Action in Victorian and Edwardian England,* Aldershot: Edward Elgar, 1991.

Library and Museum of Freemasonry. *The Hall in the Garden: Freemasons' Hall and its place in London,* London: Lewis Masonic, 2006.

Liddle, Peter H. (ed.). *Home Fires and Foreign Fields,* London: Brassey's, 1985.

Lindsay, Rev Samuel. *Coatbridge and the Great War,* Glasgow: Hay Nisbet, 1919.

Livingstone, Thomas. *Tommy's War: A First World War diary 1913–18,* ed. by Ronnie Scott with a Foreword by Andrew Marr, London: HarperPress, 2008.

Loft, Anne. 'Accountancy and the First World War', in Hopwood, Anthony G. and Miller, Peter (eds.), *Accountancy as Social and Institutional Practice,* Cambridge: Cambridge University Press, 1994.

Longbottom, F.W. *Chester in the Great War,* Chester: Phillipson and Golder, 1920(?).

Luvaas, Jay. *The Education of an Army,* London: Cassell, 1965.

Luxton, Peter. *The Law of Charities,* Oxford: Oxford University Press, 2001.

Macadam, Elizabeth. *The New Philanthropy,* London: George Allen and Unwin, 1934.

McCartney, Helen. *Citizen Soldiers: The Liverpool Territorials in the First World War* (Studies in the Social and Cultural History of Modern Warfare, No. 22), Cambridge: Cambridge University Press, 2005.

MacDonagh, Michael. *In London during the Great War: The diary of a journalist,* London: Eyre and Spottiswode, 1935.

McHugh, R.J. *The Siege of Ladysmith,* London: Chapman and Hall, 1900.

McInnes, Ian and Fraser, Mark. *Ashanti 1895–96,* Chippenham: Picton Publishing, 1987.

McKay, John J. *Bridge of Allan's Activities in the Great War: 1914–1919,* Stirling: Jamieson and Munro, 1925.

Mackenzie, John M (ed.). *Imperialism and Popular Culture,* Manchester: Manchester University Press, 1986.

Mackenzie, S.P. *Politics and Military Morale: Current affairs and citizenship education in the British Army, 1914–50,* Oxford: Clarendon Press, 1992.

McKibbin, Ross. *The Evolution of the Labour Party 1910–1924,* Oxford: Oxford University Press, 1974.

McKibbin, Ross. *Classes and Cultures: England 1918–1951,* Oxford: Oxford University Press, 2000.

Mackie, D.M. *Forfar and District in the War,* Forfar: Forfar War Memorial Committee, 1921.

Mallet, Lady Matilde. *British West Indies Regiment: Letters from the trenches during the Great War,* n.p., 1919.

Markwick, William F. *Stamford and the Great War: An authentic record of the war work of the Mayor and Mayoress and other inhabitants of the Ancient and Royal Borough of Stamford, with some account of the local conditions during the war period 1914–1919,* Stamford: Dolly Brothers, 1920(?).

Marlow, Joyce (ed.). *The Virago Book of Women and the Great War,* London: Virago, 1998.

Marr, Andrew. *The Making of Modern Britain: From Queen Victoria to VE Day,* London: Macmillan, 2009.

Marrin, Albert. *The Last Crusade: The Church of England in the First World War,* Durham NC: Duke University Press, 1974.

Marwick, Arthur. *The Deluge: British society and the First World War,* Boston: Little Brown, 1965.

Marwick, Arthur. *Britain in the Century of Total War: War, peace and social change 1900–1967,* London: Bodley Head, 1968.

Marwick, Arthur. *War and Social Change in the Twentieth Century: A comparative study of Britain, France, Germany, Russia and the United States,* London: Macmillan, 1974.

Marwick, Arthur. *Women at War 1914–1918,* London: Fontana, 1977.

Marwick, Arthur. *Britain in Our Century: Images and controversies,* New York: Thames and Hudson, 1984.

Marwick, Arthur (ed.). *Total War and Social Change,* London and Basingstoke: Macmillan, 1988.

Marwick, Arthur, Emsley, Clive and Mombauer, Annika. *Europe in 1914 (Total War and Social Change: Europe 1914–1955),* Milton Keynes: Open University, 2000.

Mason, J.M. 'The Anti-Socialist Philosophy of the Charity Organisation Society', in Brown, Kenneth D. (ed.), *Essays in Anti-Labour History: Responses to the rise of labour in Britain,* London: Macmillan, 1974.

Mason, Tony and Riedi, Eliza. *Sport and the Military: The British armed forces 1880–1960,* Cambridge: Cambridge University Press, 2010.

Masse, Lt Col C.H. *The Predecessors of the Royal Army Service Corps 1757–1888,* Aldershot: Gale and Polden, 1948.

Masterman, Charles F.G. *The Condition of England,* London: Methuen, 1909.

Matthews, Glen. 'Poverty and the Poor Law in the First World War in Worcestershire', in Ashton, Owen R., Fyson, Robert and Roberts, Stephen (eds.), *The Duty of Discontent: Essays for Dorothy Thompson,* London and New York: Mansell, 1995.

Maxtone Graham, Ysenda. *The Real Mrs Miniver: Jan Struther's story,* London: John Murray, 2001.

Mayall, Berry and Morrow, Virginia. *You Can Help Your Country: English children's work during the Second World War,* London: Institute of Education, 2011.

Mayhall, Laura E. Nym. *The Militant Suffrage Movement: Citizenship and resistance in Britain, 1860–1930,* Oxford and New York: Oxford University Press US, 2003.

Meller, Helen Elizabeth. *Leisure and the Changing City, 1870–1914,* London: Routledge and Kegan Paul, 1976.

Messenger, Charles. *Call to Arms: The British Army 1914–18*, London: Weidenfeld and Nicholson, 2005.

Messinger, Gary S. *British Propaganda and the State in the First World War*, Manchester: Manchester University Press, 1992.

Meyer, Jessica (ed.). *British Popular Culture and the First World War* (History of Warfare, Vol. 48), Leiden and Boston: Brill, 2008.

Miller, Frederick. *The Hartlepools in the Great War*, Sage, 1920.

Millman, Brock. *Managing Domestic Dissent in First World War Britain (British politics and society)*, London: Frank Cass, 2000.

Millman, Brock. *Pessimism and British War Policy, 1916–1918*, London: Frank Cass, 2001.

Ministry of Pensions. *Guide to Voluntary Organizations and Funds: Assisting officers, men and women who served in His Majesty's Forces and their dependents*, London: HMSO, 1937.

Mitchell, David John. *Women on the Warpath: The story of the women of the First World War*, London: Cape, 1966.

Mitchinson, K.W. *Saddleworth 1914–1919: The experience of a Pennine Community during the Great War*, Manchester: Saddleworth Historical Society, 1995.

Moore, Alderman H. Keatley (ed.). *Croydon and the Great War: Together with the Croydon roll of honour*, Croydon: Corporation of Croydon, 1920.

Moriarty, Catherine. 'Private Grief and Public Remembrance: British First World War memorials', in Evans, Martin and Lunn, Ken (eds.), *War and Memory in the Twentieth Century*, Oxford: Berg, 1997.

Morris, Robert J. 'Clubs, Societies and Associations', in Thompson, F.M. (ed.), *Cambridge Social History of Britain, Vol. 3*, Cambridge: Cambridge University Press, 1990.

Morriss, Henry Fuller. *Bermondsey's 'Bit' in the Greatest War*, London: Clifton and James, n.p., 1924(?).

Moss, Arthur William. *Valiant Crusade: The history of the R.S.P.C.A.*, London: Cassell, 1961.

Mosse, George L. *Fallen Soldiers: Reshaping the memory of the two World Wars*, New York: Oxford University Press, 1990.

Muddock, J.E. Preston. *"All Clear": A brief record of the work of the London Special Constabulary 1914–1919*, London: Everett, 1920.

Nesham, Felicitie (ed.). *Socks, Cigarettes and Shipwrecks: A family's war letters 1914–1918*, Gloucester: Alan Sutton, 1987.

Nevinson, Henry W. *The Diary of a Siege*, London: Methuen, 1900.

Oakley, William H. *Guildford in the Great War: The record of a Surrey town*, Guildford: Billing, 1934.

O'Day, Alan (ed.). *The Edwardian Age: Conflict and stability 1900–1914*, London: Macmillan, 1979.

Ogden, Charles. *The Bradford War Work Souvenir*, Bradford: William Byles and Sons, 1916.

Oppenheimer, Melanie. 'Home Front Largesse: Colonial patriotic funds and the Boer War', in Dennis, Peter and Grey, Jeffrey (eds.), *The Boer War: Army, nation and empire—Proceedings of the 1999 Chief of Army/Australian War Memorial Military History Conference*, Canberra: Army History Unit, 2000.

Owen, David. *English Philanthropy 1660–1960*, Cambridge: Cambridge University Press, 1964.

Pankhurst, E. Sylvia. *The Home Front: A mirror to life in England during the First World War*, London: Cresset Library, 1987 (f.p. 1932).

Parker, Peter. *The Old Lie: The Great War and the public school ethos*, London: Constable, 1987.

Pearce, Cyril. *Comrades of Conscience: The story of an English community's opposition to the Great War,* London: Francis Boutle, 2001.

Pedersen, Susan. *Family, Dependence, and the Origins of the Welfare State: Britain and France 1914–1945,* Cambridge: Cambridge University Press, 1995.

Peel, Mrs Dorothy C. *How We Lived Then 1914–18: A sketch of social and domestic life in England during the War,* London: John Lane, 1929.

Perfect, Charles Thomas. *Hornchurch during the Great War: An illustrated account of local activities and experiences,* Colchester: Benham and Co, 1920.

Philips, George. *Rutland and the Great War: A lasting tribute to a great and noble past,* Salford: J. Padfield and Co, 1920.

Philpott, William. *Bloody Victory: The sacrifice on the Somme,* London: Abacus, 2010.

Playne, Caroline E. *Society at War 1914–18,* London: Allen and Unwin, 1931.

Playne, Caroline E. *Britain Holds On 1917–1918,* London: Allen and Unwin, 1933.

Poggi, Gianfranco. *The Development of the Modern State: A sociological introduction,* London: Hutchinson, 1978.

Pope, Rex. *War and Society in Britain 1899–1948,* London and New York: Longman, 1991.

Price, Richard. *An Imperial War and the British Working Class: Working class attitudes and reactions to the Boer War 1899–1902,* London: Routledge and Kegan Paul, 1972.

Princess Mary's Gift Book, London, New York and Toronto: Hodder and Stoughton, 1915.

Prochaska, Frank. *The Voluntary Impulse: Philanthropy in modern Britain,* London: Faber, 1988.

Prochaska, Frank. 'Philanthropy', in Thompson, F.M.L. (ed.), *Cambridge Social History of Britain, Vol. 3,* Cambridge: Cambridge University Press, 1990.

Prochaska, Frank. *Royal Bounty, the Making of a Welfare Monarchy,* New Haven CT: Yale University Press, 1995.

Prochaska, Frank. *Christianity and Social Service in Modern Britain: The disinherited spirit,* Oxford: Oxford University Press, 2006.

Pugh, Martin. *The March of the Women: A revisionist analysis of the campaign for women's suffrage, 1866–1914,* Oxford: Oxford University Press, 2002.

Pugh, Martin. *We Danced All Night: A social history of Britain between the wars,* London: Bodley Head, 2008.

Purseigle, Pierre (ed.). *Warfare and Belligerence: Perspectives in First World War studies,* Leiden and Boston: Brill, 2005.

Purseigle, Pierre and Mcleod, Jenny. *Uncovered Fields: Perspectives in First World War studies* (History of Warfare, Vol. 20), Leiden and Boston: Brill, 2004.

Queen Mary's Needlework Guild: Its work during the Great War (Foreword by John Galsworthy), London: St James's Palace, 1919.

Reader, William J. *At Duty's Call: A study in obsolete patriotism,* Manchester: Manchester University Press, 1988.

Red Cross, British Joint Committee. *Reports by the Joint War Committee and the Joint War Finance Committee of the British Red Cross Society and the Order of St John of Jerusalem in England on Voluntary Aid Rendered to the Sick and Wounded at Home and Abroad and to British Prisoners of War 1914–1919,* London: HMSO, 1921.

Red Cross, Central British Committee. *Report on Voluntary Organisations in Aid of the Sick and Wounded during the South African War,* London: HMSO, 1902.

Reid, Alastair J. *Social Classes and Social Relations in Britain 1850–1914,* Basingstoke: Macmillan, 1992.

Retallack, James (ed.). *Imperial Germany 1871–1918,* Oxford: Oxford University Press, 2008.

Reznick, Jeffrey S. *Healing the Nation: Soldiers and the culture of caregiving in Britain during the Great War,* Manchester: Manchester University Press, 2004.

Richardson, R. *Through War to Peace 1914–18: Being a short account of the part played by Tavistock and neighbourhood in the Great War,* Tavistock: Joliffe and Son, 1919.

Richardson, Sir Wodehouse Dillon. *With the Army Service Corps in South Africa,* London: Richardson and Co, 1903.

Robb, George. *British Culture and the First World War,* Basingstoke: Palgrave Macmillan, 2002.

Robbins, Keith. *The Abolition of War: The 'Peace Movement' in Britain 1914–1919,* Cardiff: University of Wales Press, 1976.

Roberts, Robert. *The Classic Slum: Salford life in the first quarter of the century,* Manchester: University of Manchester Press, 1971.

Rose, Jonathan. *The Intellectual Life of the British Working Classes,* New Haven CT: Yale University Press, 2001.

Rose, Tania. *Aspects of Political Censorship, 1915–1918,* Hull: University of Hull Press, 1995.

Roshwald, Aviel and Stites, Richard (eds.). *European Culture in the Great War: The arts, entertainment and propaganda 1914–1918,* Cambridge: Cambridge University Press, 1999.

Ross, Ishobel. *Little Grey Partridge: First World War diary of Ishobel Ross who served with the Scottish Women's Hospital Unit in Serbia,* Aberdeen: Aberdeen University Press, 1988.

Rowson, John W. *Bridport and the Great War: Its record of work at home and in the field,* London: Hine and Son, 1923.

Roxburgh, Ronald F. *The Prisoners of War Information Bureau in London: A study,* London: Longmans, 1915.

Rudkin, Mabel. *Inside Dover 1914–1918: A woman's impressions,* London: Elliot Stock, 1933.

Samuel, John S. *European War: Statement of the funds raised in Glasgow for war relief purposes from August 1914 to December 1915 prepared for the Lord Provost,* Glasgow: City Chambers, 1916.

Samuel, Raphael (ed.). *Patriotism: The making and unmaking of British national identity* (3 vols.), London, Routledge, 1989.

Saunders, Nicholas J. (ed.). *Matters of Conflict: Material culture, memory and the First World War,* London: Routledge, 2004.

Scott, Ernest. *Official Histories—First World War: Volume XI—Australia during the War,* 7th ed., Sydney: Angus and Robertson, 1941.

Scott, William Herbert. *Leeds in the Great War 1914–1918: A book of remembrance,* Leeds: Leeds Libraries and Arts Committee, 1923.

Searle, Geoffrey. '"National Efficiency" and the "Lessons" of the war', in Omissi, David and Thompson, Andrew Stuart (eds.), *The Impact of the South African War,* Basingstoke and New York: Palgrave, 2002.

Searle, G.R. *A New England? Peace and war 1886–1918* (The New Oxford History of England), Oxford: Clarendon Press, 2004.

Seipp, Adam R. *The Ordeal of Peace: Demobilization and the urban experience in Britain and Germany 1917–1921,* Farnham: Ashgate, 2009.

Sell's World's Press, 34th Year, London: Sells Ltd, 1915.

Sheffield, Gary. *Leadership in the Trenches: Officer-man relations, morale and discipline in the British Army in the era of the First World War,* Basingstoke: Macmillan, 1999.

Sheppard, Thomas. *Kingston-upon-Hull before, during and after the Great War,* Hull: A. Brown and Sons, 1919.

Sherrington, Geoffrey. *English Education, Social Change and War: 1911–1920,* Manchester: Manchester University Press, 1983.

Short History of the Royal Army Service Corps, Aldershot: Gale and Polden, 1939.

Silbey, David. *The British Working Class and Enthusiasm for War 1914–1916,* London and New York: Frank Cass, 2005.

Simey, Margaret. *From Rhetoric to Reality: A study of the work of F.G. D'Aeth, social administrator,* Liverpool: Liverpool University Press, 2005.

Simkins, Peter. *Kitchener's Army: The raising of the new armies 1914–1916,* Manchester: Manchester University Press, 1988.

Simmons, Alan G.V. *Britain and World War One,* London and New York: Routledge, 2012.

Smith, Angela K. *The Second Battlefield: Women, modernism and the First World War,* Manchester: Manchester University Press, 2000.

Smith, Angela K. *Suffrage Discourse in Britain during the First World War,* Aldershot: Ashgate, 2005.

Smith, Helen Donald. *War Distress and War Help: A short catalogue of the leading war help societies,* London: John Murray, 1915.

Snape, Michael. *God and the British Soldier,* London: Routledge, 2005.

Spiers, Edward M. *The Army and Society, 1815–1914,* London: Longman, 1980.

Spiers, Edward M. *Haldane: An army reformer,* Edinburgh: Edinburgh University Press, 1980.

Springhall, John O. *Youth, Empire and Society: British youth movements, 1883–1940,* London: Croom Helm, 1977.

Stephen, Martin. *Never Such Innocence: A new anthology of Great War verse,* London: Buchan and Enright, 1988.

Stephen, Martin. *The Price of Pity: Poetry, history and myth in the Great War,* London: Leo Cooper, 1996.

Stevenson, John. *British Society 1914–1945 (Penguin Social History of Britain),* London: Pelican/Allen Lane, 1984.

Stone, George F. and Wells, Charles. *Bristol and the Great War: 1914–1919,* Bristol: Arrowsmith, 1920.

Storr, Katherine. *Excluded from the Record: Women, refugees and relief 1914–1929,* Bern: Peter Lang, 2010.

The Stroud District and Its Part in the Great War 1914–1919, Stroud: Stroud News Publishing, 1920(?).

Sunderland, David. *Social Capital, Trust and the Industrial Revolution, 1780–1880,* London and New York: Routledge, 2007.

Tate, Trudi. *Modernism, History, and the First World War,* Manchester: Manchester University Press, 1998.

Tatham, Meaburn and Miles, James E. *The Friends' Ambulance Unit 1914–1919: A record,* London: Swarthmore Press (Headley Brothers), 1919.

Teagarden, Ernest M. *Haldane at the War Office: A study in organization and management,* New York: Gordon Press, 1976.

Thane, Pat. *The Foundation of the Welfare State,* London: Longman, 1982.

Thom, Deborah. *Nice Girls and Rude Girls: Women workers in World War 1,* London: I.B. Tauris, 1998.

Thom, Deborah. 'Women and Work in Wartime Britain', in Grayzel, Susan (ed.), *Introductory Essays to the Microfilm Collection 'A Change in Attitude: Women, war and society, 1914–1918',* Woodbridge, CT: Thomson Gale, 2005.

Thompson, Andrew Stuart. 'Publicity, Philanthropy and Commemoration: British society and the war (The South African War, 1899–1902)', in Omissi, David and Thompson, Andrew Stuart (eds.), *The Impact of the South African War*, Basingstoke and New York: Palgrave, 2002.

Thompson, Paul. *The Edwardians: The remaking of British society*, Bloomington: Indiana University Press, 1975.

Todman, Dan. *The Great War: Myth and memory*, London and New York: Hambledon and London, 2005.

Trotter, Wilfred B. *Instincts of the Herd in Peace and War 1916–1919*, rev. ed., ed. by R.W. Chapman, Oxford: Oxford University Press, 1953 (f.p. London: Fisher Unwin, 1910).

Turner, E.S. *Dear Old Blighty*, London: Michael Joseph, 1980.

Turner, John. *British Politics and the Great War: Coalition and conflict 1915–1918*, New Haven CT: Yale University Press, 1992.

Tylee, Claire. *The Great War and Women's Consciousness: Images of militarism and womanhood in women's writings 1914–64*, London and Basingstoke: Macmillan, 1990.

Van Emden, Richard and Humphries, Steve. *All Quiet on the Home Front: An oral history of life in Britain during the First World War*, London: Hodder Headline, 2003.

Van Emden, Richard. *Tommy's Ark: Soldiers and their animals in the Great War*, London: Bloomsbury, 2010.

Waites, Bernard. *A Class Society at War: England 1914–18*, Leamington Spa: Berg, 1987.

Waites, Bernard et al. *The Impact of World War I (Total War and Social Change: Europe 1914–1955)*, Milton Keynes: Open University, 2001.

Walbrook, Henry M. *Hove and the Great War: A record and a review together with the roll of honour and list of distinctions*, Hove: Cliftonville Press, 1920.

Wall, Richard M and Winter, Jay M. (eds.). *The Upheaval of War: Family, work and welfare in Europe 1914–18*, Cambridge: Cambridge University Press, 1987.

Walton, John K. *Lancashire: A social history 1558–1939*, Manchester: Manchester University Press, 1987.

War Emergency Workers National Committee. *Publications, Reports and Executive Committee Minutes*, London: Co-operative Press, 1914–1916.

Ward, Edward W.D. *Army Service Corps Duties in Peace and War*, London: Brackenbury Military Handbooks, Vol. 8, 1878.

Ward, Edward W.D. *Supply and Transport on Active Service*, Dublin: Sibley and Co, 1893.

Ward, Mrs Humphry (Mary). *England's Effort: Six letters to an American friend*, London: Smith Elder, 1916.

Ward, Mrs Humphry (Mary). *Towards the Goal*, London: John Murray, 1917.

Ward, Paul. *Red Flag and Union Jack: Englishness, patriotism and the British Left 1881–1924*, London: Royal Historical Society Boydell Press, 1998.

Ward, Paul. *Britishness since 1870*, London: Routledge, 2004.

Ward, Stephen R. (ed.). *The War Generation: Veterans of the First World War*, Port Washington NY: Kennikat Press, 1975.

Wasley, Gerald. *Devon in the Great War, 1914–1918*, Tiverton: Devon Books, 2000.

Watson, A. Sydney. *The Russian French Flag Day in Walsall, July 24th 1915*, Walsall: Walsall Chamber of Commerce, 1915.

Watson, Alexander. *Enduring the Great War: Combat, morale and collapse in the German and British armies, 1914–1918*, pbk ed., Cambridge: Cambridge University Press, 2008.

Watson, Janet K. *Fighting Different Wars: Experience, memory and the First World War in Britain*, Cambridge: Cambridge University Press, 2004.

Wheeler, Capt Owen. *The War Office Past and Present*, London: Methuen, 1914.

Wilkinson, Alan. *The Church of England and the First World War*, London: SPCK, 1978.

Williams, Col G. *Citizen Soldiers of the Royal Engineers, Transportation and Movements and the Army Service Corps 1859–1965*, Ashford (Kent): Royal Corps of Transport, 1965.

Williams, Ian. *The Alms Trade: Charities, past, present and future*, London: Unwin Hyman, 1989.

Williams, John. *The Home Fronts: Britain, France and Germany 1914–1918*, London: Constable, 1972.

Wilson, John (ed.). *Grimsby's War Work: An account of the borough's effort during the Great War, 1914–1919, together with the roll of honour*, County Archives Service rpt, Grimsby: Humberside County Council, 1994 (f.p. Grimsby: W.H. Jackson, 1919).

Wilson, Trevor. *The Myriad Faces of War: Britain and the Great War, 1914–1918*, Cambridge: Polity Press, 1986.

Wiltsher, Anne. *Most Dangerous Women: Feminist peace campaigners of the Great War*, London: Pandora Press, 1985.

Winter, Jay M. *Socialism and the Challenge of War: Ideas and politics in Britain 1912–18*, London: Routledge and Kegan Paul, 1974.

Winter, Jay M. *Sites of Memory, Sites of Mourning: The Great War in European cultural history*, Cambridge: Cambridge University Press, 1995.

Winter, Jay M. 'British National Identity and the First World War', in Green, S.J.D. and Whiting, R.C. (eds.), *The Boundaries of the State in Modern Britain*, Cambridge: Cambridge University Press, 1996.

Winter, Jay M. *The Great War and the British People*, Basingstoke: Palgrave Macmillan, 2003.

Winter, Jay M. *Remembering War: The Great War between memory and history in the twentieth century*, New Haven CT: Yale University Press, 2006.

Winter, Jay and Prost, Antoine. *The Great War in History: Debates and controversies 1914 to the present*, Cambridge: Cambridge University Press, 2005.

Winter, Jay and Robert, Jean-Louis (eds.). *Capital Cities at War: Paris, London, Berlin 1914–1919*, Cambridge: Cambridge University Press, 1997.

Woods, Mike and Platts, Tricia (eds.). *Bradford in the Great War*, Stroud: Sutton, 2007.

Woollacott, Angela. *On Her Their Lives Depend: Munitions workers in the Great War*, Berkeley and London: University of California Press, 1994.

Wootton, Graham. *The Official History of the British Legion*, London: Macdonald and Evans, 1956.

Wootton, Graham. *The Politics of Influence: British ex-servicemen, Cabinet decisions and cultural change*, London: Routledge and Kegan Paul, 1963.

Worsfold, W. Basil. *The War and Social Reform: An endeavour to trace the influence of the war as a reforming agency; with special reference to matters primarily affecting the wage-earning classes*, London: John Murray, 1919.

Yapp, Sir Arthur K. *The Romance of the Red Triangle: The story of the coming of the Red Triangle and the service rendered by the YMCA to the sailors and soldiers of the British Empire*, London: Hodder and Stoughton, 1919.

Yeo, Stephen and Eileen (eds.). *Popular Culture and Class Conflict, 1590–1914: Explorations in the history of labour and leisure*, Brighton: Harvester, 1981.

Young, Michael. *Army Service Corps 1920–1918*, Barnsley: Leo Cooper, 2000.

JOURNALS AND PAPERS

Abbott, Edith. 'The War and Women's Work in England', *Journal of Political Economy*, Vol. 25, No. 7 (July 1917).

Airey, Robert Berkeley. 'The London School of Economics and the Army', *Army Review,* Vol. IV (April 1913): 465–73.

Anheier, Helmut and Kendall, Jeremy. 'Interpersonal Trust and Voluntary Associations: Examining three approaches', *British Journal of Sociology,* Vol. 53, No. 3 (September 2002): 343–62.

Ansell, C.F. 'A Trip to Kumasi', 4 parts, *Army Service Corps Journal* (November 1896–February 1897): 61–65, 97–101, 158–161, 208–12.

Atkins, A. Crofton. 'The Experimental Course at the London School of Economics and Political Science', *Army Service Corps Quarterly,* Vol. 2 (October 1907): 304–20.

Beaven, Brad. 'Challenges to Civic Governance in Post-War England: The Peace Day disturbances of 1919', *Urban History,* Vol. 33, No. 3 (2006): 369–92.

Black, John. 'War, Women and Accounting: Female staff in the UK Army Pay Department offices, 1914–1920', *Accounting, Business and Financial History,* Vol. 16, No. 2 (2006): 195–218.

Bogacz, Ted. 'A Tyranny of Words: Language, poetry and antimodernism in England in the First World War', *Journal of Modern History,* Vol. 58, No. 3 (September 1986): 643–68.

Bogacz, Ted. 'War Neurosis and Cultural Change in England 1914–1922', *Journal of Contemporary History,* Vol. 24, No. 2 (1989): 227–56.

Bourke, Joanna. 'Women on the Home Front in World War One', *BBC History,* http://www.bbc.co.uk/history/british/britain_wwone/women_employment_01. shtml.

Bryder, L. 'The First World War: Healthy or hungry?', *History Workshop Journal,* Vol. 24 (Autumn 1987): 141–57.

Carrington, Charles E. 'Kitchener's Army: The Somme and after', *Journal of the Royal United Services Institute for Defence Studies,* Vol. 123, No. 1 (1978): 15–20.

Carter, Evan Eyare. 'The Science and Art of Army Administration', *Army Service Corps Quarterly,* Vol. 3 (October 1909): 365–79.

Clayton, F.T. 'Supply and Transport Ashanti Expedition 1895', 2 parts, *Army Service Corps Journal* (September–October 1896): 221–26 and 1–6.

Coetzee, Frans. 'English Nationalism and the First World War', *History of European Ideas,* Vol. 15, Nos. 1–3 (1992): 363–68.

D'Aeth, Frederick. 'War Relief Agencies and the Guild of Help Movement', *Progress: Civic, Social, Industrial,* Vol. 10 (October 1915).

Darwin, Maj Leonard. 'Distress among the Professional Classes', *Charity Organisation Review,* Vol. 41 (May 1917): 180–92.

Daunton, Martin J. 'Payment and Participation: Welfare and state-formation in Britain, 1900–1951', *Past and Present,* No. 150 (1996): 169–216.

Davis Smith, Justin and Oppenheimer, Melanie. 'The Labour Movement and Voluntary Action in the UK and Australia: A comparative perspective', *Labour History,* Vol. 88 (2005),

Deist, Wilhelm. 'The Military Collapse of the German Empire: The reality behind the stab-in-the-back myth', *War in History,* Vol. 3, No. 2 (April 1996): 186–207.

Delaney, Liam and Keaney, Emily. 'Sport and Social Capital in the United Kingdom: Statistical evidence from national and international survey data', Department for Culture, Media and Sport, December 2005.

Demm, Eberhard. 'Propaganda and Caricature in the First World War', *Journal of Contemporary History,* Vol. 28, No. 1 (January 1993): 163–92.

Dowding, W.E. 'The Romance of Voluntary Effort', *TP's Journal of Great Deeds,* (1915).

Dowding, W.E. 'A Study of the War-Giving', *The Contemporary Review,* Vol. CVIII (November 1915): 628–34.

Englander, David. 'Soldiering and Identity: Reflections on the Great War', *War in History,* Vol. 1, No. 3 (1994): 300–18.

Englander, David and Osborne, James. 'Jack, Tommy and Henry Dubb: The armed forces and the working class', *Historical Journal,* Vol. 21, No. 3 (September 1978): 593–621.

Fair, John D. 'The Political Aspects of Women's Suffrage during the First World War', *Albion,* Vol. 8 (1976): 274–95.

Fawcett, Millicent Garrett. 'War Relief and War Service', *Quarterly Review,* Vol. 225, No. 446 (January 1916): 111–29.

Finlayson, Geoffrey. 'A Moving Frontier: Voluntarism and the state in British social welfare 1911–1949', *Twentieth Century British History,* Vol. 1, No. 2 (1990): 183–206.

Fowler, Simon. 'War Charity Begins at Home', *History Today,* Vol. 49 (September 1999): 17–23.

Fowler, Simon. 'The Origins of Flag Days', Voluntary Action History Society, Occasional Paper No. 3, June 2000, http://www.vahs.org.uk/vahs/papers/vahs3.pdf. Accessed on 28/10/13.

Fowler, Simon and Gregson, Keith. 'Bloody Belgians!', *Ancestors* (May 2005): 43–49.

Funnell, Warwick. 'Military Influences on the Evolution of Public Sector Audit and Accounting 1830–1880', *Accounting History* (Journal of the Accounting History Special Interest Group of the Accounting Association of Australia and New Zealand), Vol. 2, No. 2 (November 1997): 9–29.

Funnell, Warwick. 'National Efficiency, Military Accounting and the Business of War', *Critical Perspectives on Accounting,* Vol. 17, No. 6 (September 2006): 719–51.

Gente, Magali. 'Family Ideology and the Charity Organization Society in Great Britain during the First World War', *Journal of Family History,* Vol. 27, No. 3 (2002): 255–72.

Goodlad, Lauren M.E. '"Making the Working Man Like Me": Charity, pastorship and middle class identity in nineteenth century Britain', *Victorian Studies,* Vol. 43, No. 4 (Summer 2001): 591–617.

Grayzel, Susan R. 'The Outward and Visible Sign of Her Patriotism: Women, uniforms, and National Service during the First World War', *Twentieth Century British History,* Vol. 8, No. 2 (1997): 145–64.

Grieves, Keith. '"Lowther's Lambs": Rural paternalism and voluntary recruitment in the First World War', *Rural History,* Vol. 4, No. 1 (1993): 55–75.

Grieves, Keith. 'C.E. Montague and the Making of "Disenchantment" 1914–1921', *War in History,* Vol. 4, No. 1 (1997): 35–59.

Hall, Peter A. 'Social Capital in Britain', *British Journal of Political Science,* Vol. 29, No. 3 (July 1999): 417–61.

Hallifax, Stuart. '"Over by Christmas": British popular opinion and the short war in 1914', *First World War Studies,* Vol. 1, No. 2 (October 2010): 103–22.

Harper, Rosalyn and Kelly, Maryanne. 'Measuring Social Capital in the United Kingdom', Office for National Statistics, December 2003, harmonisation-steve5_tcm77–184072[2].pdf. Accessed on 28/10/13.

Harris, Bernard. 'Voluntary Action and the State in Historical Perspective', *Voluntary Sector Review,* Vol. 1, No. 1 (2010): 25–40.

Harris, Jose. 'Political Thought and the Welfare State 1870–1940: An intellectual framework for British social policy', *Past and Present,* No. 135 (May 1992): 116–41.

Harrison, Brian. 'Philanthropy and the Victorians', *Victorian Studies*, Vol. 9, No. 4 (June 1966): 353–74.

Harrison, Brian. 'For Church, Queen and Family: The Girls' Friendly Society, 1874–1920', *Past and Present*, Vol. 61, No. 1 (1973): 107–38.

Herbotson, A.J. 'The Geographical Training of Army Officers in the Universities', *Geographical Journal*, Vol. 21 (1903): 465–66.

Herman, Dominic. '"The Truth about Men in the Front Line": Imagining the experience of war in memoirs of the Western Front', *University of Sussex Journal of Contemporary History*, No. 2 (2001), https://www.sussex.ac.uk/webteam/gateway/file.php?name=2-harman-the-truth-about-men-in-the-front-line&site=15. Accessed on 28/10/13.

Kennedy, Thomas C. 'Public Opinion and the Conscientious Objector, 1915–1919', *Journal of British Studies*, Vol. 12, No. 2 (1972–73): 105–19.

Kent, Susan Kingsley. 'The Politics of Sexual Difference: World War I and the demise of British feminism', *Journal of British Studies*, Vol. 27, No. 3 (1988): 232–53.

Kidd, Alan J. 'Philanthropy and the "Social History Paradigm"', *Social History* (London), Vol. 21, No. 2 (1996): 180–92.

Kocka, Jurgen. 'The First World War and the *Mittelstand*: German artisans and white collar workers', *Journal of Contemporary History*, Vol. 8, No. 1 (1973): 101–24.

Kushner, Tony. 'Local Heroes: Belgian refugees in Britain during the First World War', *Immigrants and Minorities*, Vol. 18, No. 1 (1999): 1–28.

Lawson, Tom. '"The Free-Masonry of Sorrow"?: English national identities and the memorialisation of the Great War in Britain, 1919–1931', *History and Memory*, Vol. 20, No. 1 (Spring/Summer 2008): 89–120.

Lee, Janet. 'A Nurse and a Soldier: Gender, class and national identity in the First World War adventures of Grace McDougall and Flora Sandes', *Women's History Review*, Vol. 15, No. 1 (2006): 83–103.

Lee, John. 'Following "The Absent-minded Beggar": A case-history of a fund-raising campaign of the South African War', Paper given at the Voluntary Action History Society Seminar, , 22 November 2010. Podcast available at http://www.vahs.org.uk/2012/09/podcast-lee/. Accessed on 28/10/13.

Leed, Eric J. 'Class and Disillusionment in World War I', *Journal of Modern History*, Vol. 50, No. 4 (1978): 680–99.

Leon, Clare. 'Special Constables in the First and Second World Wars', *Police History Society Journal*, Vol. 7 (1992): 1–41.

Leppington, C.H.D'E. 'The War's Influence on Village Life', *Economic Journal*, No. 34 (1924): 480–84.

Lewis, Jane. 'The Boundary between Voluntary and Statutory Social Service in the late Nineteenth and Early Twentieth Centuries', *Historical Journal*, Vol. 39, No. 1 (1996): 155–77.

Li, Yaojun, Pickles, Andrew and Savage, Mike. 'Conceptualising and Measuring Social Capital: A new approach', Centre for Census and Survey Research (CCSR), Department of Sociology, Manchester University, Paper for British Household Panel Survey, 2003.

Li, Yaojun, Savage, Mike and Pickles, Andrew. 'Social Capital and Social Exclusion in England and Wales (1972–1999)', *British Journal of Sociology,* Vol. 54, No. 4 (December 2003): 497–526.

Lowe, Rodney. 'The Erosion of State Intervention in Britain 1917–24', *Economic History Review*, Vol. 31, No. 2 (1978): 270–86.

Lowe, Rodney. 'Welfare Legislation and the Unions during and after the First World War', *Historical Journal*, Vol. 25, No. 2 (1982): 437–41.

McCrone, K.E. 'Play Up! Play Up! And Play the Game! Sport at the Late Victorian Girls' Public School', *Journal of British Studies*, Vol. 23, No. 2 (Spring 1984): 106–34.

MacDonald, R.H. '"Reproducing the Middle-Class Boy": From purity to patriotism in the boys' magazines, 1892–1914', *Journal of Contemporary History*, Vol. 24, No. 3 (1989): 519–39.

McEwen, J.M. 'The National Press during the First World War: Ownership and circulation', *Journal of Contemporary History*, Vol. 17, No. 3 (1982): 459–86.

McEwen, J.M. 'Brass-Hats and the British Press during the First World War', *Canadian Journal of History*, Vol. 18 (April 1983): 43–67.

Mackenzie, S.P. 'Morale and the Cause: The campaign to shape the outlook of soldiers in the British Expeditionary Force 1914–1918', *Canadian Journal of History*, Vol. 25, No. 2 (August 1990): 215–31.

Marquis, Alice Goldfarb. 'Words as Weapons: Propaganda in Britain and Germany during the First World War', *Journal of Contemporary History*, Vol. 13, No. 3 (1978): 467–98.

Marwick, Arthur. 'The Impact of the First World War on British Society', *Journal of Contemporary History*, Vol. 3, No. 1 (January 1968): 51–63.

Mason, M.H. 'War Charities Scandals', *English Review*, Vol. 22 (April 1916): 360–72.

Masterman, C.F.G. 'The Temper of the People', *The Contemporary Review*, Vol. CVIII (July 1915): 7–11.

Melling, J. 'Welfare Capitalism and the Origins of the Welfare States: British industry, workplace welfare and social reform c 1870–1914', *Social History*, Vol. 17, No. 3 (October 1992): 453–78.

Moore, Michael J. 'Social Service and Social Legislation in Edwardian England: The beginning of a new role for philanthropy', *Albion*, No. 3 (1971): 33–43.

Moore, Michael J. 'Social Work and Social Welfare: The organization of philanthropic resources in Britain, 1900–1914', *Journal of British Studies*, Vol. 16, No. 2 (Spring 1977): 85–104.

Mosse, G.L. 'Two World Wars and the Myth of the War Experience', *Journal of Contemporary History*, Vol. 21, No. 4 (1986): 491–513.

O'Neill, James E. 'The Victorian Background to the British Welfare State', *South Atlantic Quarterly*, No. 66 (1967): 204–17.

'Orderly Room Sergeant'. 'With No. 31 Company in the Siege of Ladysmith', *Army Service Corps Journal* (June 1900): 85–91.

Osborne, J.M. 'Defining Their Own Patriotism: British Volunteer Training Corps in the First World War', *Journal of Contemporary History*, Vol. 23, No. 1 (1988): 59–75.

Panayi, Panikos. 'The British Empire Union in the First World War', *Immigrants and Minorities*, Vol. 8 Nos. 1–2 (March 1989): 113–28.

Pedersen, Susan. 'Gender, Welfare and Citizenship in Britain during the Great War', *American Historical Review*, Vol. 95, No. 4 (1990): 983–1006.

Pedersen, Sarah. 'A Surfeit of Socks? The impact of the First World War on women correspondents to daily newspapers', *Scottish Economic and Social History*, Vol. 22, No. 1 (2002): 50–72.

Porter, J.B. 'Sphagnum Moss for Use as a Surgical Dressing: Its collection, preparation and other details', *Canadian Medical Association Journal*, Vol. 7, No. 3 (March 1917): 201–7.

Price, E.C. 'The War Charities Report', *Charity Organisation Review*, Vol. 40 (August 1916): 47–53.

Price, E.C. 'War Charities and Street Collections', *Charity Organisation Review*, Vol. 42 (December 1917): 236–41.

Proctor, Tammy M. '"Patriotism Is Not Enough": Women, citizenship, and the First World War', *Journal of Women's History*, Vol. 17, No. 2 (2005): 169–76.

Pugh, Martin. 'The Rise of Labour and the Political Culture of Conservatism, 1890–1945, *History*, Vol. 87, No. 288 (2002): 514–37.

Putnam, Robert D. '*E Pluribus Unum:* Diversity and community in the twenty-first century (The 2006 Johan Skytte Prize Lecture)', *Scandinavian Political Studies,* Vol. 30, No. 2 (2007): 137–74.

'Report of the Secretary to the Local War Records Committee on the Year's Work, Sept. 30, 1920 to Sept. 30, 1921: Local war records', *History*, Vol. 6, No. 24 (January 1922): 247–58.

Roberts, James. '"The Best Football Team, the Best Platoon": The role of football in the proletarianization of the British Expeditionary Force 1914–1918', *Sport in History*, Vol. 26, No. 1 (April 2006): 26–46.

Sanders, M.L. 'Wellington House and British Propaganda during the First World War', *Historical Journal*, Vol. 18, No. 1 (1975): 119–46.

Satre, Lowell J. 'St John Brodrick and Army Reform 1901–3', *Journal of British Studies*, Vol. XV, No. 2 (Spring 1976): 117–39.

Scates, Bruce. 'The Unknown Sock Knitter: Voluntary work, emotional labour, bereavement and the Great War', *Labour History* (Australia), No. 81 (2001): 29–50.

Schneider, Eric. 'The British Red Cross Wounded and Missing Enquiry Bureau: A case of truth-telling in the Great War', *War in History*, Vol. 4, No. 3 (1997): 296–315.

Schweitzer, Rich. 'The Cross and the Trenches: Religious faith and doubt among some British soldiers on the Western Front', *War and Society*, Vol. 16, No. 2 (October 1998): 33–57.

Sharp, L.V. 'War Relief Measures in the Provinces', *Charity Organisation Review*, Vol. 36 (October 1914): 247–56.

Sheffield, Gary. 'The Effect of the Great War on Class Relations in Britain: The career of Major Christopher Stone DSO MC', *War and Society*, Vol. 7, No. 1 (May 1989): 87–105.

Sloan, Geoff. 'Haldane's Mackindergarten: A radical experiment in British military education?', *War in History*, Vol. 19, No. 3 (2012): 322–52.

Smith, H. Babington. 'Ladysmith after the Siege', *Living Age*, No. 225 (2 June 1900): 537–46.

Snook, Lisa. '"Out of the cage"? Women and the First World War in Pontypridd', *Llafur*, Vol. 8, No. 2 (2001): 75–87.

Spence, Jean. 'Gender and Class Negotiations in an Edwardian Welfare Organisation: A tale of two women', *Women's History Review*, Vol. 15, No. 2 (2006): 277–95.

Springhall, John. 'Baden-Powell and the Scout Movement before 1920: Citizen training or soldiers of the future?', *English Historical Review*, Vol. 102, No. 402 (October 1987): 934–42.

Stamper, Anne. 'Countrywomen in Action: Voluntary action in the National Federation of Women's Institutes 1917–1965', Paper given to the Voluntary Action History Society Conference '400 Years of Charity', Liverpool, 2001.

Stedman-Jones, Gareth. 'Class Expression versus Social Control? A critique of recent trends in the social history of leisure', *History Workshop Journal*, Vol. 4, No. 1 (Autumn 1977): 162–70.

Stoddart, D.R. 'Geography and War: The "New Geography" and the "New Army" in England, 1889–1914', *Political Geography,* Vol. 11, No. 1 (January 1992): 87–99.

Summers, Anne. 'Militarism in Britain before the Great War', *History Workshop Journal*, Vol. 2 (Autumn 1976): 104–23.

Sykes, Alan. 'Which War? The English Radical Right and the First World War', *War and Society*, Vol. 23, Suppl. 1 (September 2005): 59–74.

Terraine, John. 'Mortality and Morale', *Journal of the Royal United Service Institution*, Vol. 112, No. 648 (November 1967): 364–69.

Tripp, Helen. 'Mr Punch and Tommy Atkins: British Soldiers' social identity during the First World War', *University of Sussex Journal of Contemporary History*, No. 4 (2002),. https://www.sussex.ac.uk/webteam/gateway/file.php?name=4-tripp-mr-punch-and-tommy-atkins&site=15. Accessed on 28/10/13.

Tucker, Albert V. 'Politics and the Army in the Unionist Government in England, 1900–1905', *Report of the Annual Meeting of the Canadian Historical Association*, Vol. 43, No. 1 (1964): 105–19.

Tucker, Albert V. 'The Issue of Army Reform in the Unionist Government, 1903–5', *The Historical Journal*, Vol. 9, No. 1 (1966): 90–100.

Veitch, Colin. '"Play Up! Play Up! And Win the War!" Football, the nation and the First World War 1914–15', *Journal of Contemporary History*, Vol. 20, No. 3 (July 1985): 363–78.

Vellacott, Jo. 'Feminist Consciousness and the First World War', *History Workshop Journal*, No. 23 (1987): 81–101.

Vincent, Howard. 'Lessons of the War', *Army Service Corps Journal* (July 1900): 132–36.

Vining, Margaret and Hacker, Barton C. 'From Camp Follower to Lady in Uniform: Women, social class and military institutions before 1920', *Contemporary European History*, Vol. 10, No. 3 (2001): 353–73.

Voeltz, Richard A. 'The Antidote to "Khaki Fever?" The expansion of the British Girl Guides during the First World War', *Journal of Contemporary History*, Vol. 27, No. 4 (1992): 627–38.

Voth, Hans-Joachim. 'Civilian Health during World War One and the Causes of German Defeat: A re-examination of the Winter hypothesis', *Annales de Demographie Historique* (1995): 291–307.

'W.G.M.' 'War Relief Agencies', *Charity Organisation Review*, Vol. 38 (September 1915): 281–92.

Waites, Brian A. 'The Effect of the First World War on Class and Status in England, 1910–20', *Journal of Contemporary History*, Vol. 11, No. 1 (January 1976): 27–48.

Walker, Joyce. 'The British Red Cross in the Bromley Area 1910–19', *Bromley Local History*, Vol. 4 (1979): 17–23.

Walker, Stephen P. 'Philanthropic Women and Accounting: Octavia Hill and the exercise of "Quiet Power and Sympathy"', *Accounting, Business and Financial History*, Vol. 16, No. 2 (2006): 163–94.

Walter-Busch, Emil. 'Albert Thomas and Scientific Management in War and Peace, 1914–1932', *Journal of Management History*, Vol. 12, No. 2 (2006): 212–31.

Warburg, F.S. 'Work for Disabled Soldiers and Sailors', *Charity Organisation Review*, Vol. 41 (January 1917): 26–29.

Ward, Lt-Col E.W.D. 'To Kumasi and Back with the Ashanti Expeditionary Force 1895–96', *Royal United Services Institute Journal*, Vol. XL, No. 222 (August 1896): 1021–30.

Ward, Paul. '"Women of Britain Say Go": Women's patriotism in the First World War', *Twentieth Century British History*, Vol. 12, No. 1 (2001): 23–45.

Ward, Stephen. 'The British Veterans' Ticket of 1918', *Journal of British Studies*, Vol. 8 (November 1968): 155–69.

Warde, Alan et al. 'Trends in Social Capital: Membership of associations in Great Britain', *British Journal of Political Science*, Vol. 33, No. 3 (July 2003): 515–25.

Warren, Allen. 'Sir Robert Baden-Powell, the Scout Movement and Citizen Training in Great Britain 1900–1920', *English Historical Review*, Vol. 101, No. 399 (1986): 376–98.

Warwick, Paul. 'Did Britain Change? An inquiry into the causes of national decline', *Journal of Contemporary History*, Vol. 20, No. 1 (January 1985): 99–133.

Watson, Janet S.K. 'Wars in the Wards: The social construction of medical work in First World War Britain', *Journal of British Studies*, Vol. 41 (October 2002): 484–510.

Watt, Donald Cameron. 'The London University Class for Military Administrators 1906–31: A study of the British approach to civil-military relations', *LSE Quarterly*, Vol. 2, No. 2 (Summer 1988): 155–71.

Whiteside, Noelle. 'Industrial Welfare and Labour Regulation in Britain at the Time of the First World War', *International Review of Social History*, Vol. 25, No. 3 (1980): 307–31.

Whiteside, Noelle. 'Welfare Legislation and the Unions during the First World War', *Historical Journal*, Vol. 23, No. 4 (1980): 857–74.

Wilkinson, Paul. 'English Youth Movements, 1908–30', *Journal of Contemporary History*, Vol. 4 (April 1969): 3–23.

Willis, Ian. 'Wartime Volunteering in Camden', *History Australia*, Vol. 2, No. 1 (2004), http://journals.publishing.monash.edu/ojs/index.php/ha/article/view/538. Accessed on 28/10/13.

Winter, Jay M. 'Britain's "Lost Generation" of the First World War', *Population Studies*, Vol. 31, No. 3 (November 1977): 449–66.

Woollacott, Angela. '"Khaki Fever" and Its Control: Gender, class, age and sexual morality on the British homefront in the First World War', *Journal of Contemporary History*, Vol. 29, No. 2 (1994): 325–47.

Worthington, Ian. 'Socialization, Militarization and Officer Recruiting: The development of the Officers Training Corps', *Military Affairs*, Vol. 43, No. 2 (April 1979): 90–96.

Wright, D.G. 'The Great War, Government Propaganda and English "Men of Letters"', *Literature and History*, No. 7 (Spring 1978): 70–100.

Wright, Thomas A. and Goodstein, Jerry. 'Character Is Not "Dead" in Management Research: A review of individual character and organizational-level virtue', *Journal of Management*, Vol. 33, No. 6 (December 2007): 928–58.

'X'. 'The Place of Organised Charity during the War', *Charity Organisation Review*, Vol. 38 (September 1915): 292–306.

Young, Capt H. 'Practical Economy in the Army', *Journal of the Royal United Service Institution*, Vol. L (July to December 1906): 1281–85.

THESES

Higgens, Simon Giles. 'How Was Richard Haldane Able to Reform the British Army? An historical assessment using a contemporary change management model', MPhil diss., University of Birmingham, 2010.

Kimball, Charles. 'The Ex-Service Movement in England and Wales 1916–1930', PhD diss., Stanford University, 1991.

Kreis, Steven. 'The Diffusion of an Idea: A history of Scientific Management in Britain, 1890–1945', PhD diss., University of Missouri-Columbia, 1990.

Latcham, Andrew. 'Journeys End: Ex servicemen and the state during and after the Great War', PhD diss., Oxford, 1997.

Mor-O'Brien, Anthony. 'A Community in Wartime: Aberdare and the First World War', PhD diss., University of Wales, 1986.

Page, A.H. 'The Supply Services of the British Army in the South African War 1899–1902', PhD diss., Oxford, 1977.

Tadman, Michael. 'The War Office: A study of its development as an organisational system 1870–1904', PhD diss., London, King's, 1992.

Waites, Bernard. 'The Impact of the First World War on Class and Status in England, 1910–20', PhD diss., Open University, 1982.

Index

Page numbers in bold type refer to illustrations

#0109 - 221116 - C0 - 229/152/15 [17] - CB - 9780415704946